Assia Djebar

Out of Algeria

Contemporary French and Francophone Cultures 6

Contemporary French and Francophone Cultures

This series aims to provide a forum for new research on modern and contemporary French and francophone cultures and writing. The books published in *Contemporary French and Francophone Cultures* reflect a wide variety of critical practices and theoretical approaches, in harmony with the intellectual, cultural and social developments which have taken place over the past few decades. All manifestations of contemporary French and francophone culture and expression are considered, including literature, cinema, popular culture, theory. The volumes in the series will participate in the wider debate on key aspects of contemporary culture.

1 Chris Tinker, *Georges Brassens and Jacques Brel: Personal and Social Narratives in Post-war Chanson* (0-85323-758-1 cloth, 0-85323-768-9 paper)

2 Debra Kelly, *Autobiography and Independence: Selfhood and Creativity in Postcolonial African Writing in French* (0-85323-659-3 cloth)

3 Matthew Screech, *Masters of the Ninth Art: Bandes dessinées and Franco-Belgian Identity* (0-85323-938-X cloth)

4 Akane Kawakami, *Travellers' Visions: French Literary Encounters with Japan, 1881–2004* (0-85323-811-1 cloth, 0-85323-730-1 paper)

5 Nicki Hitchcott, *Calixthe Beyala: Performances of Migration* (1-84631-028-8 cloth)

JANE HIDDLESTON

Assia Djebar
Out of Algeria

LIVERPOOL UNIVERSITY PRESS

First published 2006 by
Liverpool University Press
4 Cambridge Street
Liverpool L69 7ZU

Copyright © 2006 Jane Hiddleston

The right of Jane Hiddleston to be identified as the author
of this work has been asserted by her in accordance
with the Copyright, Designs and Patents Act, 1988

British Library Cataloguing-in-Publication data
A British Library CIP record is available

ISBN 1-84631-031-8 cased
ISBN - 13 978-1-84631-031-7 cased

Typeset in Sabon by Koinonia, Manchester
Printed and bound in the European Union by
Biddles Ltd, King's Lynn

Contents

Acknowledgements

Some of the material in Chapters 2, 3 and 4 originally appeared in *French Studies, Research in African Literatures* and *Law and Literature*. I would like to thank the editors and publishers of these journals for allowing me to reprint these sections. I am also grateful to Anthony Cond and Andrew Kirk at Liverpool University Press for their efficiency and support in bringing the book to fruition. I would like to thank members of the Department of French Studies at the University of Warwick, who managed not to overburden me in my first years as a lecturer, so that I was able to find time to work on the book. Assia Djebar herself engaged with work related to the book, and I am grateful to her for her encouragement. Finally, I am indebted to various friends and colleagues who supported my work on this project generally, or who offered advice on particular sections: Andy Merrills, Nick Harrison, Colin Davis, Azzedine Haddour, Sam Haigh, Charles Forsdick, Emma Wilson, John Harrington, Helen Watanabe. My family has also, as ever, been a constant source of strength.

J.H.
Exeter College, Oxford
January 2006

Introduction

L'expatriation au présent ne peut être objet d'écriture, ni point
d'appui: elle est son contraire; son mouvement aveugle, ses élans
contrariés et multiples figent l'intérieur de l'être alors que le corps
marche, que le regard quête, que le dos se courbe ou se redresse...[1]

Assia Djebar: Out of Algeria is a book about expatriation, and the
constant, necessary revisiting that follows. Algeria remains a focus,
an object of desire throughout Djebar's corpus, but it is also a point
of departure, and excludes the writer more often than it grounds or
defines her. Her only locus of identification or belonging, Algeria is at
the same time figured as broken, war-torn, unfamiliar and irrevocably
lost. A potential symbol of difference in contradistinction to colonial influence, Djebar's Algeria is also diverse, divided and ultimately
destroyed. Driven by the urge to recover her country's history, Djebar
repeatedly returns to Algeria's past only then to interrupt the narrative of its shaky development. The native land is the object of a quest,
inciting the writer to invent an identity and a genealogy, but it also
resists and eludes that quest. It offers glimmers of familiarity, hints
of a home, but under closer inspection shatters and disseminates the
cultural security that Djebar strives to create and represent. As the
quotation reproduced above suggests, this sense of alienation may
not be a straightforward or completed movement of expatriation, but
the writing is constantly jolted by its movement, by a sense of doubt
concerning its author's enclosure within a secure set of borders or a
defined locus of identification.

At once preoccupied with and severed from her native land,
Djebar writes from within this tension. Her novels all set out to tell
the story of Algeria's experiences of colonialism and postcolonialism,
but the writing at each juncture falls short of its task. Djebar hopes
to trace through the writing process the line of her country's trajectory, a meaningful narrative of its battles against colonialism, and
latterly, resurgent Islamism, but the possibility of a coherent, ordered

version eludes her. Although she is educated in the French system, and is only able to write in detail using the French language, she finds that this language glosses over the multiple, intricate Arab and Berber resonances of her cultural history. Anti-colonial narrative becomes deformed and indeed compromised when created in the language of the coloniser. In addition, the increasing instability of Algerian society, and her personal sense of exclusion from its newly Islamicised culture, disrupt the positioning of her narrative voice. Djebar's 'expatriation' cannot be a secure, logical stage in a reasoned chronology, but the vanishing point in her evolution, the reminder that the narrative of her country's history necessarily circles around experience and finishes by excluding it. In searching for a new history of Algeria, then, and in hoping to chart the development of Algerian women's roles, Djebar gradually, increasingly, finds that her native land is lost to her. Algeria turns out to be plural, fractured, composed of multiple conflicting voices, and its contemporary society is ravaged both by the traumatic aftermath of colonialism, and by the recent emergence of Islamic terrorists seeking to reshape Algerian identity according to new oppressive ideals. Furthermore, the writer's experience of losing any sense of possession and belonging means that her writing too becomes an artifice disconnected from the land she sought to recreate.

I want to conceptualise Djebar's progressive struggle and dissatisfaction with the notion of Algerian identity by referring to a number of contemporary theoretical concepts. Currently living and working in New York, Djebar participates in francophone, Arab and Berber, and Anglo-American schools of thought, and it is this crossroads between French philosophy, multiple Algerian traditions and Anglo-American postcolonial theory that will shape my analysis of her gradual, partial 'expatriation' in this book. Most importantly, my investigation will situate Djebar's thinking in relation to recent French philosophy, and make connections between her understanding of subjectivity and individuation and those produced by contemporary thinkers working in France. Despite her affiliations with Arab Algerian culture, and her obvious use of local oral tradition, some of Djebar's most visible reference points are French influences gleaned from her education in the French colonial system. Her works are littered with references to European literature and thought, as well as to Arab and Berber sources, and her self-conscious essays in *Ces voix qui m'assiègent* name writers such as Derrida, Camus, Blanchot, Duras and Irigaray more often than Algerian figures such as Mohammed Dib or Kateb Yacine. References such as these show that her anxieties about the writing process derive not only from her sense of alienation in the colonial system, but also from her readings of metropolitan thinkers who problematise notions of language and subjectivity more broadly. Such engagements may be seen by some readers to compromise her position, demonstrating her affiliation with the colonial culture, but her European heritage is itself a crucial part of her ambivalence. Analysis of the connections between her work and French philosophy will also help to conceptualise Djebar's evolution in terms that develop and critique notions of postcolonial individuation prevalent in existing criticism.

I intend to argue that Djebar's depictions of Algerian history can be seen to display both Foucault's critiques of societal influence, and Derrida and Nancy's more elusive conceptions of the disseminated subject. Her trajectory dramatises a struggle between a search for specificity in Foucault's sense, and an increasing awareness of the dissolution of any such specificity as a result of the ruptures and discontinuities of Algerian history. Foucault argues that the specific subject is constructed by the power relations operating on him or her at any one time.[2] Although he rails against these determinations and promises that such constituted subjects also resist their imposing limits, he concentrates on processes of classification and social organisation as well as on what lies beyond. It is important that this model of individuation is not necessarily determinist, since although individuals are shaped by networks of social relations, these do not necessarily succeed in pinning being down to a single, immutable position. Subjects are 'specific' because they continually renegotiate their relations with social imperatives rather than adhering automatically to set patterns. In Peter Hallward's words, 'Foucault moves away from an impossibly literal or immediate experience of a singular "outside" [*dehors*] (madness, death, language-in-itself), toward the composition of specific histories of how our experience has been *specified* and confined'.[3]

Unlike Foucault, however, philosophers such as Derrida, Lacoue-Labarthe and Nancy stress the limits of the concept of the subject and of our possible knowledge of its coordinates. For Derrida, processes of *différance* mean that the singular being is infinitely shifting away from its classification in language, and the attempt to determine subjectivity results in a sense of absence and lack. The subject is dislocated in language by the double forces of 'temporisation' and 'espacement'. The unstoppable spatial and temporal movements of *différance* mean that the being is continually self-singularising, it is never wholly anchored in a determinate location or moment.[4] Derrida also in this essay conceptualises the deferral and displacement of *différance* with reference to Freudian notions of the unconscious, which names not a hidden self but a web of singular traces. Subjectivity, in all its layers, is never present to itself but, like meaning, is passed continually along the chain of associations. Singularisation in this sense is also not absolute, as Peter Hallward understands it, but it is a process of movement away from language or linguistic definition. Next, building on Derrida, Nancy argues that since singularities are not self-consistent and self-present, they are continually exposed to an outside, to that which is not themselves, and they necessarily emerge out of this very process of exposure. The singular-plural being is situated in an ongoing series of relations and interactions, yet this focus on relationality, unlike in Foucault, in no way helps to pin the subject down. Being is born into relation and its singularity is the result of its multiple encounters and combinations, but this relationality has no substance of its own:

> le *co-* lui-même et en tant que tel la co-présence de l'être, n'est pas présentable en tant que l'être qu'il 'est', puisqu'il ne l'est qu'en l'écartant. Il est imprésentable, non pas parce qu'il occuperait la region de l'être la plus reculée et la plus mysérieuse, voire celle du néant, mais parce qu'il n'est pas soumis, tout simplement, à une logique de la présentation.[5]

Djebar does not write explicitly about such philosophers, but I want to suggest that her work implicitly juxtaposes comparable models of subjectivity, intensifying and dramatising the stakes of their construction by transferring them to postcolonial Algeria. She demonstrates how our sense of ourselves is always divided between knowledge of our situatedness (in her case, in relation to Algerian history, colonialism or Islam) and resistance to the tyranny of such determined positioning. Her literature forms a site of experimentation, where diverse models are tried out and thrown into confrontation with one another in order to demonstrate the very difficulty of theorising postcolonial Algeria in terms of any single, straightforward framework.

My reading of Djebar's relationship with French philosophy will portray her evolution (her partial 'expatriation') as a gradual shift away from a positioned Algerian identity or genealogy, through a discovery of Algeria's singular-plurality, and ultimately to an ongoing preoccupation with its loss.[6] Key texts such as *Femmes d'Alger dans leur appartement* and *L'Amour, la fantasia* juxtapose the search for specificity in Foucault's sense with reflections both on Derridean self-singularisation, and on the endless plurality of Algerian culture, in a way that recalls Nancy's *Être singulier pluriel*. Later works then testify to an increasing sense of despair with regard to the relocation of any identity or specificity at all. *Femmes d'Alger* and *L'Amour, la fantasia* struggle to conclude their search for Algerian identity, and feminist works such as *Vaste est la prison* and *Loin de Médine* seek to uncover women's lost voices while admitting to the impossibility of that project. The works all seek to negotiate between conflicting influences, between various social, political, religious and historical movements, but they also find that the narration of that specificity dissolves into a discovery of the processes of singularisation that exceed the grasp of any such positioned framework. The later texts, moreover, reflecting on the outbreak of civil war in Algeria in the 1990s, go on to abandon the search for the specific and try to mourn its frustrated shadow. In *Le Blanc de l'Algérie*, Djebar writes about the deaths of her friends, and of a number of great Algerian writers assassinated by Islamists, and uncovers the difficulty of writing a collective, 'national' liturgy for the singular-plural deceased. Finally, the recent works present postcolonial Algeria in even more fraught and complex terms, and the author at this point appears to reject the specific and to explore her country's internal otherness according to Derrida's ethics and poetics of hauntology.[7] *La Femme sans sépulture* and *La Disparition de la langue française* present Djebar's native land not only as singular-plural but as 'spectral', haunted by the differential traces of a colonial past that is still both there and not there. *La Disparition* forms a culmination, in that in this epoch still haunted by colonialism and ravaged by the newly oppressive Islamist culture prevalent in Algeria, both identity and language are figured as ghostly, dispossessed, beyond the grasp of the francophone writer who is no longer in command of her project. As a result of her ambivalent relationship with colonial culture, and the resurgence of an Islamist belief-system she struggles to recognise, Djebar's position in relation to Algeria becomes dislocated and ultimately dissolved.

Djebar's early works, written in the late 1950s and 1960s, begin her tentative quest to make sense of women's positions in contemporary Algeria. Although the earliest texts, *La Soif* and *Les Impatients*, remain somewhat disengaged from the political troubles unfolding at the time and do not contain the same sort of historical analysis found in the later works, they do investigate modern Algerian women's struggle to create a role for themselves. In this sense they inaugurate the search for a feminine genealogy, sorting through the conventions and norms that shape women's lives in Algeria at the time of the war of independence while also charting individuals' resistance to such norms. Evidently less sophisticated than Djebar's highly intricate later works, the early pieces are worthy of attention since, through an exploration of young girls' turbulent love affairs, the texts focus on the question of what it means to be a woman in Algeria at a time of political upheaval. Furthermore, *Les Enfants du nouveau monde* and *Les Alouettes naïves* combine a similar examination of women's positions in relation to patriarchal society with exploration of the effects of the war on feminine agency. In *Les Enfants*, the conflict leads not so much directly to female political activity as to an initial sketch of women's potential resistance to the roles imposed upon them by their husbands. In *Les Alouettes*, Djebar begins her ongoing reflection on the memory of the war and on women's place within that fraught process of recollection.

It is in *Les Alouettes* that Djebar first starts to trace the difficulties of creating a coherent narrative of Algeria's war-torn history, and it is this realisation of the disjunction between memory and narrative that silences her for the following ten years. Using the time to make the films *La Nouba des femmes du Mont Chenoua* and *La Zerda et les chants de l'oubli*, Djebar temporarily halts her novel-writing in order to explore the potential of real-life testimony and the visual image. The films will not be analysed in detail in this book, however, since my concern is above all the evolution of Djebar's fiction, her changing perception of the writing process, and the films constitute in some respects a separate investigation of the relation between word and image. In addition, the films are difficult to access and less widely known than the novels, and show less evidence of the engagement with philosophy and theory that I hope to track here. The pause in her writing career, however, is significant as it engenders an alternative approach to novel-writing, and a heightened self-consciousness with regard to its traps. The frustrated search for history at the centre of *La Nouba des femmes du Mont Chenoua* leads to the invention of an alternative form of writing in the novels that follow. With *Femmes d'Alger* and *L'Amour, la fantasia*, then, the quest for a meaningful Algerian history, and for an understanding of women's roles within that history, is expressed explicitly in terms of the simultaneous, inevitable dissemination of that historical narrative. The search for a specific identity is met immediately with the discovery that the women's voices that she thought might produce that specificity are all endlessly singular, resistant to categorisation, and at the same time relational or composite. If, for example, *L'Amour, la fantasia* begins with the inaugural moment of the French invasion in 1830, and juxtaposes scenes of colonial violence with visions of resistance during the war of independence, it fails to invent as a result of that juxtaposition a sense of continuity or progress. At the same time, the scenes focusing on the narrator's childhood, and later, her love affairs, seem to want to position her in relation to various traditions, but here too she flounders between incompatible influences. As for *Femmes d'Alger*, Delacroix's painting of the same name appears to instigate the narrator's investigation of the treatment of Algerian women, their silencing and eventual 'coming to voice'. Nevertheless, the collection in the end offers a diversity of fragmented, uncertain and anxious voices, which have lost any sense of their country's direction and purpose.

The next group of works, *Ombre sultane*, *Vaste est la prison* and *Loin de Médine*, express this tension more particularly, and more acutely, in the context of Algerian women's social experiences and their relationships with men. In these texts Djebar combines influences of Western and Arab feminism, and troubles the notion of an Algerian feminine collective by juxtaposing conflicting strands of each genre. While Western feminism is stereotypically often seen to be concerned with either introspection or individual agency, Arab feminism, in keeping with Islamic tradition, is thought to foreground collectivity. Djebar problematises the polarity of this debate as she upholds feminine solidarity while also dissociating that solidarity from any notion of sameness or belonging. She champions feminine collective agency as a means of political resistance, but she also presents feminine experience as endlessly variable and impossible to access using the French colonial language. In *Ombre sultane*, for example, Djebar counterbalances depictions of Isma and Hajila, two wives of the same man. The text focuses on feminine subordination and the subsequent process of liberation, intertwining these two stages by flitting disconcertingly back and forth between the characters. Most significant, however, is the relationship between the two women, their mutual identification and conflict. The characters are at times presented as doubles or shadows of one another, while at others they seem to be in competition, and myths of feminine harmony are punctured. In *Vaste est la prison*, Djebar sets out to evolve a genealogy of Algerian women, paradoxically stressing singular resistance to imposed frameworks as well as shared experiences. She also explores the notion of a 'feminine language', hoping to recreate lost specific idioms while finding that singular echoes slip between the lines of her own narrative. *Loin de Médine* raises similar questions, drawing attention to the power and agency of Islamic women in the past while suggesting that their contingent experiences escape our knowledge in the present. Depictions of a specific feminine identity construction are coupled with an exploration of the plural relations and influences that trouble that initial position.

Although *Loin de Médine* was written in response to the resurgent Islamist violence at the end of the 1980s and the beginning of the 1990s, it is the next set of texts that mark the real turning point in Djebar's trajectory as a result of this latest upheaval. With *Le Blanc de l'Algérie*, Djebar bears witness to a political and cultural crisis in modern Algeria and expresses disillusionment towards the possible redefinition or repossession of her native land. It is here that Djebar begins to write most explicitly from a position of partial 'expatriation', since the assassination of scores of Algerian writers and thinkers on their own territory tears the country apart and makes her a stranger within its borders. Algeria is figured as pale, bloodless, hollowed out, unrecognisable. Furthermore, in attempting to mourn the loss of her friends, Djebar struggles to locate an appropriate language of commemoration and laments the imposition of artificial, grandiloquent Islamist rhetoric. She seeks in the face of this imposition to retrieve what she terms the 'dedans de la parole', to infuse language with the singularity that it so frequently occludes, but the text also records the impossibility of attaining that ideal. Similarly, in *Oran, langue morte* Djebar tries to encapsulate the shared experience of bereavement, but once again, the language of mourning splits and breaks down. Memory is juxtaposed with oblivion, and Djebar depicts modern Algeria as a society ruptured by a series of losses with which it is unable to come to terms. Next, *Les Nuits de Strasbourg* traces the shadows of colonial violence that underpin modern inter-cultural communication and 'métissage'. Djebar experiments here with the potentially enriching celebration of 'hybridity', though she finishes by presenting no smooth amalgam but, again, the threads of a set of communities torn apart by loss.

The final chapter of Djebar's work moves from the attempt to mourn the loss of Algeria's victims to the reconfiguration of the country itself as ghostly, at once dead and alive, and beyond the writer's grasp. Any sense of the specific, of a determined history or particular genealogy of Algerian women, evaporates and Algeria is figured as insubstantial, lost or torn apart. Algeria is in these texts not only bereaved, struggling to mourn its most talented creators and commentators, but also spectral and divided from itself. In *La Femme sans sépulture*, the ghost of Zoulikha, a resistance fighter during the war of independence, resurfaces to haunt the memories of her friends and relatives and reminds them of the persistent shadows of colonial violence. Yet the narrator's attempt to retell her story and to make sense of her trajectory results in her extinction; writing resuscitates her only to bury her again and to remind us both of her absence, and of our ignorance regarding her fate. *La Disparition* forms, as I have suggested, the culmination of Djebar's writerly journey, since it is here that Algeria, symbolised by the Casbah, is portrayed as pure artifice, a fetish that covers over the lack of an identifiable and secure referent. The text also offers a conclusion to Djebar's writing project because it reconfigures not only Algeria, but also the French language and francophone narrative as objects of loss. The language is bound up with the ghosts of colonialism while also reinventing itself as the antidote to Arabic monolingualism. The French language is haunted, uneasy, different from itself, and Djebar seems by now pessimistic regarding its ability to capture and encapsulate her lost native land. Nevertheless, as for Derrida, from whom she derives her thought of a haunted, 'spectral' Algeria, attention to that which is both absent and present, the shadows of the past, remains an obligation and does not signal the end of the quest. For Derrida,

> il faut parler *du* fantôme, voire *au* fantôme et *avec* lui, dès lors qu'aucune éthique, aucune politique, révolutionnaire ou non, ne paraît possible et pensable et *juste*, qui ne reconnaisse à son principe le respect pour ces autres qui ne sont plus ou pour ces autres qui ne sont pas encore *là, présentement vivants*, qu'ils soient déjà morts ou qu'ils ne soient pas encore nés.[8]

Djebar's later work expresses disillusionment, but retains a sense of the ongoing necessity of attending to Algeria's past using an alternative conceptual framework of spectrality and partial memory. Post-coloniality in Algeria is this anxious shifting between past and present, the haunting of other epochs and other cultures, the disjointed, Derridean trace that supplements contemporary ideology.[9]

In presenting the evolution of Djebar's trajectory as a movement out of Algeria, as a partial expatriation haunted by the apparition of an Algeria that she cannot grasp, I hope to offer a new reading of her career as a story of its own. A number of critics have focused their attention on the writing of Djebar, and numerous papers exist exploring the tension in her work between the quest for Algeria and the demands of a francophone narrative. Books such as those by Jeanne-Marie Clerc and Mireille Calle-Gruber explore Djebar's fraught relationship with the language in which she writes, unpicking the association between self-expression and veiling, or testimony and silence.[10] Calle-Gruber interestingly characterises Djebar's quest as a discovery not of identity, but, as I also suggest, of 'la singularité *dans* l'altérité'.[11] Both Calle-Gruber and Clerc see the writer as suspended between cultures and influences, attempting to twist and rework the French language so as to account for the multiple experiences of Algerian women through history and to signal the presence of Arabic and Berber customs alongside the colonial influence. Debra Kelly analyses Djebar's creation of an autobiographical perspective, her sifting through existing historical accounts to elucidate the forgotten perspective of various generations of women, and she argues that Djebar's project is an attempt to situate herself in time and space.[12] In addition, John Erickson, in his *Islam and Postcolonial Narrative*, reads Djebar's novels as the attempted 'coming to voice' of Algerian women, and Hafid Gafaïti similarly conceives Djebar's appropria-tion of the first person as a defiant performance of feminine agency and newly found self-expression.[13] Commentators such as these frequently seem to stress the confidence and self-assertion of Djebar's project, however, and at times risk downplaying her ongoing struggle with writing.[14] Furthermore, few critics have noted the shift occur-ring during the course of Djebar's development away from the search for a voice and towards an acceptance of Algeria's loss. The synthetic special issue of *World Literature Today* (70.4, 1996), published after Djebar won the Neustadt International Prize for Literature, exposes the range of Djebar's engagements, and helpfully explores various currents in her feminist and anti-colonial critique. But the journey of her creativity has not been charted in detail, and though critics have identified the development of certain issues across the different texts, there is no clear demonstration of her changing trajectory.

One alternative view of Djebar's *œuvre* worth noting is that offered by Clarisse Zimra. A leading critic of Djebar's work, Zimra has produced numerous articles analysing not only the texts as individual units, but also their interconnections with other sources.[15] Most importantly, Zimra's contribution to the recent collection *Assia Djebar: Nomade entre les murs…Pour une poétique transfrontalière* argues that Djebar's works should not be read in isolation, each covering a separate, succinct period or theme, but on the contrary, they should be understood as a network of intertextual references. Each text engages in processes of projection and retrojection, picking up and reinventing earlier preoccupations while foreshadowing new developments to be explored in later works. The conceptual framework for this reading is derived from Bakhtin's theory of dialogue, according to which all voices are shaped by their interaction with other voices, bearing the trace of that other influence. In Zimra's words, Djebar's is a

> jeu d'écriture qui demande une lecture en rappel: relire, repartir en amont, retrouver l'endroit où cette image, ce cri, ce détail ont surgi; mais alors, les reprendre en aval, un tel mouvement modifiant l'autre sens. Bref, se déploie alors un régime du sens multiplié, symphonique; ce que Bakhtine nommait «polyphonie».[16]

Characters in the early works resurface in altered form in later texts, and scenes of trauma, resisting resolution, are repeated and re-enacted to produce varying effects. For Zimra, this continual reformulation and reinvention figures Djebar's resistance to containment, her unease with regard to the categories into which readers have attempted to force her. It is as if she never wants a particular version of a scene to be taken as definitive, and she rewrites problematic moments so as to prevent their false resolution. In portraying the prevalence of such reworking, however, Zimra does not pinpoint the changing dynamic of Djebar's engagement and her gradual withdrawal from any possible identification with Algeria as a knowable point of reference.

Taking into account Zimra's contribution, I nevertheless want to read Djebar's journey as a movement through a series of different understandings of subjectivity, while noting that this movement is not a steady and unidirectional unfolding. Djebar juxtaposes conceptions of Algerian identity as 'specific', 'singular' and 'singular plural', and many of the works explore the tension between these distinct ways of conceiving of the writer's subjectivity. She does not argue straightforwardly in the early works for a categorical understanding of Algerian essence, and nor does she leave Algeria definitively in the most recent texts. Zimra's emphasis on repetition, dialogue and re-enactment serves to remind us that Djebar's evolution is not unequivocally linear. Her exploration of Algerian polyphony and diversity is also clearly influenced by the multiplicity of oral, Arabic and Berber traditions that she uses, and her engagement with these traditions is as important as her dialogue with French philosophy. However, I do want to underline the significance of the turning point affecting Djebar's career that coincides with the explosion of violence in Algeria in the 1990s, and the increasing impact that the witnessing of this trauma bears on her work. The notion of an Algerian identity, however elusive in the earlier works, fades even more disturbingly in the later works; and the poetics, and ethics, of hauntology proposed in *La Femme sans sépulture* and *La Disparition de la langue française* offer a new vision of Algeria as a partially lost memory, a present-absent trace. These later works constitute a distinct development in that they leave behind the search for identity once and for all, and replace any lingering desire for an identifiable Algerian culture and genealogy with an awareness of the persistent resonance of the past as well as of its elusive intractability. Reflection on postcolonial Algeria requires a movement outwards, the opening up of categories and the interpenetration of present, past and future, rather than the straightforward swapping of old for new.

I intend in this way to demonstrate how Djebar's reworking of philosophical concepts, together with her progressively more urgent questioning of the identity of the postcolonial Algerian nation, helps to test and challenge notions of positionality, of the specific. Djebar's own history, moreover, is highly unusual, and her position between France and Algeria, colonialism and anti-colonialism, itself shapes her philosophical and cultural engagement. Born in Cherchell in 1936, the daughter of a primary school teacher, Djebar enjoyed the unusual privilege, as a girl, of attending the institution where her father taught, and she gained the sort of education ordinarily available only to boys. She then went to a girls' boarding school in colonial Algeria, where she was one of three or four Algerians out of four or five hundred girls. She was educated in the French system, and remains highly influenced by it, though she keeps a strong sense of the importance of local tradition and, interestingly, compares the closeted atmosphere of the lycée with that of the harem. After graduating from university in Algiers, Djebar proceeded to the khâgne at the Lycée Fénelon in Paris, and was the first Algerian woman to be admitted to the Ecole normale supérieure at Sèvres in 1955. She abandoned her studies before finishing in order to return to Algeria and to write for the Algerian FLN newspaper *El moudjahid*, publishing interviews with Algerian refugees in Tunisia and Morocco during the war of independence, and later teaching history and literature in Rabat and Algiers. Now based in New York, Djebar's trajectory in this way incorporates influences from both France and Algeria, from a colonial, as well as an Islamic, Arabic and Berber, heritage. Elected as a member of the Académie française in 2005, she works securely within a metropolitan literary and philosophical tradition, but strives at the same time to represent the intervention of local oral and Islamic cultures. Her work explores the history of her native land, using at the same time literary and philosophical references from France, and in this sense she is both far from exemplary, and uniquely subtle.

Djebar's journey, through both life and work, combines multiple affiliations with a sense of scepticism, of discomfort, with categorisation and positioning. Hiding behind her pseudonym, which Kelly shows to be etymologically connected to 'healing' and 'consoling', Djebar troubles the identification of her writerly voice rather than offering us a vision of a secure self.[17] Affected by a plurality of cultural currents, she writes in order to sift through their contradictions and interrelations while refusing to amalgamate their influences into an identifiable, fused hybrid. Cramming her texts with literary and cultural references from all over the world, she refrains from adhering to any single inheritance but plays with fragments from different sources. Her tentative 'expatriation', then, is not a refusal but a process of questioning, a challenge to modern Algeria and a drive to open up its borders. Djebar retains Algeria as a reference point, a focus for her search for a sense of history and belonging, but she also continually tries to broaden that focus and to escape the constraints of existing versions. Algeria turns out to be more divided, more conflicted and more multifaceted than expected, and in the later works in particular, becomes ravaged to the point of disintegration. If, in producing an extended and erudite corpus of novels, Djebar hoped to work through the confusion of Algeria's trajectory, from colonialism to civil war and terrorism, she progressively finds that the writing process frustrates her and refuses to offer any clarity or resolution. The French language itself separates her from her Algerian compatriots and places her in an ambivalent position in relation to colonialism, and to Arabisation. But the turbulence of her country's history is such that any narrative of its evolution becomes fragmented, disjointed and ultimately artificial; it is not only the colonial language, but also, on another level, language as such, that distances the writer from the culture she sought to determine. Multiple singular moments in Algeria's war-torn past haunt and elude Djebar's anxious, irresolute project.

Djebar and Postcolonial Theory

Djebar's modulating conceptions of processes of individuation in Algeria also offer a substantial contribution to contemporary postcolonial thought, and it will be worth sketching this background before embarking on an analysis of the novels themselves. Postcolonial thinkers rethink the modes of subjectivation invented by the philosophers discussed earlier, and Djebar's anxious questioning of the status and position of the Algerian subject tests the conclusions of various thinkers. While some commentators, for example, argue that the affirmation of a particular subject position is the only means of resisting (neo)colonial domination, others assert that the dissolution of identitarian categories serves to criticise entrenched hierarchical structures and relations of power. Conceptions of postcolonial resistance waver between the urge to privilege concrete agency and subjectivity on the one hand, and liberation through the deconstruction of all specified subject positions on the other. Djebar's alternating configurations bring out the insufficiencies of both sets of arguments, and propose a more subtle dramatisation of the interaction between a specific identity, singularity and the singular-plural. The opposition between identity and its dissolution can be reformulated as a necessarily simultaneous, multi-layered engagement with these distinct modes of individuation. Postcoloniality is not one position, and indeed, Djebar herself does not use the term, perhaps in the attempt to avoid the creation of a fixed theory. The experience of postcoloniality is changeable, modulating, and demands both engagement with a series of models and a questioning of their status.

First of all, I want briefly to look at Djebar's relationship with the processes of hybridisation championed by Bhabha as characteristic of 'the postcolonial condition'. Weaving through the chapters of *The Location of Culture* is a reflection on *différance*, on temporal and spatial disjunction that learns much from the conclusions of Derrida. Bhabha's deconstructed subjects are disjoined from discourse, they linger in a no-man's land in the interstices between signifier and signified, and in this sense they are singular and changing beings residing outside the national framework. Although national discourses work to position them definitively within a circumscribed category, the hybrid postcolonial subjects discussed by Bhabha become indeterminate shadows hovering in the 'in-between'. This 'in-between' is conceived early on in Bhabha's work as a 'Third Space' that severs the process of enunciation. While 'official' discourses seek to contain their subjects in language, Bhabha reminds us that the framework of the speaker's positionality is dissociated from the actual enunciation produced, leaving an ambivalence at the heart of discourse: 'the pronominal I of the proposition cannot be made to address – in its own words – the subject of enunciation, for this is not personable, but remains a spatial relation within the schemata and strategies of discourse'.[18] The intervention of this Third Space into discourses of specificity means that the representation of that specificity is disjointed and displaced, hovering over without encapsulating the subject's continual self-reinvention.

As in Derrida's work, the relation between discourse and its elusive 'subject' is temporally as well as spatially dislocated. The subject of the enunciation is split by interruptions in both time and space, and there is a lag or discrepancy which means that discourse is never able to catch up with the continually shifting singular moments that it set out to encode. The Third Space detaches the subject from the proposition and artificially freezes it in time. Unlike Derrida, however, Bhabha's orientation here is emphatically cultural. It is particularly discourses of national culture that gloss over the interstices of the singular, and it is our own idiosyncratic experience of culture, resultantly, that resists being unified or fixed. Precisely because any discourse, including that of nationalism, inserts a gap between proposition and referent, any attempt at cultural identification finishes by leaving behind the diverse and changing people it seeks to determine. Thus in 'DissemiNation', a chapter that again owes much to the philosophy of Derrida, the excess of discourse is explored in the context of the disjunctions of national time. What Bhabha terms 'the shreds and patches of cultural signification' exceed the presumed certainties of a nationalist pedagogy, and multiple local temporalities remain discrepant from the broader framework of national time. Furthermore, notions of a shared national past offer a vision that diverges from that of the heterogeneous people, who must constitute themselves without reference to a mythical origin or prior presence. The cultural differences of these people, who split and disintegrate the national discourse, are also themselves emergent, incomplete and evolving rather than adhering to a specified position.

This emphasis on excess and self-differentiation clearly aligns Bhabha with Derrida, as I have suggested, but it is also at this point worth recalling the difficulties associated with his championing of deconstruction and his abandonment of the specific. Certainly the particular workings of national or colonial discourse are a little unclear, since Bhabha at times argues, with Derrida, that all discourses gloss over the vagaries of the singular, while at others he seems specifically to refer to the minority peoples caught between colonialist and nationalist demands. His reflections on the intervention of the Third Space risk getting caught up in an abstract realm that excludes any possibility of a specific engagement with colonial or neocolonial influence in a particular historical context. Djebar's simultaneous dramatisation of Derridean self-singularisation and the demands of a specific engagement with colonial and national history helps to avoid these difficulties of abstraction and historical occlusion. Djebar contextualises and concretises Derrida's theorisation of excentricity by exploring the particular demands of colonial history and demonstrates the need to take a position in relation to that history, despite the difficulties involved in such a process. Moreover, Bhabha's understanding of interaction and plurality lacks some of the nuances of Nancy's, and indeed Djebar's, thought. Whereas Nancy and Djebar both stress the contingency of relations between singular beings, their rupture as well as their recreation, Bhabha seems to champion hybridity as a value in itself. Bhabha's Third Space names a hybridity that becomes too established in its (transcultural) position, and it takes on a determinism of its own. It could be seen to connote fusion, or a completed state of disorder. In this sense Bhabha at times contradicts his own singularising project.

Against Bhabha, another group of postcolonial critics point out the problematic political implications of eradicating any specific subjectivity in favour of a focus on linguistic différance. One of the main objections of thinkers such as Aijaz Ahmad, Benita Parry and

Arif Dirlik is that the rhetoric of theory, of linguistic play and the dissolution of the subject in the *abyme* of representation, is both abstract and self-perpetuating. The emphasis on the floating singular being in the interstices between discourses shifts attention away from the real material conditions of the colonial, and the anti-colonial, project. A thoroughgoing understanding of colonial and postcolonial politics is exchanged, according to Ahmad, for an excessive celebration of the interstices of discourse. As a result, Ahmad's summary of the proposals of poststructuralist theory suggests that 'any attempt to *know* the world as a whole, or to hold that it is open to rational comprehension, let alone the desire to change it, was to be dismissed as a contemptible attempt to construct "grand narratives" and "totalizing (totalitarian?) knowledges"'.[19] Theory as 'inquiry' is replaced by theory as 'conversation', the suggestion of possibilities and the exploration of available narratives rather than an investigation of real events. Ahmad also believes that thinkers such as Bhabha reject Marxism outright without considering the ways in which it can help us to understand colonial ideology. Issues of class are dissolved into issues of culture and representation, and economic factors become masked by discussions of 'the interminable whisperings of Discourse'.[20] Theory itself becomes a commodity, an object of exchange in the marketplace of ideas where empirical reality and materiality are ignored.

The most significant difficulty associated with the emphasis on singularisation and *différance* is the possible eradication of the very notion of conflict. Benita Parry criticises Bhabha's *The Location of Culture* for writing out the inscriptions of conflict in the real world, and for representing colonialism as a space of ambivalence rather than of antagonism.[21] The disintegration of any possible subject position neutralises the confrontations of colonialism, effacing the stark rigidity of colonial manicheism and its paralysing effects. Similarly, the replacement of the subject position with ongoing self-singularisation makes it difficult to conceive of political agency. The invention of a specific position, and in some cases a belief in national determination, is often a powerful and necessary tool for resisting colonial and neocolonial imposition. Even more, for Azzedine Haddour the deconstruction of the binary forms part of the politics of assimilation imposed by the French in Algeria, and it helps to efface the native's difference. The real segregationist politics of colonialism become dissolved, and Haddour argues against the effacement of specified positions by suggesting that 'to reduce difference to a play through which the subject of Western metaphysics is constituted is to deny difference its agency and subjectivity'.[22] Lastly, Arif Dirlik reiterates many of Ahmad's neo-Marxist points, but stresses crucially that the problem with the use of deconstruction by postcolonial critics is that it confuses politics with culture. For Dirlik, oppositional politics do not rely on a conception of oppositional cultures, and a nuanced reflection on questions of identification and self-representation does not preclude the active formation of a resistant subject position.[23]

The difficulty with some of these points is that at times they appear to denounce theory per se without considering the specificity of its intellectual work, and without exploring the subtle differences between the philosophies of singularity outlined in the present introduction. At the same time, the criticism of deconstructive thinking and the celebration of more materialist scholarship rests on the assumption that there is only one way of describing colonialism and its effects. The distinction between political and cultural analysis, however, is perhaps a crucial one that these thinkers themselves ignore when denouncing deconstructive thought. While reflection on historical agency, on the confrontation between subjects in the colonial system, does seem necessary to our understanding of the politics of that system, this does not mean that the underlying processes of self-differentiation or singularisation cease to have relevance. Rather, 'postcolonial subjects' may position themselves in certain ways politically and historically, while remaining uneasy with the ways in which language, and in particular colonial languages, gloss over plural influences and affects. The assumption of a political position does not necessarily imply unequivocal cultural identification, and an awareness of the processes of linguistic *différance* does not foreclose the strategic taking of sides.

Finally, in some senses like Djebar, Gayatri Spivak's work seems to shift between an understanding of the specifications of colonial confrontation and an analysis of the slippage of 'the subaltern', of the minority subject, between identificatory discourses. Her work contains a residual uncertainty regarding the status of the specific subject, as she hesitates between on the one hand emphasising the excess of the singular in relation to discourses that endeavour to pin it down, and on the other describing the implacably confrontational structure of colonial ideology. First, reading *De la grammatologie*, Spivak shows how Derrida's critique of the subject expresses the (perhaps continually unsatisfied) need to preserve an alterity that is 'both ineffable and nontranscendental'. She argues that the logocentrism of European thought has always resulted in this exclusion of the Other, and we need to attend to this 'inaccessible blankness', the singularity that exceeds our grasp, rather than using postcolonial theory to circumscribe its identity.[24] Postcolonial critique is for Spivak not a question of retrieving the Other's voice, of locating a foreign but self-same position. It consists in an appeal to a 'tout autre' that is not self-consolidating but endlessly internally different. Spivak's 'subaltern' is not an oppressed yet self-contained subject; instead it is singular and its contingency resists delimitation or definition.

From one perspective, then, 'Can the Subaltern Speak?' emphasises the contingency of the subaltern and its resistance to identitarian frameworks. The voice of the subaltern seems to be troubled because of its own internal difference, in Derrida's words, 'rendering *delirious* that interior voice that is the voice of the other in us'.[25] At the same time, however, Spivak's emphasis on the incompatibility between the cultural community of the Western reader and that of the writer implies that some sort of specified, identitarian category persists. Spivak's postcolonial critic at times seems to be excluded from the text not because the latter is resistant to totalisation but because of the cultural specificity of both parties. Spivak's famous calls for 'strategic essentialism' contain the same ambivalence, as she seems both to claim the importance of affirming a particular identity or essence and to trouble the very possibility of 'essence' (using the term 'strategic' to distance herself from its implications). She oscillates between underlining the intractable singularity of the subaltern on the one hand, and inserting the text into a binary opposition between self and other, or Western reader and 'postcolonial' writer, on the other. Despite her desire to deconstruct straightforward forms of identity, she at times preserves the opposition between inside and outside, native and non-native, and emphasises the political determinations of each side.

Some readers may see this as an inconsistency in Spivak's work. Indeed, her predilection for the singular sits uneasily with some of the more materialist arguments she asserts, and she repeatedly criticises the application of Western models to other cultures while apparently persisting in using European deconstruction to describe the experience of the native. Even more, Peter Hallward reads both strands of her work, her reflections on 'non-narrativisable subaltern insurgencies' and the critique of the Western institution, as politically vague, 'contra-dictory and aporetic'.[26] Certainly, the slippage between philosophical reflection and political argument can result in some confusion, and her points on minority resistance to Western theoretical doctrine are somewhat unsettled by her ongoing insistence on the inaccessibility of the subaltern subject. The point I would like to make here, however, is that these two modes of thought always and inevitably exist in tension with one another, and neither structure finishes by abolishing the need for the other. Postcolonial thinking requires an awareness of both possibilities in order to evoke adequately the genuine contradic-tions involved in the identification of the postcolonial subject.

Djebar's work provides insight into the persistence of this tension between specificity and self-singularisation. As I have suggested, her texts initially strive to unveil or conceive a specific feminine Algerian identity, rescuing Algerian women from occlusion both by colonialism and by Islamic law, and giving voice to this particular oppressed group. This does not mean that they are passively speci-fied, but that they are positioned in relation to a series of specific influences and negotiate between them. Despite Djebar's belief in the necessity of this project, however, she then troubles the determina-tions of that position. She couples the search for the specific with an investigation of the singularities that resist circumscription, that lie beyond the framework of any particular structure. Furthermore, the singularity she uncovers turns out to be not isolated but plural, as the erasure of the subject is coupled with a proliferation of diverse traces and echoes. Djebar offers no single 'postcolonial theory', but a series of possible models, each of which operates on a different level and none of which can conceptualise postcolonial Algeria in a secure and determinable way.

CHAPTER ONE

The Early Years

Assia Djebar wrote four novels during the first phase of her career between 1957 and 1967. After leaving the Ecole normale supérieure at Sèvres during the war of independence, she worked for the national newspaper *El moudjahid* conducting interviews with Algerian refugees in Tunis and Morocco, before going on to teach history in Rabat and later in Algiers. The novels consist at this stage in a form of experimentation, and the period can be seen as one of apprenticeship in the strategies and techniques of writing. At times highly naive and a little self-indulgent, Djebar's early novels set out to identify her specific concerns as a writer and to develop a sense of the position of women in Algerian society. Occasionally simplistic and often tentative, these works nevertheless testify to a gradual dawn of consciousness, and Djebar creates through the writing of these early texts the seeds of the philosophical and political meditations on specificity and its limits that will characterise her later work. Most importantly, it is possible to chart through the works an awareness of some of the tensions and contradictions that will be developed in her later writing. The women's romantic tribulations recounted in *La Soif* become, by the time of *Les Alouettes naïves*, a far more sophisticated set of reflections on memory, on the relationship between self and other, and on the confused intermingling of the war effort with changes in sexual and gender norms. If at the outset the young author seems preoccupied above all with women's roles and their relationships with men, by the end of this initial phase she adds to such reflections a greater understanding of her political context, and of the broader stakes involved in narrating Algerian women's lives. This awareness is simultaneously coupled with an increasing sense of the difficulties associated with translating into linguistic form some of the singular memories and affects provoked by the complex political and social changes occurring as a result of the war.

The transition from *La Soif* to *Les Alouettes naïves* also inaugurates Djebar's gradual evolution of a philosophy of singularity that will continue to mutate throughout her career. Both *La Soif* and *Les Impatients* remain relatively straightforward in their assessments of female agency and women's gradual evolution of a sense of independence in a society governed by patriarchal convention. Yet the works do already betray a preoccupation with the multifarious relationship between the individual and the collective, the effects of social demands in Foucault's sense, and the simultaneous resistance of the subject to confinement by those demands. Foucault examines the capacity of individuals to transform and remodel themselves, but he also stresses the insidious forces that tyrannise over that process of change, and he shows how society encourages individuals to submit to a whole gamut of dominant forces and ideologies.[1] Foucault's writing on sexuality shows how the self is fashioned in relation to a prescriptive system, propagated by centres of power, and even transgression is shaped by and conceived in relation to that system. Djebar's characters in these works are similarly seeking to establish a mode of behaviour that reconciles personal demands with contemporary social expectations, but their unease in relation to these also suggests that that process of negotiation is an ongoing one, and their 'specificity' is not so easy to define. In experimenting with a variety of preconceived roles, the characters come to realise their own indefinable difference from these roles. It is in *Les Enfants du nouveau monde* and, even more prominently, in *Les Alouettes naïves*, however, that these concerns become explicit, as Djebar starts to dissect more carefully the modulating interplay between singularisation and social or collective demands. In *Les Enfants*, women subtly balance the search for a self with an ongoing engagement with social conventions, and with the construction of a network of activists transforming their patterns of interaction as a result of the war. Female characters question the entrenchment of traditional relationships and begin to redefine themselves by establishing alternative connections with a more open-ended community akin to Nancy's conception of the open-ended encounter between singular, evolving beings. In *Les Alouettes naïves*, this reassessment of patterns of interaction between men and women is combined with a sense of unease regarding the translation of singular wartime encounters into a reliable narrative offering a specified, collective 'national' history. Memories of resistant activity are presented as partially inaccessible and intractable, and the relationships formed during this period of transformation and trauma also serve to destabilise the narrator's search for a secure position both within contemporary society and within a recognisable narrative of Algeria's past.

La Soif

Djebar's first novel, *La Soif*, is a tentative study of the processes by which a young woman achieves self-awareness and a sense of her position in relation to others. Though published in 1957, reflection on the war of independence is surprisingly absent from the text, and the young Djebar, just twenty years old at the time, focuses above all on intimate relationships and on the central character's evolving sense of self. Djebar later disowned *La Soif* as a result of criticisms levelled by the Algerian intelligentsia, who accused her of ignoring the reality of contemporary Algeria, though more recently she has explained her creation as 'une sorte de rêve', an account of her intimate and personal preoccupations at the time.[2] The narrative follows closely the thoughts and actions of a single character, Nadia, and investigates her changing perception of her social role rather than looking beyond the immediate context at historical movements and ruptures. At the outset, Nadia is depicted as somewhat narcissistic. Preoccupied with her own self-image, she seeks the attention of male admirers without consideration for the damage she might inflict. Enjoying the affections of Hassein, she nevertheless becomes bored by his devotion and creates as a more challenging goal the seduction of her friend Jedla's husband, Ali (in order to give her grounds for a divorce). The execution of this project, however, coincides with Jedla's unhappiness at the discovery that Ali fathered a child before marrying. Plagued with further doubts, the newly pregnant Jedla decides to have an abortion and dies during the operation. Pained by the loss of her friend, Nadia by the end of the novel perceives her own selfishness, settles with Hassien and is further reconciled both to her own limitations and to the demands of both society and the other.

In some senses, the novel is a fairly straightforward meditation on youth, social convention and the negotiation of a social role. Djebar portrays Nadia's steady journey towards self-knowledge and seems to conclude that an acceptance of one's own limitations, and an ability to concede to the demands of social interaction as opposed to normativity, are necessary to prevent a descent into narcissism.

Despite the traditional novelistic structure, however, Nadia's character does at the same time seem slippery; the extent of her learning is not really made clear and the narrative refrains from judging her position overtly. While on one level we seem to be witnessing Nadia's self-discovery, on another level it remains uncertain what the nature of that discovery is, and Djebar simultaneously exposes her continual strategies of self-delusion. *La Soif* raises questions regarding the possibility of genuine learning or self-knowledge, displaying and critiquing the roles we enact while also suggesting that we cannot exist independently of those roles. At the end of the novel, Nadia's behaviour is in some ways as artificial or self-conscious as at the beginning, and the 'self' she seemed to be looking for remains as elusive, as singularly evasive, as ever. Though she clearly makes a journey of sorts, Nadia's subjectivity does not achieve the consistency that she had, perhaps, desired.

The novel opens with a tone of apparent profound introspection. Nadia observes the seemingly carefree celebrations of the summer holiday-makers and immediately distances herself from their activities. Detached from the scene and looking in from the outside, she stresses her languid dissatisfaction and contrasts their futile amusements with her own ironic indifference: 'je trouvais je ne sais quel goût amer à ce mois de juillet et à cette plage épanouie comme une femme'.[3] This self-involved detachment characterises much of the narrative, whose perspective remains narrowly focused on Nadia's reactions and thoughts. The early chapters run through some of her relationships with other characters, and her attitude seems frequently to be one of narcissistic disregard. Scorning her sister's acquiescence during pregnancy, she comments 'je n'aimais pas l'air absent, que prenait alors son beau visage', and her judgement of Myriem's husband is equally unremitting.[4] Similarly, she is disdainful towards Jedla and Ali's marriage, mocking their apparent conformity and, after breaking off her own engagement, cherishing her independence and solitude. Djebar focuses on Nadia's sense of herself as an individual, on her refusal of the social roles of marriage and motherhood and her need for isolation and personal self-invention. Reacting against conventions, Nadia expresses no sense of belonging with her community and her perspective is highly individualist. At the same time, however, her gestures of refusal seem excessively self-serving, and her self-description as despondent and 'désabusée à vingt ans' is a cliché, or a constructed image.[5]

While resisting playing conventional social roles, Nadia thus invents an alternative series of guises that, despite their ingenuity, are exposed as equally disingenuous and artificial. Though Djebar champions Nadia's self-assertion, the recurrence of the language of theatre and gaming reveals the character's underlying uncertainty about her identity and her anxious desire for a sense of self that is always missing. Straining against norms in the Foucauldian sense, Nadia tries to locate a secure place for herself only to find that this place is equally conventional. She rejects the demands of her Muslim heritage and celebrates her European appearance, but the positions she invents for herself are no less constricting. For the most part artificial and insincere, she plays a series of roles aimed at seducing Hassein or Ali. In an early scene with Hassein, for example, she claims that she ended her engagement because of him, observing with pleasure and on the sly that 'parce que sa voix seule était ironique, parce que son regard me guettait, me guettait comme un chat, je sus alors que le jeu reprenait'.[6] This notion of gaming or performance recurs in a further episode with Ali, where, in the style of Madame Bovary, Nadia writes the narrative of their relationship using the conventions and tropes of a novel.

> Je m'imaginais déjà les scènes, avec des souvenirs de romans et de films à l'appui. Je jouerais à la petite fille ingénue, provocante à peine, admirant follement Ali. Hassein ne serait pas dupe de mon rôle; il me verrait en train de provoquer le mari infidèle, de tromper l'amie d'enfance confiante.[7]

Here she seems to construct her persona in layers, as she imagines acting out a position within the very confines of a narrative that is itself fictional and performative. Moreover, as in Flaubert, Djebar's ironic reference to novelistic tropes exposes the folly of the search for such a particular, constructed identity and reveals the novel's own structures to be fabulous or self-deluding. If Nadia's fiction of her seduction of Ali is both artificial and convention-bound, then perhaps the fiction of *La Soif* represents the trajectory of its heroine by means of a similar set of normative tropes.

These roles, then, portray Nadia as self-conscious to such an extent that she rejects not only social norms but also any relationship with the other. Her games are self-seeking, undertaken in the name of pride and self-gratification, and her solipsism divorces her from any sense of her possible dependence on others. Her pursuit of self-assertion leads her to ignore the ways in which she relies on and is formed by the relationships she creates with other people. In her games she takes advantage of them and enlists their affections in order to prop up her own self-image. Just at the moment when Jedla offers her Ali, for example, she runs to Hassein in order to conquer the next challenge. Equally, when Ali asks for her support when Jedla is suffering, she confesses that she only despises Jedla, and her relationships serve only to reinforce her vanity and pride. In the place of friendship and openness, she finds a disturbing vacancy, 'de moi, au fond de moi, tout était calme, plein, grave, comme une mer étale'.[8] Significantly, moreover, other characters' perceptions of her leave her indifferent and unperturbed. Hassein observes the shallowness of her preoccupation with herself, noting 'malgré votre émancipation et votre liberté, que les autres filles vous envient, je pense que vous n'en êtes pas arrivée là', and he understands her narcissistic need for admiration better than she does.[9]

Nadia's apparent advancement, at the end of the novel, consists in a realisation of her need for Hassein despite the convention-bound nature of this relationship. If Djebar initially criticises her character's solipsism, by the end we are presented with a humbled version of the heroine who learns to understand herself through her relationship with her partner, with the family and with the community in respect of which she has certain duties. From this perspective, the text moves from a heightened sense of individualism towards a more subtle understanding of the ways in which the individual lives as part of a wider collective framework and must negotiate with the demands of society, even if these remain oppressive. An awareness of the subject's position within a community and a social context troubles any vain quest for self-affirmation. In her final conversation with Jedla, Nadia loses her sense of the distinction between performance and reality, and claims that despite her machinations: 'au fond, on dit de moi que je suis sans patrie. Mais à cette heure, je me sens comme toutes les autres femmes de ce pays, nos mères, nos grand-mères: pourvu qu'elles aient leur foyer, qu'elles puissent servir, obéir à leur époux, c'est tout ce qu'elles demandent...'[10] Nadia's rejection of a motherland, a community and a home ends with this apparent recognition of the impossibility of detaching herself from society. She still abhors its oppressive conventions, but her narcissism has been somewhat tempered.

As I suggested, however, Nadia's evolution and revelation remains open to question. While she is humbled by Jedla's death, the self that she seems to have found through this bereavement remains artificial. Her initial reaction to the tragedy is as self-conscious as any of her roles, as she reflects 'je m'empêtrais dans les mots de responsabilités, de remords, de conscience. Ce n'étaient que des mots.'[11] Furthermore, though her description of her life with Hassein stresses reconciliation, maturity and a movement away from childish ideals, the repeated assertion of her newly found calm suggests that this is another guise that she has chosen to assume. At one moment, she admits that she is still afraid, still troubled by the past, and that the personas she adopts with her husband are falsely acted out: 'c'était si facile d'accueillir joyeusement Hassein tous les soirs, de jouer les rôles qui le séduisaient, ceux de la coquetterie ingénue, de la jalousie têtue ou de la gravité émouvante'.[12] When he asks her what is troubling her, she self-consciously uses the terms that she knows will encourage him to be attentive towards her, and her behaviour remains programmed by created designs. The final pages of the novel draw out this unsettling duality in Nadia's development. Realising her need for Hassein, she endeavours to anchor herself in a secure family environment and to negotiate with the conventions of society. At the same time, she is unable to escape from the confines of her own self-consciousness, and the identity she builds remains disturbingly unreal.

The extent to which Djebar intended to expose this duality remains unclear, and such a persistent anxiety towards identity construction may not initially have been at the forefront of the author's project. Much of the text does seem naive and a little simplistic, and certainly the disregard for the upheavals of 1950s Algeria betrays a somewhat narrow field of vision. *La Soif* was clearly written before Djebar reached maturity and the focus on the self-seeking intrigues of seduction seems trivial in the context of the war. What the text demonstrates, however, is the difficulty involved in escaping conventions and locating a position of one's own. Nadia's movement towards self-understanding remains incomplete and the artifices of identity construction continue to impede her sensitivity to her own mutability. Djebar shows that even when we believe we can save ourselves from the traps of role-playing, Foucault's determinist paradigms come to programme our experience in advance. The desire for freedom and self-invention can be impeded by self-conscious reference to stereotypical models and tropes. Our experience will continue to be shaped by the images and preconceptions that we inherit from both society and fiction. If we dare to look behind these artifices, we risk finding only inconsistency and uncertainty, a process of singularisation that cannot be defined and that it is easier to mask with role-playing.

Before moving on to *Les Impatients*, it is worth considering whether this exploration of models of identity construction might also, obliquely, reflect an unwitting sense of unease with regard to the political situation in contemporary Algeria. Djebar certainly does refrain from speaking out politically here, and the text for the most part seems alarmingly ahistorical. An apparently throw-away comment on colonial language, however, provides additional insight into the exploration of social positionality discussed above. When discussing his ambition to become a journalist, Ali asserts that debates in Algeria have always focused on the position of the colo-niser and on the colonial project, rather than on the mentality of the colonised. Ali concludes that it is this colonised position that requires further reflection, and he affirms 'c'est cela qu'il faut secouer, c'est ce qu'il faut leur dire dans notre langue'.[13] Ali diagnoses the absence of a language in which to express the identity and concerns of the colonised as the principal ill affecting contemporary Algeria. In this way then, although much of the text ignores such political questions, the anxiety regarding identity construction could be read as a char-acteristic of the Algeria of the 1950s, as well as the concern of Nadia herself. The heroine's lack of a genuine sense of self mirrors the coun-try's loss of a language of identity, and her preconceived patterns of behaviour could be mapped onto the imposition of colonial models on a society ill at ease with itself. The absence of a powerful sense of self, and of a language in which to express it, afflicts both Nadia and Algeria more broadly.

Les Impatients

Published just a year after *La Soif*, *Les Impatients* reflects similarly on notions of identity construction, or the search for the specific, in particular in the context of women's subordination and revolt. Once again paying little attention to contemporary political upheavals, the text nevertheless constitutes a subtle exploration of the position of women in modern Algeria and exposes some of the ambiguities underpinning processes of resistance and self-affirmation. Criticising on the one hand the social conventions that imprison women within the confines of marriage and family duty, Djebar nevertheless demonstrates the difficulties involved in creating an alternative position and reveals how an attitude of unthinking defiance can also lead to the re-entrenchment of normative positions. Dalila, the text's heroine, begins by overtly rejecting the demands of her brother, Farid, and her stepmother Lella, to conform to social expectation and uphold the honour of the family. In the absence of the father, Farid occupies the position of the authoritative patriarch, and both he and the other members of the family seem preoccupied above all with the maintenance of traditional custom and the avoidance of scandal or dishonour. Angered by the oppressive rigidity of this social structure, Dalila secretly begins a relationship with Salim, whom she meets on the sly before eventually following him to Paris, against the wishes of the family. Having defied convention in this way, however, Dalila, now engaged to Salim, struggles to reconcile herself with her new position. Though she maintains fictional ideals of romantic love, by the end of the novel she is forced to question her fantasies, to accept the consequences of her actions and to re-evaluate her position in the family.

As in *La Soif*, the text's conclusion remains somewhat ambiguous, conveying once again the problems involved in processes of identity construction and the contradictions inherent in the desire for revolt. Like Nadia, Dalila in some senses evolves as a character and reaches by the end of the text a position of increased maturity and understanding. During her time in Paris with Salim, she gradually recognises the folly of believing that a fictionalised version of romantic love would rescue her from subordination and provide her with a fuller sense of self. And certainly Salim's sudden departure, his accidental death at the hands of Lella's irrationally jealous husband, and her subsequent return to her family, leave her stripped of her whimsical ideals. Nevertheless, the reader of *Les Impatients* is left with a sense of uncertainty regarding Djebar's stance towards the possibility of feminine resistance. While normative social conventions are clearly the focus of Djebar's critique, it remains unclear to what extent Dalila might have been lulled into a disturbingly passive acceptance of her family duty, and to what extent she has succeeded in achieving self-knowledge. Furthermore, Dalila may understand the superficial nature of her initial resistance, but we are left with a sense of doubt about the evolution of any alternative strategy. Djebar does express her dissatisfaction with oppressive conventions in this

novel, but her position with regard to Islam and feminine independence remains indeterminate. Again, her characters work against the
norms of Foucault's 'specific', but struggle nevertheless to accept the
disturbing intractability of the singular.

At the start of the novel, Dalila's distaste for Lella and her conformity with ordinary social expectations is shown clearly. If Lella calls
her a 'sauvage' for not wanting to attend a wedding party, Dalila in
the end acquiesces but once there leaves her companions in order to
lose herself sensually in the dance. Revelling in finding herself outside
the stifling claustrophobia of the cramped family home, Dalila allows
her body to take on a form of autonomy, succumbing to the rhythms
of the music in order to forget the specificity of her environment.
Gradually shifting away from her companions, she moves freely
and as if unconsciously, and subsequently leaves the party in order
to enjoy a solitary journey home. Similarly, in her initial meetings
with Salim, Dalila relishes her departure from social constraints and
notes the natural spontaneity of their connection. Recalling that she
is from a bourgeois Muslim background, she nevertheless finds that
her interaction with Salim is unselfconscious, and she takes pleasure
in knowing that her clandestine meetings with him fly in the face of
convention. Dalila also shuns her friend Mina's women's gatherings,
expressing her lack of interest in 'ces questions qui passionaient les
jeunes lycéennes et étudiantes: problème de l'évolution de la femme
musulmane, problème du mariage mixte, problème des responsabilités
sociales de la femme, problème…'[14] Detaching herself from the Islamic
women's community, Dalila scorns those wives, such as Zineb, who
are controlled by their husbands and criticises not only patriarchal
authority but also women's complicity in the structures that restrict
them. It is also significant that Dalila refuses to wear a veil, even to
ensure entry to a wedding to which she is not invited: 'non. Je n'en
avais pas envie. L'idée de mettre un voile comme un masque puisque,
contrairement à Lella et à Zineb, il ne nous était pas nécessaire, me
répugnait.'[15] Associating the veil with obscurity and occlusion, Dalila
instead defiantly asserts her own agency and desires.

Dalila's relationship with Salim is as a result calculated to serve
as a symbol of resistance. If for the most part she denounces the
constraints of conventional relationships and champions the liberation of women from the demands of patriarchy, she sees her interaction with Salim as an emancipated, life-giving gesture of refusal
towards such demands. Fascinated with the reflected image she

perceives of herself and Salim as a couple, she enjoys the relationship precisely because she imagines that, in its secrecy, it disrupts her family's expectations. It is in this sense, then, that her understanding of her actions is self-contradictory. On the one hand, Dalila celebrates feminine solitude, and observing Zineb's serenity during her pregnancy, she notes: 'j'eus l'intuition que nulle part plus que dans le bonheur, dans la plénitude, la femme ne se sent seule, paisiblement seule, dans une tranquillité riche d'où l'homme est exclu'.[16] She also criticises Arab women's unquestioning submission before their husbands. On the other hand, however, her decision to use Salim as a tool for revolt finishes by reinstating the very repressive structure she set out to overthrow. Having rejected the demands of her family, and having revelled in the 'désordre', the 'scandale' she has caused, her behaviour with Salim is once again submissive.[17] Switching from one convention-bound structure to another, Dalila's search for agency remains unsatisfied and, like Nadia, she loses herself behind the surface of the roles she plays.

As in *La Soif*, a vocabulary of performance and artifice pervades the text, implying once more the difficulty of achieving a genuinely emancipated position of self-assertion. Dalila's project of resistance is couched in theatrical, fictional language that betrays the inevitably stereotypical nature of her gesture and the all-pervasive influence of preconceived models. Even at the moments when she affirms most confidently her individualism, Dalila's behaviour colludes with models gleaned from social myths. After her first argument with Salim and her ensuing accident, for example, she notes the irony of his disappearance, observing that it is 'tel le comparse d'un drame sur lequel le rideau était tombé', and this theatrical vocabulary aptly conveys her self-consciousness, her understanding of her experience in terms of accepted dramatic tropes.[18] Equally, her vision of love is informed by the romantic adventures of novelistic heroines, and at this point her self-satisfaction, like that of Nadia, recalls the idealistic fantasies of Emma Bovary. In an exchange with her sister Chérifa, for example, Dalila glorifies her own embrace of artifice: 'c'était vrai; c'était du romanesque. Je le savais et j'en étais heureuse. Elle, elle serait toujours privée de ce qu'elle me reprochait: du plaisir pétillant d'audace et d'ardeur, des rires, de la jeunesse.'[19] Dalila savours the mythical structure of her self-understanding and rejects the role imposed on her by her family precisely in order to comply with another normative and regulated pattern of behaviour. Most disturb-

ingly, during Salim's absence she remarks 'comme cela était roman-
tique de me vouer à ce rôle de fiancée pure, attendant le retour de
son bien-aimé!' Here, her initial goal of self-affirmation is entirely
subsumed by her desire to play the role of a suffering, tragic heroine.
The position she carves out for herself is as constrained as that from
which she set out to escape.

Dalila's life in Paris with Salim is double-edged. On the one
hand, she strives to believe in the romanticism of their relationship,
and delights in the apparent strength of their passion. She seems
to enjoy the *idea* of an all-encompassing engagement and for this
reason celebrates Salim's exacting power over her. Having earlier
admitted that she would welcome subordination if her 'master' were
a loving husband rather than her duty-bound family, she notes 'je me
délectais des teintes brutales que prenait notre amour'.[20] Moments
of resistance, such as when she goes out without telling Salim, are
juxtaposed with episodes of supplication, where she begs her lover
to continue watching over her and speaks to him in soft, concilia-
tory tones. At the same time, however, while conforming to this role
of the submissive fiancée and allowing this model to programme her
behaviour, Dalila also intermittently rejects this position and questions Salim's authority. Periods of acquiescence are interspersed with
moments of resistance, and after Salim discovers the time she has
spent with Gilberte, she answers in riposte: 'ce que je ne supporte pas,
ce sont tes airs de maître; c'est toi qui m'as obligée à mentir'.[21] Dalila's
attitude to feminine subordination is in this sense riven with contradictions, as she revolts against the role expected of her by her family
and attempts to assert her own needs and desires, only to find herself
once again in a subordinate position. Attempting to find a voice for
herself, Dalila still struggles to negotiate the preconceived patterns
and tropes that determine the different ways in which women and
men interact.

The final pages of the novel seem increasingly ambiguous in this
sense. After discovering Salim's death and returning to her family,
Dalila seems to have reached further maturity, recognising the importance of home after the upheavals of her relationship with Salim.
Finding the old patterns disrupted and upset, with Lella killed and
Farid in prison, Dalila is concerned to help rebuild the family community and to create security for the new generation. The closing motif
of the little boy caught stealing nevertheless leaves Dalila ambivalent and unsure. Hearing the child repeatedly cry out 'ils mentent'

in lyrical Arabic tones, she reflects not on the verity of his crime but on the poetry of his revolt. She perceives in his intonation the trace of her own former rejection of authority, and the repetition of the term 'mentir' is once again suggestive of the falsity and artifice of social roles. Witnessing his quasi-heroic demand for justice, she reconsiders her own uncertain position and contemplates the extent of her compromise. Later on, lying awake and listening to the sounds of the town outside her window, she notes the imprint of the past on the patterns of the present, bringing to the forefront traces of memory that she had believed to be buried: 'les passions que l'on croit mortes et l'orgeuil qu'on croit vaincu, laissent sur leur visage un écho qu'on ne sait définir'.[22] In this sense, Djebar draws attention to the coexistence of reconciliation and revolt, and suggests that both impulses linger within the banks of Dalila's unconscious. Maturity and self-knowledge are subtended by an ongoing sense of dissatisfaction with social demands, and the text concludes by affirming again the illusions and myths of social convention.

If *La Soif* offered us some fleeting insight into Djebar's reactions to colonial imposition, then perhaps *Les Impatients* introduces her readers to what will become an urgent preoccupation with the position of women in contemporary Algerian society and in Islam. In this early and under-developed text, the author voices her rejection of social structures of repression and invites us to reflect on the importance of self-assertion in contradistinction to normative demands. *Les Impatients* exposes some of the myths and stereotypes that inform female behaviour and criticises not only the enforcement of family duties but also the authoritarianism of men over their partners or wives. Nevertheless, the process of carving out an alternative position is portrayed as uncertain and irresolute. Djebar does reinforce the importance of community and leaves open the question of what sorts of female agency can be maintained. Foreshadowing texts such as *Ombre sultane* and *Vaste est la prison*, *Les Impatients* asks how Algerian women position themselves in relation to Islam and social convention without providing a definitive response. If this early text is in this sense somewhat tentative and inconclusive, this unease points precisely towards the difficulty involved in modern Muslim women's search for a position and a sense of self. This engagement with the specific, with social norms and their limits, results not in self-definition but in the discovery of the impossibility of such a definition.

Les Enfants du nouveau monde

Les Enfants du nouveau monde constitutes Djebar's first step towards a more political mode of reflection. Published at the end of the war in 1962, the work marks the beginning of a prolonged interrogation concerning the nature of women's contributions to the war effort and the effects of the conflict on their processes of self-construction and individuation. Though tentative, Djebar builds on her existing reflections on women's uneasy struggles against traditional or preconceived roles, and couples this uneasiness with an exploration of emerging conflicts between more overtly political, as well as social, demands. Most importantly, the text develops further the search for an alternative form of identification in contradistinction to that imposed by patriarchal norms and family life. Djebar notes that the war heralds new forms of questioning, and the text uncovers diverse forms of feminine resistance, both overt and tacit, forgotten by more mainstream accounts both of Algerian women's position during the war and of the experiences of the maquisards. The work also champions solidarity between women in defiance of their husbands and challenges the uncomplicated celebrations of communal resistance upheld in the discourse of the Front de Libération Nationale in order to emphasise the female characters' differing, independent reactions to the cause. This investigation of singular disengagement from familiar roles nevertheless does not herald the unmediated embrace of individualism and self-knowledge. The text foregrounds the network of connections between characters while also stressing that they cannot be known as wholly self-contained and self-present agents (as Nancy told us, such a completed subject does not exist). Women learn to step outside the communal norms imposed on them by society, but this process of singularisation and relational self-construction remains tentative and incomplete rather than assured. The new forms of sharing between different women with varying backgrounds also bear the traces of the more normative social demands they wanted to leave behind.

Before embarking on a reading of *Les Enfants du nouveau monde*, it is worth noting that the role of women during the Algerian war of independence is a subject of much contention. It is not something that is discussed in detail in French histories of the conflict, and in the aftermath women's contributions were similarly very much played down by Algerian public memory. As Michèle Perrot points out in her preface to Amrane-Minne's collection of interviews with women combatants, these courageous individuals have subsequently been forgotten at once by politics, by social organisation and by collective memory. Although Fanon predicted in 'L'Algérie se dévoile' that women's active contribution to the war effort would lead to their increased and long-awaited emancipation in Algerian society, successive governments since independence have limited rather than promoted the liberation of women. Social expectations regarding women's roles in the home and their rights in relation to their husbands have become more rather than less restrictive. Ironically, though they helped to free their country from occupation and oppression, the activity and agency of the female combatants was quickly seen as a threat to Islamic values and as a collusion with what was seen as Western individualism. As a result, after the war women were forced back into traditional roles, their achievements were forgotten, and they became again invisible. Critics have begun to explore this phenomenon and to uncover the lost traces of female testimony, but multiple singular experiences remain overshadowed by grand, patriarchal narratives of insurrection produced by both French and Algerian politicians and historians.

Fanon's famous essay 'L'Algérie se dévoile' focuses on one aspect of women's participation in the resistance movement: the use of the veil and the new connotations it acquires. First, Fanon notes how the French colonisers believed that by denouncing the veil as a symbol of oppression, they would win over Algerian women and convince them of the benefits of the colonial presence. Contrary to this expectation, however, Algerian women instead sided with their compatriots and turned the erroneous expectations of the colonisers to their advantage. Without arousing suspicion, they were able to transport money and weapons, and conveyed messages to the guerillas. This activity, according to Fanon, took two different forms and evolved during the course of the war. Initially, women shed their veils and calmly walked the streets carrying information and helping to plan individual attacks. Presenting themselves in European style, they hid bombs in handbags that French soldiers omitted to search. Later, however, women again took up their veils and used the excess folds of the fabric they wore to conceal bombs, grenades and machine-gun clips. This project is for Fanon doubly subversive, since it contributes practically to the war effort, while also symbolically denying the value of the imposed cultural practices of the coloniser and affirming Algerian (and Islamic) difference. Finally, Fanon celebrates the truly revolutionary nature of this moment, since it constitutes the separation of the veil from tradition and signals its redeployment as a tool for liberation, both of Algerian society and of women. Confident in his affirmation of the progress and innovation symbolised by this redeployment, Fanon optimistically, though prematurely, predicts 'ce sont les exigences du combat qui provoquent dans la société algérienne de nouvelles attitudes, de nouvelles conduites, de nouvelles modalités d'apparaître'.[23]

Crucially, however, works by Djebar and research by historians and militants such as Amrane-Minne highlight not just one type of contribution, but a whole variety of strategies undertaken by women in their desire to participate in the war effort. If Fanon stresses the subversive bravery of urban women helping to plant bombs and hiding weapons beneath the folds of their veils, these other sources emphasise how women's resistant activity was diverse and multifaceted, and was not limited to urban areas. Their participation in the conflict was shaped by, and in turn helped to refashion, their existing relationships with each other and with men. Fatima Benosmane, for example, interviewed in Amrane-Minne's collection, was a militant activist and a nationalist before the war began, and helped to form the *Association des femmes musulmanes algériennes*. Her testimony notes the diverse forms of the contributions made by women, such as those who housed militants from other regions when they came to meetings in Algiers, and she underlines at the same time the important sense of solidarity she derived from meeting other radicals, even in prison. Other witnesses demonstrate the ways in which women were emancipated through their work with the maquis, where relations between women and men were more egalitarian than in other sectors of society, but where women were also subjected to torture in the same unspeakable ways as their brothers. A further example is that of the famous Zohra Drif, who helped in the plotting of the Battle of Algiers, yet who similarly celebrated women's courage and defiance in the face of adversity: 'nous étions conscients de notre faiblesse, mais nous avions la conviction terrible que tous les paras du monde n'arriveraient à rien contre nous'.[24] Such statements testify to the extraordinary determination of the combatants, despite their limited resources.

Few of Djebar's characters exude the confidence of a fighter such as Zohra Drif, but it is significant that *Les Enfants du nouveau monde* paints women gradually learning to carve out a political role. Chérifa, for example, though tentative and secluded, makes a vital transition from acquiescence with her role as a cloistered wife to an increased understanding of her relationship with society and contemporary politics. Djebar's text charts the moment of her awakening, where 's'empare d'elle un désir étrange et qui l'inquiète, de faire quelque chose, quelque chose d'audacieux dont l'éclat étonnerait Youssef'.[25] While the moment is at the same time one of confusion, it marks the crucial instant of her shift away from passivity into more positive action. Even if her initial gesture of resistance consists merely in leaving the house unsupervised, the courage of her decision is emphasised almost as much as that of women such as Salima, who undergo torture at the hands of the French. Similarly, Lila's decision to live alone signifies a considerable step towards liberation and independence, and her desire to 's'ouvrir au nouveau monde qui ne serait plus seulement celui des autres' is at once anti-patriarchal and anti-colonial.[26] Djebar seems to imply that the war saw the emergence of a new set of configurations in relationships both between men and women and between coloniser and colonised. More radically, Salima's engagement in the independence movement is linked to her role as a protector within the family and her resolution to 'se conduire comme un homme' in both contexts.[27] For Hassiba, working in the mountains with the maquis is a sign of defiance and power.

In this way, *Les Enfants du nouveau monde* serves to uncover the multiple facets of the characters' engagements and informs us that there is no single version telling the truth of women's activity during the war. Tracing the events of a single day, the novel juxtaposes sections featuring its manifold characters in order to dramatise the simultaneity of their divergent experiences. In doing so, it presents a set of alternative histories to those sanctioned by either French or Algerian dominant discourses and reveals how women's multiple singular involvements resist categorisation according to familiar expectations and roles. If war has typically been seen as masculine territory, Djebar displays all the myriad events and experiences that such a perception ignores. As Miriam Cooke argues, this multiplicity of feminine experiences is also itself something that was crucial in particular to the Algerian war of independence, as stereotypes of the masculine coloniser versus the feminine oppressed were prevalent in both colonial and anti-colonial discourse. Cooke points out precisely that Fanon's 'stratégie femme' did not consist in women playing the roles of men but in a new, unprecedented type of warfare relying on women's underground help, but it is important now that such roles are not conceived as newly deterministic or stereotypical.[28] As a result, in presenting a plurality of differing feminine viewpoints on the war, Djebar represents both the unique nature of the Algerian combat and the importance of remembering the diverse forms that the combat took. In resisting the entrenchment of stereotypes dictating men's roles as heroic soldiers and women's passive observance, the text portrays multiple unprecedented anti-colonial strategies and the singularity of their diverse agents. Djebar challenges assumptions concerning war and divisions of gender, and she depicts the ways in which the Algerian conflict affected men and women and their roles in both the public and the private sphere.

In noting the beginnings of women's political activism and posi-tive contribution to the struggle for independence, however, Djebar, unlike Fanon, is not prematurely celebratory of their emancipation. Characters such as Salima and Hassiba actively participate in the fighting, but their stories are not central to the novel, and much more time is spent unpicking the complex intricacies of Chérifa and Lila's relationships with their husbands. Both characters take steps to affirm their independence and seek to transgress the limits of the social roles they are expected to play, but Djebar is very hesitant in suggesting their liberation and ultimately stresses the continued subjugation of women in modern Algerian society. Chérifa does question her rela-tionship with Youssef, but he continues to dominate her thoughts, and it is difficult to forget the initial descriptions of her powerlessness in the face of his sexual desire: 'elle savait, depuis le début, qu'elle n'aimait pas cet homme; elle savait aussi effacer de sa mémoire tout souvenir de leurs furtifs contacts nocturnes, «son devoir d'épouse», disait-on'.[29] Later in the novel, when Youssef departs to the mountains, Chérifa remains in the passive position of waiting for him alone, even if she also tacitly rejects that position. In the case of Lila, Ali's desire to idealise her is clearly itself a means of exerting power over her, and though it is also a sign of his own weakness, Lila experiences it as a threatening expression of foolish male pride. Her gradual, periodic ruminations on her position in relation to him then constitute less a refusal than a realisation of her own needs and desires. Though frus-trated by his intransigence, she nevertheless acknowledges the depths of their bond.

The transformations undergone by characters such as Lila and

Chérifa constitute not a straightforward celebration of individual agency and emancipation, but rather a gradual process of negotiation between the singular self and various collective demands. Djebar traces here not the straightforward 'coming to voice' of a single character but the simultaneous shifts experienced by a group of characters learning to reconcile private goals with common visions and needs. In this sense, her exploration is not a simple rejection of a stereotypically Muslim form of communitarianism, nor is it an uncomplicated embrace of European individualism, but a complex attempt to combine aspects of both positions. As the critic Gordon Bigelow points out in his article on *Les Enfants du nouveau monde*, while Djebar is apparently building on the modernist tenets of Fanon and Bourdieu in her investigation of her characters' sense of agency, at the same time she underlines both the ongoing influence of the traditional community and the necessity for new sorts of links.[30] The novel questions entrenched patterns of kinship and dwelling, but it refrains from rejecting them outright, and instead combines aspects of habitual forms of communal interaction with increased stress on relationships between women. Characters start to doubt the suitability of conventional family structures and forge new sorts of relationships, without, however, leaving their old bonds entirely behind. Reflections on women's changing status, and their degree of self-awareness, are interspersed with an acceptance of the lingering effects of the traditional past.

Djebar's subtle musings on relationships within and between the sexes are reflected in the manner in which she hesitantly unveils their intimate form. On one level, *Les Enfants du nouveau monde* consists in a revelation of its female characters' inner ruminations; it uncovers hidden aspirations and longings that do not fit in with traditional social conventions regarding women's roles. Djebar allows her characters to express intimacies that would usually have remained taboo, she provides insight into their private reflections, and in so doing partially lifts the veil on their dissatisfaction, their sense of unease with outworn patterns of behaviour and interaction. At the same time, however, Djebar's disclosures are hesitant and fleeting and her insights take the form of brief scenes interrupted before any falsely reassuring conclusion is reached. The novel dwells on each character only briefly and intermittently, cutting between chapters entitled with different characters' names, and the exposure of their inner reflections takes the form of a succession of incomplete fragments. The text covers only a moment in their fraught and complex lives, offering glimpses of past events and future expectations while refusing to put forward too clearcut an image of their fate. On one level, this fractured structure sketches the very form of the open community of singular beings, interacting with one another without presenting themselves as wholly secure or self-present agents. The novel offers a collective vision of modern Algerian women but structurally refuses to present their multiple voices as definitive or fully evolved. On another level, it suggests that Djebar also remains ambivalent regarding the future emancipation of Algerian women and seems cautious of celebrating their liberation prematurely. Wary of predicting too radical a change, she prefers to hint at a shift in modes of perception while refusing to categorise and determine that shift from the outside. Chérifa and Lila also remain partially 'veiled', both because they do not separate themselves definitively from the authority of their husbands, and because their lives resist evaluation by Western or European readers who cannot grasp and appropriate the precise dilemmas they each, in their singular ways, are forced to face.

Like *La Soif* and *Les Impatients*, *Les Enfants du nouveau monde* focuses on women's roles during a period of radical revision and change. All three of these early works expose the inequality and injustice of entrenched patterns of behaviour for men and women, and they tentatively set about proposing alternative modes of life for the heroines on whose experiences they dwell. Highly uncertain of the potential nature of any alternative practice, the novels nevertheless depict women experimenting with various strategies, working through the limitations of those strategies, and struggling to surmount the contradictions underpinning their desired critique. It is *Les Enfants*, however, that explicitly combines this inquiry into gender roles with political reflection on the position of Algeria during the war of independence and with an overt denunciation of the French colonial project. In this text, Djebar critiques *both* the subordination of women in Algerian society *and* the violence inflicted upon Algerians by colonisers fighting to retain control of the territory. She exposes the dislocation experienced both by women reassessing their relationships with their husbands and by a nation of Algerians struggling to evolve a politics of resistance in response to a colonial project that dispossessed them of their land.

This double critique demands, however, perhaps a final word of caution. A characteristic of much of Djebar's work in the later period, the simultaneous denunciation of colonialism and patriarchy never-theless risks conflating two distinct sources of oppression and two contrasting strategies of resistance. As we shall see, in texts such as *L'Amour, la fantasia*, Djebar explicitly combines colonial and femi-nist critique, most notably in the opening image of the invasion of Algiers, described in terms of the violation of a bride on her wedding night. Though the text is subtle and telling in its dissection of diverse discourses of oppression, passages such as this do require careful unravelling of the different forces of subjugation at play. Similarly, *Les Enfants du nouveau monde* is enthusiastic in its exploration of Algerian women's 'prise de conscience', but the very notion of the new world seems to conflate the birth of independent Algeria with the social emancipation of women. Certainly, as Fanon told us, the war did herald a unique moment of questioning, but of course this vision turned out to be an illusion, and decolonisation did not bring a radical improvement in the equality of social relationships. Characters such as Salima and Hassiba do actively engage in the combat, speaking out in the name of national liberation, but we need to preserve a sense of the difference between the colonial enemy and the social apparatus that restricts Chérifa and Lila as they interact with their husbands. Women's struggle, as Djebar shows, involved a set of singular-plural strategies and processes, and the overly facile conflation of these with the nationalist cause risks eliding the complex conjunction of singular difference and supportive interaction that Djebar set out to uncover.

Les Alouettes naïves

The last of the novels written in the early period, *Les Alouettes naïves* again focuses on Algerian identity and the increasingly troubled evolu-tion of its conceptualisation as a result of the war of independence. Djebar develops her analyses of women's roles during the conflict and further tests the limits of social conventions in positioning and circumscribing their individuation, but she also considers more broadly the memory of the trauma of the war and the disorientation of postcolonial Algeria. The leading narrator, Omar, is a man, and the focus shifts between his own past experiences in the maquis and his relationship with Nfissa, the girlfriend of his brother Rachid, with whom he is also in love. Omar struggles to grasp the fraught connec-tion between his fractured memories and the patterns of interaction occurring in the present day, and the work is constantly interrupted by the haunting resurgence of a past that resists rationalisation and resolution. Omar's own memories are also interspersed with references to and insertions from Nfissa and her sister Nadjia's lives, and Djebar evokes their singular struggles as women making sense of the political and social changes occurring at the time. In both cases, the novel combines concern for the actual, 'specific' changes undergone by men and women during the war with examination of the resistance of singular past events to a linear narrative sketching a clear process of development or change. Foreshadowing the concerns of *Le Blanc de l'Algérie*, Djebar shifts in this novel away from social and cultural analysis towards a more complex investigation of the sense of temporal disjunction, retrojection and revenance that impedes the invention of a postcolonial Algeria for men and, perhaps in different ways, for women. The text is uneasy about its capacity to represent the unsettling events of the past and to explain the positioning of characters in the present, self-consciously moving back and forth in time while displaying the traps and loopholes that disrupt the smooth progress from one epoch to the next. In this way, the search for the specific, the working through of social determinations in Foucault's sense, gives way at times to a Derridean investigation of the singular excess of narrative and the shadows of the past, the other, that it excludes.

The title of the novel itself evokes some of the difficulties involved in this process of narrating Algeria's past, and perhaps in particular the singularity of Algerian women. Djebar explains in the preface that French soldiers referred to the dancers of Ouled-Naïl as 'les Alouettes naïves', mispronouncing their unfamiliar name. She goes on to note that these prostitute-dancers existed only for the soldiers and tourists, but that nevertheless, they remain 'fidèle encore (oh! si confusément, si faiblement) à un rythme ancien, et à l'ombre de notre vrai style'.[31] This suggests that what is striking about the dancers and their renaming by the French is the combination of exoticism and rewriting with traces of an original, ancestral past. The French soldiers on the one hand deform the name of the dancers, distorting it so that the sounds become familiar in their own language. They eradicate linguistic difference by appropriating the name of the other and adapting it so that it fits within their own framework of knowledge. Furthermore, their enjoyment of the dancers is bound up with their desire to control the territory, and the possession of Algerian women functions as a symbol of continued French power over the colony. On the other hand, however, Djebar points out that the elusive past of the dancers is something that will always escape the French imaginary, since it subsists only in the form of fleeting rhythms and movements imperceptible to the untrained eye. The movement of these dancers mimes both French control over Algeria and the limits of that control, the recesses of memory that it is unable to incorporate into its own narrative of the nation's past. This coupling of reinvention with the hazy resurgence of lost rhythms also ultimately structures the novel as a whole, as the narrator attempts to come to terms with the immediate past of the resistance movement. The image figures the conjunction of the francophone narrative with a set of memories foreign to that language.

Before moving on to discuss the representation of women in the body of the novel, however, it is worth dwelling on the male narrator's own sense of unease as he recalls his activities in the maquis. In this sense, the initial impetus of the writing is the occlusion effected by colonial power rather than patriarchy, and Djebar analyses an Algerian male perspective on the trauma of resistance and the halting process of reinvention before returning again to the question of femininity. Descriptions of meetings and events in the present, then, are frequently and intermittently interspersed with images of significant moments from Omar's past, and he seems on one level to want to hold on to these memories, to mark their importance and to incorporate them into a meaningful narrative of progress. The novel opens, for example, with a description of Omar's arrival at a refugee camp shortly before reaching the border. The passage begins with the question 'comment oublier le spectacle?', and is followed by the enumeration of a series of details, as he examines the atmosphere, the expressions on people's faces, observers' comments.[32] While noting the theatricality of his reconstruction, Omar wants to pinpoint every aspect of the scene, to note each detail in such a way that the moment transcends its temporality and achieves further resonance in the present. Similarly, Omar's memories of his brother Rachid are minutely detailed and he lingers on each aspect of his figure as if in an attempt to recapture the absolute singularity of the moment:

> Il me suffit de fermer les yeux pour retrouver l'allure de sa démarche qui m'avait frappé avant que je le reconnusse. Il avançait, silhouette haute, léger balancement des épaules qu'il avait larges, un peu courbées toutefois d'une façon esquissée qu'on ne remarquait que

> lorsque ainsi il se hâtait, ressemblant, je perçois à présent, à quelque
> oiseau des mers du large frôlant les flots dans un vol orgueilleux:
> derrière la protection des ailes amples, dans le sillon tracé au sein
> de l'azur, d'autres oiseaux le suivent, prêts, sinon, à se laisser fléchir
> de lassitude.[33]

In this passage, Omar dwells at length on the subtle tonality of
Rachid's gesture, in the hope of encapsulating its multiple layers
and implications. He at once cherishes the contingency of the ineffable moment and, curiously, strives to identify its transcendence. In
isolating Rachid's silhouette in this way, Omar extracts the moment
from its temporal context and seeks, paradoxically, to recreate its
intractable singularity in permanent form.

Les Alouettes naïves is littered with such moments, where the
narrator piles up the details of his memories in an attempt fully to
grasp their resonance. Moreover, interspersed with recollections of his
friends' and compatriots' actions and emotions are more disturbing
evocations of experiences that re-emerge in the present because their
trauma resists the reassuring patterns of chronological progression.
Some of these fragments reconstruct scenes from the prison. In one
episode, Omar tells his companions in Tunis of a game he played in
his cell, whereby he would hold his face up to the light of the window
only to turn away so quickly that the dark room itself seemed to
be bathed in light.[34] This moment evokes Omar's desire to illuminate the shadows of his confinement, to establish clarity in the hazy
unease of a moment of despair. A similar search for clarity or understanding characterises Nfissa's recollections of Karim's death, as the
text retraces the details of his passing and the reactions of friends
and bystanders to the loss. As in the description of Rachid, minute
details follow one another in quick succession and fleeting observa-
tions are piled on top of each other in a proliferating sequence with
no resolution. Women's cries and chants, the agitation in the village,
the distant light of a fire all mark the moment of trauma and, in the
absence of a proper burial assuring formal commemoration, echo or
flicker hauntingly in the present.[35]

The repeated resurgence of such irresolute memories is juxtaposed,
however, with a persistent sense of loss. If the novel intermittently and
obsessively returns to the past in order to hold on to its singularity,
or to attempt to confer sense on the intractable, it also represents
that past as always partially inaccessible to the present. Revocations
of significant moments are frequently frustrated, interrupted by the

demands of present circumstances and resistant to recreation through language. Omar's reminiscences about his time with Rachid in the maquis are interspersed with confessions of amnesia, and he wilfully recreates selected details by conflating them with other moments:

> Oui, j'ai tout oublié: les premiers mots de Rachid, mon élan; cette hésitation dont je parle, j'insiste pour dire que je la reconstitue comme il m'arrivera de reconstituer d'autres éléments de cette histoire en m'appuyant sur les couches de notre passé, en spéculant sur ce fonds commun que, jamais comme en cette rencontre imprévue, je n'avais senti aussi important pour moi.[36]

Passages such as this remind us that the memories recounted are incomplete shadows that fail in their project to revivify the past and to transgress the boundaries between epochs. Memory is bound up with myth, or with fiction, and the indistinct traces of past affects and moments only re-emerge as a result of the writing process. The text recreates not the precise activities of the maquis but the murky trauma of their effects, as an intervening narrator reflects: '*ce n'est point le passé qui revient, seulement sa moiteur; ce n'est pas le gloire d'autrefois et les pas des combattants de la nuit qui remontent, mais la montagne par-dessus la ville nue qui gémit*'.[37]

The relocation of memories, and the realisation of their loss, results in a text that both explores and unsettles temporal sequence. The narrative shifts back and forth in time and the narrators remain uncertain of how to figure the relation between past and present. Traces and hints of lost moments interrupt Omar's experiences and activities in the present day, and these at once unsettle the expected progression of sequential time *and* remind us that the recesses of the past are never wholly accessible. Contingent moments at times expand beyond their contexts and resurface in the present day with defiance. Foreshadowing Djebar's much later reflections on spectral resurgence in *La Femme sans sépulture* and *La Disparition de la langue française*, such moments undermine any efforts at secure resolution, they stretch the limits of contemporaneity and haunt present experience with ghosts that refuse to be buried. At other times, these ghosts seem more tentative and figure only their own absence so as to reinforce the irrevocable separation between distinct periods in time. The transfer of memories across temporal boundaries is revealed as an unsatisfactory and incomplete process, announcing not a renewed connection but irrevocable loss. In both cases, however, temporal progression is not rhythmic and predictable but insecure, lurching, subject to sudden movement in either direction. Chronology is not steady but disturbingly uneven, broken by abrupt shifts, projections and retrojections, as well as gaps. In describing how he shares memories with his 'brothers' or compatriots in Tunis, for example, Omar admits 'je trace ces lignes non pas, comme je le souhaiterais, chaque jour, mais par à-coups, une fois tous les mois, tous les deux mois, dans ces éclaircies écrivant toutefois deux, trois ou plusieurs soirées consécutives'.[38] Reconstruction consists of sudden rushes of memory disrupted by bouts of amnesia and loss.

Recurrent images of frontiers serve to delineate this uncertain relationship. First, the text is divided into sections entitled 'autrefois', 'au-delà' and 'aujourd'hui', as if to separate past from present in a neat and ordered way. The 'autrefois', for example, names another time, apparently distinct from the present day. Despite these headings, however, the narrative of each section does not adhere to a single epoch but itself moves backwards and forwards in time. In this way, the reader is at once reminded of the distinct phases of Omar's experience and confronted by their curious blurring. The division of past from present becomes, as I have suggested, not a secure ordering but part of a struggle between amnesia and uncontrolled resurgence outside the patterns of ordinary sequence. The 'aujourd'hui' is by no means simply the present, but projects both backwards and forwards, and each moment is shadowed by traces of other times. Moreover, the 'au-delà' evokes a beyond that exceeds categorisation; it names not a specified moment or experience but a further process of projection. The 'au-delà' is temporal excess, it is composed of reconstructions that do not fit into a single framework but that stand apart, either because they remain intractable or because they defy the secure resolution implied by linear time. On a further level, the novel hovers not only at the borders between epochs but also in the in-between space separating Algeria from Tunisia. These frontiers are, similarly, not neat geographical divisions but spaces of insecure transition, demarcating the limits of the nation but also opening out onto its spectral other. In passing between Algeria and Tunisia, characters enter a space of exile haunted by the uncertain history of their native land, itself in its moment of creation. The geographical border also connotes a temporal disjunction, not so much a separation, but a point at once of projection and reversal.

This complex interplay between memory and loss, between presence, absence and the 'au-delà', also figures women's occluded contribution to the Algerian conflict, and Omar's narrative both contains, and is interrupted by, glimpses of the war from a feminine perspective. Djebar focuses in this novel not only on Omar's own unsettled relationship with the past, but also, as in *Les Enfants du nouveau monde*, on the representation of women's roles within that past, and it is women's memory in particular that slips outside reconstructed narratives of events. Djebar is certainly fascinated by the psychological mechanics of Omar's sporadic recollections, but the text also engages in particular with women's exclusion from history books on the war and with the subsequent denial of their contribution within Algerian society. As the title of the novel itself suggests, women's activities have been twisted and appropriated by various discourses of oppression. Nfissa, for example, though a source of fascination for Omar, is portrayed more as Rachid's lover than as a resistance fighter and much of her experience in the maquis is shrouded by amnesia. The narrator reminds us that her reaction to events consists in turning resolutely towards the future, but the result is also that her personal history of this period becomes lost to the text. Her sister, and to some extent her alter-ego, Nadjia, continues to work for the war effort carrying bombs, and it is through the inclusion of just a few fragments describing Nadjia's experiences that Djebar draws attention both to her contribution and to the lack of public knowledge regarding such activities. Brief sections in italics allude to her bravery and suffering at the hands of the French, offering a glimpse of her trauma while refraining from inserting that trauma into a complete and falsely resolute history:

> *Bien sûr, c'était visible, elle avait simulé la folie, muette à travers les crochets de toutes leurs questions, invulnérable en dépit de leurs tristes stratagèmes, tendue dans le silence, mais celui-ci était devenu voyage fluide, depuis ce jour où elle avait cherché à s'échapper, où la sentinelle avait tiré et où elle s'était effondrée dans son sang.* [39]

Sections such as these break up Omar's reflections on his own past and voice hints of a woman's narrative for the most part shrouded from view. As Emily Tomlinson argues in her article on *Les Alouettes naïves*, these passages give voice to 'the living dead', Algeria's unburied, those alienated from the scene of both political and philosophical representation but who in Djebar's narrative refuse to remain packaged away in the past.[40]

Omar's self-conscious musings on the relationship between past and present are in this way interrupted by brief fragments of alternative realities unrecognised by patriarchal discourse. Women's histories are included as curtailed interjections, partial glimpses that stand apart both from official narratives and from Omar's own hesitant life story. Images of Nadjia's courage, and her trauma after being tortured by the French, are the most disturbing of such passages, and their brevity and opacity contribute to the reader's sense of the resistance of such violence to forms of linear explanation appropriate to French history books. Other passages, however, are curtailed not because they speak of repressed horrors but because they evoke a women's world of rituals, belonging and complicity, with a language or idiom foreign to that of the patriarchal society. Certain sections dwell on the intimate relationship between Nfissa and Nadjia, for example, and convey a subtle sense of female solidarity. In one fragment, Nadjia remembers the village where they spent their childhood, the movement of the dancers and the young girls' silent dreams, created as they sit and observe.[41] Other passages offer visions of the life of Omar's mother, Lla Toumia, and they recount the hidden, unspoken effects of the war on local women. French soldiers tell the villagers to dance for them, for example, and take photographs in order supposedly to educate their compatriots on the minutiae of local custom, though as the title of the novel indicates, it is evident that in so doing they reappropriate those practices for their own purposes.[42] The inserted descriptions in italics, in response to this reappropriation, attempt to recount such events from the stolen perspective of the women themselves. Women's resistance during the war, termed by Fanon the 'stratégie femme', is translated here into a women's language, akin to Irigarary's 'parler femme'. As Tomlinson points out, these are points of rupture that creep in between the lines of the main text and convey an idiom or syntax of their own.

This 'parler femme' expresses most importantly an alternative language that refuses to conform to the demands of historical narrative and that supersedes Omar's own struggle with memory. It is not necessarily proper to women as opposed to men, and does not designate a distinct feminine specificity, but rather evokes a diverse set of rhythms and traces excluded from official accounts. It reflects feminine complicity, not in order to demarcate male and female communities, but to give voice to subjects who have for the most part been deprived of expression and whose broken memories lie beyond the frontiers of accepted historical knowledge, as a result of both colonialism and patriarchal custom. Like Omar's recollections, these sections disrupt temporal linearity and explore the complex processes of projection and retrojection that structure singular memory narratives, but while Omar still searches for order and understanding, the interjections in italics contain no such struggle. Djebar presents a series of singular viewpoints without attempting to rationalise and contextualise their content, and she refuses to conclude or resolve the experiences they convey. Irigaray's language of the 'parler femme' is appropriate here then, not so much because it defines feminine specificity, but because it connotes singular movement rather than the construction of a rational grounded subject. The 'parler femme' allows different speakers to blur with one another, and it expresses dialogue or exchange as opposed to self-knowledge. Irigaray describes women's symbolic 'value' in terms of this sort of sharing or complicity, arguing: 'la valeur d'une femme échappe toujours: continent noir, trou dans le symbolique, faille dans le discours... Ce n'est que dans l'opération de l'échange entre femmes que quelque chose – d'énigmatique, certes – peut s'en pressentir.'[43] Similarly, Djebar's inserted narratives interrupt Omar's symbolic search for the past with echoes of shared women's idioms irreducible to his tentative history of progression.

Intermittent images of veiling, unveiling and partial disclosure further develop this reflection on the halting resurgence of hidden memories and the dangers of trying to appropriate and secure Algerian women's positionality. The resonance of Islamic practices, and the multiple connotations of the Islamic veil, are a focus in many of Djebar's later works, and we have already seen how, in *Les Impatients*, she seems ambivalent in her assessment of possible modes of resistance to Islamic patriarchy. In *Les Alouettes naïves*, this analysis becomes less a political critique than a subtle investigation of the play of the veil and its twin associations of suggestion and concealment. Foreshadowing at this point *Ombre sultane*, Djebar refers to the varying implications of the use of the veil as a means of exploring the game of exposure or revelation, and presents Islamic practices as multifaceted and complex rather than determined. In this sense the text complicates our attempts to interpret the symbol of the veil and challenges Dalila's rather simplistic rejection in *Les Impatients*. Nfissa's attitude to the veil, for example, seems highly ambivalent and variable, as at times she rejects its oppressive implications while at others she celebrates the wearer's empowerment. In an early passage, she revels in her freedom when walking to classes at the university, she enjoys her unrestricted ability to observe others in the street while nevertheless empathising with the veiled women who recall her heritage.[44] In spending the summer with her aunts, Nfissa decides to wear the veil again, but she arranges it in a way that both masks and reveals: 'Nfissa montrait avec fierté qu'elle savait, d'un geste sûr, relever le pan du voile: elle ramenait les deux coins inférieurs du rectangle de soie sous le menton et le drapé se faisait, ample au niveau des hanches et des coudes, en fuseau contre les jambes à mi-mollet.'[45] This gesture demonstrates both Nfissa's determination to wear the veil in such a way that it expresses her own singular form and her understanding of its capacity to expose as well as to conceal. The veil is portrayed not as a homogenising symbol of oppression but as an infinitely flexible fabric, connoting not necessarily occlusion but also suggestion. The manipulation of the veil is itself an expression of the uniqueness of the wearer, implying that revelation is necessarily partial and incomplete. In a similar way to memory narratives, then, the play of the veil promises tentative forms of suggestion while shying away from excessive exposure. Djebar's novel offers glimpses of hidden experiences rather than explaining them with a clarity that would distort their intractable substance, and similarly Nfissa's veil neither masks nor denudes her but hints at the singularity of her form.

This play of suggestion, this amalgamation of revelation and dissimulation, structures not only the process of recollection but also the mechanics of desire, of the relationship with the other. Omar's descriptions of Nfissa, like those of Rachid evoked at the beginning of this section, couple a desire for knowledge or revelation with a sense of bewilderment and separation. The narrator wants to possess and encapsulate Nfissa in language, but he also finds that she slips beyond his reach. Like his memories of resistance and comradeship, Omar's evocations are punctuated with confessions of uncertainty, again suggesting that total revelation is impossible and that both the other and the past can be known to us only as partial fragments. In describing his desperate prostration at her feet, for example, the narrator recalls:

> Il est des moments dans la vie qu'on voudrait une fois pour toutes oublier, et peut-être renier – qui persistent pourtant en suspens, durcis d'interrogations et dont la richesse, ou simplement l'opacité, reste inexpliquée. Ce qui suit est pour moi l'un de ces instants. Comme si l'amour pour cette femme sort de moi, va se dissiper, mais que demeurent dans son village des ombres dernières.[46]

In this passage, though Omar focuses on his inability to forget, it is clear that the memory is opaque, irrational, incomplete and decontextualised. Furthermore, the experience of love that Omar is remembering is itself formless, indistinct and impossible to pin down in language. The memory of love is merely a shadow, a hazy outline that resists stark unveiling or coherent explanation. Once again, Djebar is showing how the woman's singularity exceeds the grasp of male desire, of patriarchal language, and though she is fascinated by the patterns of Omar's struggle, she stresses at the same time his inevitably limited success.

In conclusion, by dissecting Omar's desire in this way, Djebar again brings up the question of women's roles during the war, as fighters and as lovers or wives, but here the anxiety concerning narrative itself betrays a growing sophistication and self-consciousness. As in *Les Enfants du nouveau monde*, Djebar explores women's potential active involvement in the conflict, but also their relationships with men and the ways in which society encourages men to seek to control and dominate them. In the former novel, Djebar investigates the tentative emergence of female agency in her transcription of women's dialogues both with one another and with themselves. Yet in *Les Alouettes naïves*, this investigation takes the more subtle form of a study of women's elusive representation in language, of their exposure and silencing through narrative. From one perspective, it can be argued that Nfissa does finish by playing a conventional role as a wife and mother, and she exchanges her active role in the maquis for a more comfortable position adhering to traditional social expectations. From another perspective, however, Djebar's portrait of her heroine itself functions as a symbol of resistance to straightforward explanatory narratives that claim unequivocally to grasp and reveal their subjects. The uncertainty surrounding Omar's apprehension of Nfissa, her changeable nature and ambivalence towards both modernity and tradition, serve to deflect attempts falsely to categorise her or to appropriate her character in the service of a single ideology.

Les Alouettes naïves inaugurates many of the most complex concerns of Djebar's later works, in that it explores not only the specificity of Algerian history and society but also the difficulties involved in reconstructing and narrating the vicissitudes of these in a straightforward, linear way. Memory turns out to be disjunctive and unreliable, and the women's experiences, occluded by official and patriarchal accounts, are in turn presented as partial fragments resisting the appropriation of the male narrator. Like the 'alouettes naïves' of the title, Djebar's female characters are distorted by narratives imposed from the outside, and their own interjections confound expectations of linearity and resolution. Ultimately, Omar's text consists not in a coherent, ordered exposition of either his own past or that of his beloved Nfissa, but in his inevitably confused and singular apprehension of these. He does not 'specify' his position in relation to the war and to the future of Algeria; instead his narrative is underpinned by traces of Derridean *différance*. As in the essay 'La Différence', referred to in my introduction, subjectivity is both deferred and displaced by the singular shadows of potential alternative incarnations. Furthermore, Omar's memory narrative clearly emerges as a result of his relationships with his compatriots, but the text is nevertheless punctuated with realisations of his isolation, his detachment from any reassuring communal discourse that would confer a secure meaning and structure upon his experiences. Reconstruction turns out to be bound up, paradoxically, with amnesia or concealment, and unfolds not progressively but in anxious fits and starts. Evocations of the war, and the changes in relationships between men and women engendered by the period, emerge as singular patterns and unusual rhythms, rather than as ordered narratives of continuity and progress.

CHAPTER TWO

War, Memory and Postcoloniality

After completing *Les Alouettes naïves*, Djebar temporarily stopped writing and remained silent for twelve years, before publishing one of her most famous collections, *Femmes d'Alger dans leur appartement*. The reasons for this silence are evidently manifold and testify to the difficulties associated with locating and describing a position in the aftermath of the upheavals of the war. Having struggled to create a meaningful narrative reconstructing her characters' experiences in the maquis in *Les Alouettes*, Djebar temporarily abandoned the use of written language as a means of making sense of colonial violence and instead experimented with film. After battling with the disjunctions of writing in French, Djebar turned to cinema in order to search for an alternative to the obfuscation of written language, and to explore the contrasting potential of visual imagery while reassessing the implications of her novel-writing practice. Written francophone narrative perhaps seemed insufficient as a tool for expressing both the traumas experienced by war victims and the unstable position in which they found themselves after decolonisation, and Djebar chose to investigate the potential of both filmic dramatisation and documentary to access her forgotten subjects. This medium also allowed her to include directly the voices of the women interviewed without the influence of transcription or translation.[1] I shall not investigate the subtlety of Djebar's filmic techniques here, however, since her experimentation both with live witnesses and with camera work in *La Nouba* and *La Zerda* lies beyond my primary concern with the writing process.[2] This period, however, was evidently not an admission of defeat but part of a process of reflection that gave rise to alternative modes of writing, ultimately more self-conscious than that of the four early novels. *Les Alouettes* dramatised the immediate tension in the aftermath of the war between the demands of a chronological narrative progressing through time and the resistance of the country's unhealed wounds to suture within such a structure. Djebar's subsequent works, such as

Femmes d'Alger, conceive this tension in philosophical rather than clearly autobiographical terms and they theorise explicitly both the search for an appropriate, 'specific' narrative and the impossibility of determining the singular postcolonial subject in language.

This process of withdrawal and renewal has several implications, which go on to influence the form of many of Djebar's subsequent works and will be explored in detail in this chapter. On one level, her silence clearly arose out of an inability to locate the Algerian subjects of her work in a francophone narrative. After the dramatic changes of the war of independence, the writer struggles to create and define a new 'Algerian identity', and as *Les Alouettes* reveals, the search for a memory narrative that would make sense of the past and situate the postcolonial Algerian subject in the present remains unsatisfied. The period of silence and reflection could on this level be read as a part of an endeavour to re-establish an alternative identity out of the ruined traces left after the war. On another level, however, Djebar's silence at the same time seems itself to perform her important and ongoing sense of the insufficiency of French narrative in describing the excess of female subjectivity. In the essay 'Les enjeux de mon silence', she refers to 'ces réticences', 'ces retenues' and 'ces litotes du parler des femmes', and she alludes to an elusive residue of singular idioms, excluded from the French language even in her later works, and containing no substance of their own.[3] She conveys the singular idioms of Algerian women's self-expression, describing it as a resistant stain untranslatable to the French language, but with no determined cultural character of its own. They are traces or supplements, to use Derrida's language again, inaccessible singularities that Djebar can hint at but that get lost in the chain of new associations that her French narrative brings. Finally, and this is the aspect that the author describes most explicitly, Djebar's period of introspection leads to a discovery of the plural rhythms and inflections of postcolonial, Algerian women's identity, of the multiple forms that its singularisation might take. While *Les Alouettes* contains, according to the author, a few passing echoes of the Arabic language, her later works both incorporate and celebrate the manifold dialects and idioms that contribute to her own singular-plural mode of expression. Nancy's thinking in *Être singulier pluriel* is developed here by Djebar's conception of language usage as at once idiosyncratic or idiomatic, and heterogeneous or plural. She recognises the necessity that 'l'espace en français de ma langue d'écrivain n'exclut pas les autres langues maternelles que je porte en moi, sans les écrire'.[4] Her narrative carries within it hesitant traces of multiple other voices that both interrupt and structure her perception of her own, and Algeria's, past.

Femmes d'Alger dans leur appartement

Djebar's ground-breaking collection, *Femmes d'Alger dans leur appartement*, sets out to theorise the implications of her post-war 'silence' and dramatises the confrontation between distinct modes of individuation in the aftermath of colonialism. The texts explore the representation of Algerian women, both after the violence of the insurrection and during the years of colonial imposition, and they question the possibility of recreating a specific feminine voice. Like the following text, *L'Amour, la fantasia*, the portraits of the women contained in the stories are to some extent framed as affirmative alternatives to residual colonial and Islamic, patriarchal versions that reduce and stultify the subjects they claimed to encapsulate. Following her own silence, Djebar's fragments now seem to want to 'give voice' to generations of Algerian women who have been denied the privilege of self-expression; they appear to invoke a particularised feminine language that would accurately convey experiences that slip beyond the limits of sanctioned history. If Islamic law in Algeria recommended that women refrain from using the first person, and French colonial discourse portrayed them using a series of distorted metaphors and images, Djebar's short stories seek to invent a more appropriate collective idiom that might resuscitate the idiosyncrasies of this forgotten community.

In introducing the stories, however, Djebar first stresses the difference between her search for a mode of representation and the trap of 'representativity', and this distinction already reveals her reservations towards the notion of a specified identity. Nick Harrison discusses this issue extensively in his *Postcolonial Criticism*, where he warns against the dangers of confusing *darstellen* (representation as depiction) with *vertreten* (political representation), and concludes that the writer's examination of his cultural community should not be mistaken for a universal indicator of the nation's 'postcolonial condition'.[5] In the case of Djebar, although she clearly is concerned in particular with Algerian women and on a number of occasions invokes their 'genealogy', she stresses that the characters in her texts are not exemplary and cannot define a generalised, specified identity as such. The collection may be overtly concerned with the discovery or invention of a feminine Algerian 'voice', but from the beginning the author tries to prevent her readers from reading any of the multiple, singular narratives and idioms recorded as part of an established or unified category. Multiple women's voices offer hints of memory, or partially fictionalised experiments, rather than testimonies to the experiences of an entire community. Djebar writes:

> Ne pas prétendre «parler pour», ou pis «parler sur», à peine parler
> près de, et si possible tout contre: première des solidarités à assumer
> pour les quelques femmes arabes qui obtiennent ou acquièrent la
> liberté de mouvement, du corps et de l'esprit. Et ne pas oublier que
> celles qu'on incarcère de tous âges, de toutes conditions, ont des
> corps prisonniers, mais des âmes plus que jamais mouvantes.[6]

Already, then, the author is revealing her anxieties concerning the relation between the collective subject of her work and the narrative that she is able to produce. She is acutely aware of the constructed nature of the voices of her text and warns against conflating these with a real collectivity outside the space of her fictional creation. Although at the end the narrator triumphantly expresses the hope that the text might liberate women from their history of oppression, she struggles to fulfil this promise by actively recapturing their singular histories and charting the genealogy of their suffering. The collection, despite its apparent aims, will not be an uncomplicated description of a specified community, but a suggestive indication of the indeterminacy and dynamism of postcolonial Algerian women.

Crucially, Djebar's preface also presents this as a question of language, and the hypothetical, particularised feminine voice splits into a series of idioms, each of which is self-singularising rather than determined. Much of this initial section is concerned with dissimulation, with silencing and with the impossibility of giving form to echoes that have been lost. The narrator wonders 'comment œuvrer aujourd'hui en sourcière tant d'accents encore suspendus dans les silences du sérail d'hier?', and multiple 'accents' or idiolects struggle to resonate in a narrative necessarily separated from its forgotten past.[7] The original inflections of her characters' narratives remain indistinct echoes, subtly reconfiguring the rhythms of the text while subverting its urge to define. The question quoted here betrays an awareness of singular traces, produced in a fleeting moment, resistant to the permanence of the printed form. Moreover, as I have suggested, this attention to the singular is coupled with recollection of the plural inflections that simultaneously shape her francophone written text. The stories are not translated from a specific language, such as Arabic, but contain hints from diverse sources: 'son arabe, iranien, afghan, berbère ou bengali, pourquoi pas, mais toujours avec timbre féminin et lèvres proférant sous le masque'.[8] The point here is not only that the Arabic language has multiple forms, but also that the voices and influences that interrupt her writing are plural and do not derive from the framework of a national culture. Various echoes intervene in her prose and they belong neither to a single originary language nor to a particular, rooted culture.

Djebar is looking for an appropriate language or set of languages that would avoid national or cultural determination and that would not be seen artificially to encapsulate an entire community. She does investigate the possible specificity of such a language, in that she does seek to define it in relation to particular influences, and it is supposed to offer a mode of expression to a certain under-represented group. Djebar does at this stage cling to the idea that her writing will somehow 'give voice' to this multiplicity of disenfranchised women, and this very notion of an active voice connotes agency, knowledge and self-determination. At the same time, however, this notion of specificity is continually underpinned by a sense of the elusive singularity of the multiple idioms spoken by that group, and it is this elusive quality that disrupts and fragments the final version of the collection. The essays of *Ces voix qui m'assiègent* theorise in detail this tension introduced in *Femmes d'Alger*, and it is worth analysing Djebar's own explicit comments here before turning to the fabric of the text itself. In a section entitled 'Etre une voix francophone', for example, she considers the extent to which she can be seen precisely to 'be' a francophone voice, questioning whether she 'is' what she says. She investigates her specificity as Peter Hallward conceives the term, and wonders whether the term 'francophone' might offer an appropriate definition of her transcultural position. She uses it to examine her relationship with existing cultural frameworks, stressing at the same time that the negotiation of such relations should be conceived as active rather than passive. Despite her frequent categorisation according to such labels, however, she almost immediately distances herself from them, suggesting that the notion of a voice implies a form of self-presence, while the term 'francophone' connotes both classification and demands of representativity. Recalling Derrida's examination of the distinction between speech and writing in *De la grammatologie*, Djebar implies that the voice connotes presence or immediacy, while her writing on the contrary conveys above all the absence of the author. Djebar's voice is impossible to locate, and instead her writing connotes silence and indeterminacy: '*j'écris à force de me taire*'.[9] The emphasis on silence and absence implies not specificity but singularity, a self that is always in excess of the language used to describe it. This dissociation from the notion of a self-present voice troubles her sense of belonging to any preconceived 'francophone' category.

Alongside this sense of a singularity that is buried by the language in which she writes is an emphasis on profusion and the impossibility of containment. The metaphors that Djebar uses to describe her writing imply not only silence or absence but also overflowing, a material force that explodes any imposed framework or particularised structure: 'mon écriture sort, surgit, coule soudain ou par moments explose'. The focus is not on signification, on writing as the medium or conveyor of a particular sense. On the contrary, writing is a substance that the writer struggles to manipulate but fails to control. Metaphors of surging, flowing and spilling over convey fluidity, as if meaning continually forms and reforms itself rather than solidifying its referents. Djebar affirms that she uses:

> *Langue mais ni gel, ni glace, ni même encre*
> *Langue qui coule*
> *Et qui coud les blessures.*[10]

Language is not a gel that provides cohesion, nor is it ice that freezes meaning in time, nor ink that leaves an indelible mark. Instead it is a formless form that exceeds boundaries while creating links and suturing over rifts and scars. Djebar's emphasis on materiality is also significant here, as she describes the consistency and texture of writing rather than its sense.

This impression of overflowing is finally combined with a proliferation of multiple echoes that cannot be confined by any identitarian framework. Specificity dissolves into singular-plurality in Nancy's sense, as the self is figured as a unique composition that cannot be described according to existing cultural categories. Djebar asserts that the French language does not provide her with a specific voice, both because French is associated with the coloniser and because her sense of singularity is excluded by language *tout court*. Furthermore, this singularity is plural in that it is composed not only of absence but of a proliferation of different voices, dialects and influences, all of which continually underpin her usage of French and form a unique composition. A multiplicity of languages subtends the narrative that she writes, troubling the borders of the colonial language as well as the apparent particularity of the colonised. She elucidates her aims in the following terms:

> Oui, ramener les voix non francophones – les gutturales, les ensauvagées, les insoumises – jusqu'à un texte français qui devient enfin mien. Ces voix qui ont transporté en moi leur turbulence, leur remous, davantage dans le rythme de mon écrit, dans le style de narration que je ne choisis pas vraiment, dans la non-visualisation qui serait ma tentation, dans le cadrage des corps, dans...[11]

Here the interruption of the sentence at the end of the paragraph further emphasises her resistance to containment, and the notion of a hidden plurality of voices expresses both impenetrability and profusion. The languages Djebar investigates constitute at once a 'parole plurielle' and a 'parole perdue', as if multiple hints and traces circulate around an elusive and intractable core.[12]

Returning to *Femmes d'Alger*, here it is the aftermath of the war of independence that problematises the representation process, and it is particularly women who struggle to create a meaningful or determined narrative of their postcolonial experience. The collection as a whole concentrates on the difficulties experienced by generations of Algerian women who have been excluded from history. Yet above all, the traumas of the physical violence of the war, of exile and bereavement, disable the women of contemporary Algeria from producing a coherent testimony linking present and past. As I suggested in relation to *Les Enfants du nouveau monde* and *Les Alouettes naïves*, women's participation in the conflict was played down after the war and public discussion of their suffering was inadmissible. The collection thus on one level seeks to correct the distortions of existing versions, to give voice to women silenced by oppression, and to offer an alternative mode of expression that might make sense of their position. Disillusioned with conventional history, Djebar sets out to expose the sorts of experiences that official narratives gloss over or leave out. She implicitly denounces versions of the revolution that subsume moments of women's resistance beneath the veneer of a patriarchal grand narrative, and she offers fragments of women's hidden memories. These present an 'unofficial' picture of Algerian experience, a set of forgotten moments in women's lives, or a series of incomplete images unaccounted for in mainstream historical texts. The volume gathers together heterogeneous traces and presents them as an alternative collective, the shadow of the unknown feminine community lingering behind more familiar accounts of masculine activity. Notably, twenty years after its initial publication Djebar also adds a further intervention to this collectivity of women's voices, 'La nuit du récit de Fatima', bearing witness to renewed controls over women's movement as a result of the tensions of the 1990s. This added contribution has the explicit purpose of linking three generations of women's suffering 'pour éclairer la solidarité de toute parole féminine, notre survie'.[13]

On one level, then, Djebar seems to argue that ongoing communication and dialogue will be necessary for women's further emancipation. Djebar is acutely conscious of the limitations of her project, but the stories all contain characters intent upon finding alternative ways to talk about both the present and the past. Sarah, in 'Femmes d'Alger', passionately affirms that 'je ne vois pour les femmes arabes qu'un seul moyen de tout débloquer: parler, parler sans cesse d'hier et d'aujourd'hui, parler entre nous, dans tous les gynécées, les traditionnels et ceux des H.L.M.'.[14] The story is concerned above all with dialogue between women, with the difficulty of locating the appropriate words (such as when Sarah refrains from explaining her scar to Anne), and with the attempt to discover or invent a set of singular feminine idioms. Sarah's research on the hawfi women's songs is part of this project, and Djebar includes some of the fragments that Sarah unearths in an attempt to relocate the lost traces of a past language. The oral form is important here, since the dynamism of women's sung and spoken idioms is precisely what the printed history books fail to convey. Women's experience is more likely to be known through the passing on of musical rhythms or fragmented rumours than through published narratives on the Algerian past. In addition, the scene in the hammam is full of signs even of non-verbal modes of expression that do not conform to the demands of a rationalised or linear narrative. Cries, whispers, echoes and shouts convey a singular language where the link between signifier and signified is not convention-bound but more immediate, closer to the rhythms and movements of the body. The scene is constantly interrupted by 'chuchotements', 'sons creusés', the 'brouhaha des voix entrecroisées', and 'conversations ou monologues déroulés en mots doux, menus, usés, qui glissent avec l'eau'.[15]

Throughout the collection, excerpts in italics or with wide margins introduce new perspectives or idioms and help to stretch the narrative beyond the control of any single authoritative voice.

The collectivity explored in the text is, however, far from unified, but consists of a diverse, disjointed conglomeration of scenes and images. Women's memories of the war of independence are presented not in the form of a complete history but as a series of incomplete, allusive flashbacks. These are not resolved into a secure and meaningful continuity but continue to stand out, since the occluded horrors of which they speak resist straightforward resolution. There can be no collective narrative of women's experience, then, since each testimony is a fragment that resists incorporation into a broader meaningful structure. The nightmare passage at the beginning of 'Femmes d'Alger' demonstrates this broken structure, and reveals the difficulty of determining or coming to terms with experiences recalled from the war. The passage seems to evoke a torture scene, starting with the disturbing description of a 'tête de jeune femme aux yeux bandés, cou renversé, cheveux tirés'.[16] It then becomes apparent that this is Ali's, Sarah's husband's, dream and that he is confusing his work as a surgeon with horrific memories of the tortures inflicted on resistance fighters. The passage is itself fractured, stilted and frequently opaque, juxtaposing a series of details and features without explaining the links between them, nor the background to the scene. It intermingles torture and the everyday, irresolute wartime memories with Ali's professional life, and blends past and present while omitting to determine cause and effect. The presentation of the image as a fractured dream sequence demonstrates its resistance to rationality and logic, and the troubled amalgamation of Ali's imaginings with the unspeakable traumas experienced by Sarah reinforces the sense that the original moment is inaccessible.

The violent, halting resurgence of Leila's memories demands a similar, disjointed narrative form. At the time of narration, Leila is in a psychiatric clinic undergoing treatment for her drug addiction, but her conversations with Sarah are constantly interspersed with sudden and fleeting recollections of horrific wartime scenes. These are presented as brief, disjunctive interjections, not part of a chronological sequence but nightmarish visions that resist the ordinary demands of narrative progression. She laments the occlusion of women's contributions to the war effort, and conjures up terrifying images of explosions killing or injuring the bomb-carriers:

Où êtes-vous les porteuses de bombes? Elles forment cortège, des grenades dans les paumes qui s'épanouissent en flammes, les faces illuminées de lueurs vertes… Où êtes-vous, les porteuses de feu, vous mes soeurs qui aurez dû libérer la ville… Les fils barbelés ne barrent plus les ruelles, mais ils ornent les fenêtres, les balcons, toutes les issues vers l'espace…[17]

As the passage continues, Leila seizes on more and more of the scene's details, and her narrative shifts disconcertingly back and forth in time. References to destruction and mutilation are scattered among lamentations on the inevitable amnesia surrounding such events, and the structure becomes increasingly chaotic until the language falters and breaks down. This breakdown of linguistic explanation is perhaps most radical in the face of physical pain, since, as theorist Elaine Scarry argues, it has no referential content.[18] Leila's stilted, staccato testimony offers hints of the violence of the scene but never fully articulates the intractable suffering of the women. Such haunting moments are singular in the sense that they cannot be pinned down by narrative but can be apprehended only in the form of partial, flickering traces.

In the later stories, 'Jour de Ramadhan' and 'Les morts parlent', discourses of mourning and commemoration similarly struggle to catch the singular moment in language. In the former, women frequently allude to the war, but such references generate anxiety and are subsequently curtailed. In 'Les morts parlent', the scene of the wake of the old woman is interrupted by Aïcha's subjective thoughts, as well as by fleeting traces of memories and anxieties from the past, but none of these add up to a coherent history. The text deals explicitly with bereavement, but it also charts the fraught resurfacing of difficult moments, such as the disappearance of Hassan at the time of his work with the maquis. The death of the old woman gives rise to reflection on the family's moments of communality and rupture during the war, but Aïcha's memories are also always incomplete or curtailed. Disturbing wartime memories are also interspersed with moments indicating the oppression of women in Algerian society, again alluding to the particularity of feminine experience during the war without succeeding in presenting their roles in a clear or affirmative form. Aïcha's mourning, for example, is juxtaposed with disjointed fragments of her own traumatic wedding and subsequent repudiation, the implications of which seem not to have been 'worked through'. Furthermore, Djebar makes some overt criticisms of public, ritualised forms of commemoration, and she reveals Hassan's perception of the hollow centre of narratives celebrating the glory of the war. He laments the emptiness of neat formulae summarising 'la guerre de Sept Ans', or 'la guerre de libération', and questions, 'libération du décor et des autres, mais...'[19] Hassan formally addresses the gathering at the wake, but the inserted section in italics dissociates the character from his ceremonial language. The reader is distanced from the rhetoric of commemoration and reminded that *'en son coeur à lui règne une étendue aride. Pire que l'oubli.'*[20] If, then, Leila's memory narratives are themselves violently ruptured as if to mimic the destruction of the war, Hassan's are more coldly removed from the singular substance they may have wanted to convey. The passage reinforces in this haunting manner the deferral of the singular moment and the inadequacy of narrative in specifying its meaning.

Djebar's exploration of women's singular wartime memories is coupled with an investigation of female subjugation throughout the history of colonial oppression. It is true that the male characters do not form a stronger, more resolute community than the women; they often seem isolated, and Djebar is at pains to stress that her focus on women's alienation does not mean that her male characters were in any way less disorientated by the ambivalent effects of the conflict. Ali and Sarah's relationship in 'Femmes d'Alger', for example, suffers from an absence of satisfactory communication, and Ali's understanding of the past is perhaps no less troubled than that of the female characters. Nevertheless, Djebar's primary focus does remain on women and she examines not only the difficulty of identifying and narrating Algerian women's multiple postcolonial experiences, but also their systematic misrepresentation through history. 'La nuit du récit de Fatima', for example, traces a series of episodes of active mistreatment in a patriarchal society, both during and after the colonial period. Djebar focuses here on relationships between women, on the importance of solidarity but also on loss, and the sacrifices endured when the individual bids for freedom. The transfer of the narrative voice between different feminine narrators promises dialogue between them, a sense of historical continuity despite the restrictions placed on women's self-expression. The promise of freedom, however, is accompanied by the severing of relationships between mother and daughter, and the process of narrating these losses itself becomes oppressive and inappropriate: 'le fil de la narration ne va-t-il pas me serrer, m'enserrer, m'emprisonner?'[21] Similarly, in 'Il n'y a pas d'exil', loss and exile experienced during the war of independence are explored against the background of a history of female disenfranchisement, and the family still seems to be governed by the authoritarian father arranging his daughters' futures and allowing himself to be waited on by them. Present experiences of feminine suffering are framed by entrenched social customs, and the women's expression of their losses is bound up with their relegation to domestic space. In addition, the women's reactions to traditional forms of mourning, such as the bereaved women next door wailing in unison, differ, and Djebar seems to imply once again that the notion of a feminine community, with a specific set of roles, remains a myth.

If most of the stories of *Femmes d'Alger dans leur appartement* concentrate on women's negotiation with colonial and patriarchal oppression both before and after the war of independence, the final section 'Regard interdit, son coupé' presents this as part of an even broader history of silencing and misrepresentation. Here, Djebar explains the reference in the collection's title to Delacroix's famous painting depicting three Algerian women and their servant in the private and enclosed space of their chamber. Djebar alludes to the painting in order to denounce Delacroix's invasion of the women's quarters and his drive to encapsulate these women's unfamiliar lives in the form of a portrait. Delacroix's penetration is a 'regard volé', and the act of entering into this private space and attempting to seize and recreate its singular detail is to a certain extent itself an act of colonial violence. The work is, according to Djebar, on one level 'Orientalist', since it exoticises its subject, associating the women with an artificial aesthetic ideal. It fictionalises and reshapes both the individuals and the interior, and evokes an 'instant fugitif d'une révélation évanescente se tenant sur cette mouvante frontière où se côtoient rêve et réalité'.[22] Such rhetoric clearly allies Delacroix's work with a tradition of exoticisation and idealisation, whereby Oriental women were associated with a colourful sensuality in order to suit the demands of the colonial libidinal gaze. Malek Alloula's *Le Harem colonial* explores the evolution of this vision through colonial post-cards and photographs, and Djebar's collaboration with Alloula in *La Zerda et les chants de l'oubli* further explores the alliance of such portraits with fantasies of sexual exoticism.

Despite the possible violence of Delacroix's wilful incursion into the women's segregated space, however, and despite his embellishment or appropriation of their experience, Djebar at the same time examines the painting precisely because it raises the same questions regarding representation and singularity that her own work addresses. She notes how he longs to hold on to the scene he discovers, but also how he grapples with the sense that it will always exceed his grasp. The painting alludes to what we cannot, as spectators, hold onto or appropriate. The women are presented as 'à la fois présentes et lointaines', both restricted or contained by their environment, and somehow distant, absorbed in another world. The painting is full of suggestion, hinting at the women's internal reveries while denying both painter and spectator access to their singular thoughts. Djebar's reading of Delacroix emphasises the limitations of his work and interprets those limitations precisely as enriching, as crucial signals of the difficulties associated with representing such intractable subjects. The painting ultimately separates us from the women rather than simply granting us entry into their world:

> Ces femmes, est-ce parce qu'elles rêvent qu'elles ne nous regardent pas, ou est-ce parce que, enfermées sans recours, elles ne peuvent même plus nous entrevoir? Rien ne se devine de l'âme de ces dolentes assises, comme noyées dans ce qui les entoure. Elles demeurent absentes à elles-mêmes, à leur corps, à leur sensualité, à leur bonheur.[23]

This description of the painting reinforces the sense that the Algerian women of both Delacroix and Djebar's work resist determination and knowledge. The work explores on yet another level the tension between representation and the excess it can never encapsulate. Djebar discusses Delacroix, then, not simply in order to criticise him but to demonstrate the distortions inherent in the way women are perceived from both inside and outside.

Djebar's interpretation of Delacroix may be controversial, and certainly critics such as Marnia Lazreg have criticised Djebar for glossing over the obvious violence, at once colonial and patriarchal, of the painter's gesture.[24] Nevertheless, the stakes of *Femmes d'Alger*, and of Djebar's reading of the Delacroix painting, are an important reflection on the silencing and occlusion of Algerian women and the search for a mode of expression that would evoke the singular-plurality of their community. Delacroix's work may indeed be an act of appropriation or fetishisation and his painting is certainly not an unmediated or 'realistic' portrait. But it offers insight into women's representation throughout the history of Algeria and provides a link

between the silencing, or false representation, of the postcolonial feminine subjects explored in 'Femmes d'Alger' and the double heritage of
colonial and patriarchal oppression. As Nick Harrison argues, both
works informatively 'draw attention to a certain "gaze", and to the
way that the "image" of woman is, at a second remove, "perceived",
an image with its own history that is somewhat independent from the
fluctuating and variegated historical reality to which it is applied'.[25]
Djebar is therefore neither accusing nor correcting Delacroix directly,
but reflecting on layers of misrepresentation and occlusion. Her reference to what might be seen as Delacroix's Orientalism implies not a
recuperation or collusion, but an understanding of the interpenetration of representation, ideology and violence in existing perceptions
of Algerian women.

   Djebar's engagement with the history of representations of Algerian women is in this way double-edged. She sets out both to record
the traps and lures of Delacroix's representation and, perhaps futilely,
to correct this legacy of distortion. On the one hand, alongside her
reading of Delacroix, Djebar does go on to retrace moments of feminine self-affirmation and agency from the period of the French invasion in 1830 to the war of independence, and the collection does
remind its readers of the multiple ways in which women have participated in, or been affected by, political struggle. Djebar draws an
oblique comparison between the heroism of Messaouda, who when
her tribe's fort was besieged in 1839 climbed onto the ramparts to
call her brothers to arms, and the bomb-carriers of the war of independence. On the other hand, however, despite her recollection of
such moments, Djebar repeatedly reflects self-consciously on the
tyranny of representation, on the absence of a language in which to
describe their singular unfolding. Existing representations, such as
that of Delacroix's painting, only suggest or skirt around the inaccessible subjects they set out to evoke. The final section of the text
reflects on the evacuation of women's actions, of their bodies, from
history, and on the forgotten multiplicity of women's roles beyond
their traditional position either as sexual objects or as mothers. Yet
such unique and unconventional moments of resistance are known
only through the residual traces of oral history, the idioms of which
Djebar is at pains to recapture, but which are necessarily fleeting and
indistinct. Even Picasso's version of *Femmes d'Alger*, which seeks to
liberate the women from their confinement by depicting the 'renaissance de ces femmes à leur corps', risks denuding them and reshaping

them according to the artist's own desires.[26]

Djebar's *Femmes d'Alger dans leur appartement* performs the play between the potential revelation of the singular feminine subject and the destructive, distorting effects of the representation process. Throughout the collection, images of veiling and unveiling recur, not in the form of a binary opposition but as coexistent facets of the process of exposition. The text seems to want to reveal the substance of a community that has been denied the means to express itself. It explores and pinpoints the various external factors acting on the community, such as colonialism and Islamic patriarchy, and attempts to establish a meaningful position for generations of oppressed women through the invention of an alternative narrative. Djebar's francophone text, her manipulation of the language and her use of an allusive, polyphonic and fragmented form set out to uncover experiences and identities that have been either forgotten or misrepresented. This very 'unveiling', however, is itself seen as destructive, failing to capture the multiple singularities the author may have set out to reveal and distorting them by imposing another artificial representational code. Djebar's critique of Delacroix is as a result not a straightforward affirmation of her own successful representation, as some critics have argued, but the trigger for an exploration of her own struggle.[27] Djebar's discussion of Algerian women's literal shedding of the veil serves as a metaphor for this tension, and indeed for her own writing project. Observing that women increasingly leave their homes unveiled, Djebar comments not only on the liberatory implications of such a bold act, but also on its dangers:

> Le corps avance hors de la maison et pour la première fois il est ressenti comme «exposé» à tous les regards: la démarche devient raidie, le pas hâtif, l'expression du regard contractée.
>
> L'arabe dialectal transcrit l'expérience d'une façon signicative: «je ne sors plus *protégée* (c'est-à-dire voilée, recouverte)» dira la femme qui se libère du drap; «je sors *déshabillée* ou même *dénudée*». Le voile qui soustrayait aux regards est de fait ressenti comme «habit en soi», ne plus l'avoir, c'est être totalement exposée.[28]

From this point of view, a certain refusal of disclosure, of completed representation, serves as a means of protecting the elusive singularity of the plural subjects of the work. Djebar's desire to uncover the hidden experiences of her characters and to 'give voice' to generations of oppressed women is inevitably subtended by this reluctance to reveal too much, or to allow her own representation to determine and reduce its subject. Using language not to provide knowledge, not to reduce the subject, but to allude to those aspects of experience that cannot be fixed in narrative, Djebar conveys a sense of the ongoing singularisation of her characters.

Femmes d'Alger enacts a theoretical drama between distinct conceptions of individuation and their relationship with the writing of the text itself. The stories seem to want to situate Algerian women in relation both to their past and to the uncertainties of the present. Yet at the same time, the text refuses to fix the specific position of its female characters, and it couples a depiction of their circumstances with confessions of anxiety concerning the limits of the specific and the resistance of multiple intractable moments to representation in narrative. Singular experiences resist categorisation in language and the community of women Djebar seems to want to create instead turns out to be singular-plural, composed of relations between beings that are in turn different from themselves. The narrator at times promises to provide information about the history of Algerian women, but she always almost immediately withdraws and admits that even her own alternative structures and idioms cannot catch up with the manifold unique moments that at once comprise and fracture their genealogy. Self-conscious worries and doubts sever the construction of any specific portrait and remind us that determined knowledge about the intractable collectivity of Algerian women is illusory. This project of rewriting history and of seeking alternative narratives evoking singular women's experiences is continued in *L'Amour, la fantasia*, where the writing process is theorised even more frequently, and where the narrator's tension in relation to her project seems even more explicit and acute.

L'Amour, la fantasia

Djebar's next major novel, the first of the Algerian quartet tracing the genealogy of her female compatriots, is one of her best-known works and develops some of the reflections of *Femmes d'Alger* into a more expansive engagement with her country's history. In *L'Amour, la fantasia*, she attempts to write a collective autobiography of the women of Algeria, interweaving accounts of the invasion of Algiers in 1830 with testimonies from the war of independence and with scenes from her own childhood and youth. She sets out to investigate both her own sense of self and the genealogy of Algerian women to which she might be seen to belong, and she strives to understand the composite influences of the colonial heritage, of Berber traditions and of Islam. Memories of her own past are interspersed with interjections, fragments of narratives by women of different epochs as well as self-conscious musings on the difficulties of the very project on which she has embarked. The novel is overtly concerned with collective identity, seeking to establish parallels between past and present and to elucidate once again the experiences of a forgotten community. Nevertheless, Djebar again shuttles between a series of provisional identity constructions and a more uneasy sense of the impenetrability of singular existence, and this sense is heightened in turn by the chaotic mass of influences that drift around the intractable core.

In *L'Amour, la fantasia*, conflicts between the specific, the singular and the singular-plural are demonstrated by the text's complex relationship with the genre of autobiography. First, Djebar seems to want to narrate specific experiences that determine her character, fixing on a series of moments during her evolution that might help to define her position in relation to French, Algerian and Islamic cultures. As Clarisse Zimra argues, the text situates the author in relation to a set of central categories: 'Woman. Writer. Moslem. French-speaking. French-writing'.[29] The opening sequence painting the 'fillette arabe allant pour la première fois à l'école', for example, is rich in cultural implications, as Djebar considers the specificity of her position as a young Arab girl who is educated and who knows how to write. In other scenes, she analyses her reactions to Muslim and French customs with regard to love, marriage and male/female relationships, identifying the ways in which she inherits beliefs from both traditions. Her aim seems to be to articulate her complex negotiation with the different cultural paradigms that circumscribe her identity. Despite this project, however, Djebar's 'position' is also so fraught with contradictions that she finds that the attempt to delimit it precisely in the end results in the occlusion of parts of the self. As both Nick Harrison and Debra Kelly point out, the use of the first-person pronoun, or at least a clear concern with oneself rather than others, has also been seen to be inimical to Islam, particularly for women, and Djebar struggles to use it here to describe her experience of growing up influenced at once by French culture and by Islam.[30] Djebar's paradoxical relationship with the French language means that while she is allowed to express herself in ways that were not usually permitted, she also simultaneously cuts herself off from singular memories that cannot be contained within the colonial language, associated with myths of self-assertion, as well as with clarity and logic.

Djebar's autobiographical project is also, perhaps appropriately for an Islamic writer, a collective one, focusing specifically on feminine Algerian identity. In an interview with Mildred Mortimer, Djebar overtly describes the text as 'une quête de l'identité', and she hopes to give voice or agency to Algerian women at various moments in history since 1830.[31] Just as she spoke of how she wanted to identify the 'parler des femmes' in *Ces voix* and *Femmes d'Alger*, here too Djebar hopes to delineate the specificity of Algerian women, oppressed at once by colonialism and by Islamic patriarchy. The text contains fragments of women's lives from various epochs, creating links and associations over time and attempting to construct through these connections some sense of a collective feminine voice. Critics have repeatedly emphasised the importance of this communal voice and the search for an identifiable position. Hafid Gafaïti, for example, asserts that

> from the beginning, her work also inscribes the individual in a specific social or cultural setting. From this perspective, the quest for identity can be conceived only through one's situation in the socio-cultural context on the one hand, and, on the other hand, in the structure of global history.[32]

History and society come to determine and define a highly specific position. Similarly, John Erickson emphasises the notion of '*being woman*' in *L'Amour, la fantasia*, situating Djebar's voice within a greater sisterhood of oppressed women.[33]

Certainly, parts of Djebar's text themselves stress this search for a collective identity. Scraps of recent memories, for example, focus on the nature of Arab women's speech. In one passage, Djebar considers the difficulty of translating the Arabic word 'hannouni' used by her aunts and cousins, underlining the curious particularity of their idiom.[34] Djebar also addresses her female ancestors, hoping to locate suppressed echoes and unspoken narratives and juxtaposing these with the struggles of women in the present day. The 'aïeules' of the 1840s are also portrayed alongside Chérifa, a resistance fighter during the war of independence, and Djebar notes the patterns of continuity and change that characterise their relationship. The novel on this level sets out to draw up a genealogy of Algerian women's suffering and resistance, and identifies the specific effects of colonialism on notions of femininity and women's roles. In moments of self-confidence then, Djebar claims that her writing succeeds in incorporating the voices of Algeria's forgotten women, and she asserts: 'écrire ne tue pas la voix, mais la reveille, surtout pour ressusciter tant de soeurs disparues'.[35] Passages such as this celebrate the potential of her exposition to resist centuries of oppression by both Islamic tradition and colonial imposition.

Most importantly, however, while Djebar strives to locate a sense of feminine specificity, the text also splits and fragments the collective identity that it wants to evoke. Differences between women are as notable as similarities and the nature of their oppression is shaped by historical events in contrasting ways. Not only does language gloss over the temporal and spatial displacement of each singular being, but also the collective feminine voice hides multiple differences, contradictions and contrasts. Various speakers interrupt the text, but their reflections take the form of incomplete fragments that tail off before establishing an identity or a position. Multiple whispers leave their trace within the text, without the narrator being able to reconstruct and gather them together, and she reflects: '*chaîne de souvenirs: n'est-elle pas justement «chaîne» qui entrave autant qu'elle enracine?*'[36] This sense of fragmentation is further heightened by Djebar's replication of the structure of a musical 'fantasia' as an alternative to producing a unified, teleological account. The 'fantasia' is broken by sudden interruptions and irregular rhythms, echoing at the same time the running and firing of the cavaliers. Djebar records this cacophony of cries and chants, and she juxtaposes discordant voices that preside over any desire for a smooth harmony. Sections entitled 'voix', 'murmures', 'clameurs' and 'chuchotements' break up any sense of connection or linearity, and they offer a multiplicity of divergent traces rather than conforming to a coherent or ordered pattern. These interjections are not narratives in the conventional sense, but they intimate sounds, idioms and modes of language excluded from 'official history' and resisting any alternative chronology or telos of their own.

Autobiography, as both a singular and a collective project, turns out for Djebar to be an unsatisfied quest, a partial fiction, or a 'preparation' rather than a completed work.[37] As Celia Britton has argued, a number of recent postcolonial critics have associated autobiographies by silenced female writers with a process of 'coming to voice', and the search to uncover hidden feminine voices is certainly an explicit motivation behind *Femmes d'Alger*.³⁸ Yet, just as Britton argues that Daniel Maximin's text refuses to posit a consistent subjectivity or voice, Djebar too never harnesses together the plural contingent voices that appear in her work to form a cohesive sense of self. Instead the text presents layers of possible selves, all of which remain partially opaque and irrevocably fragmented by the language in which they are constructed. The text attempts to position both the author herself and, more broadly, feminine Algerian identity, but the French language of agency seems to confer an excess of clarity that ends in annihilation and betrayal. Autobiography becomes a sort of dissection, cutting open the singular being with the hope of revealing and defining her substance while destroying her in the same process. For Djebar, 'tenter l'autobiographie par les seuls mots de français, c'est, sous le lent scalpel de l'autopsie à vif, montrer plus que sa peau. Sa chair se desquame, semble-t-il, en lambeaux du parler d'enfance qui ne s'écrit plus.'³⁹ Clarity of expression is experienced as destructive, attempting to fix and reduce those very singularities that by definition remain infinitely contingent and resistant to knowledge. If in *Femmes d'Alger* unveiling results in a loss of protection, here, even more, self-exposure leads to violent deformation. Djebar also reflects that 'me mettre à nu dans cette langue me fait entretenir un danger permanent de déflagration', reinforcing this tension between revelation and dissemination or even physical disintegration.⁴⁰ Autobiography turns out to be as much about insufficiency and fragmentation as about identification.

This tension is played out in Djebar's narratives of both war and love. First, the text at times sets out to situate her female characters in relation to history, mapping the position of particular women with regard to the political upheavals of the nineteenth century and the war of independence. The initial description of the invasion of Algiers is full of metaphors evoking the oppression of women, and the scene sets out to re-describe this inaugural moment in a feminine language, as if to recover the lost suffering of a nation of women subjugated at once by colonialism and patriarchy. This early scene figures Algeria itself as a woman, as if the atrocities committed during the nineteenth century were akin to those inflicted on women silenced by men. The scene opens, for example, with a standard Gregorian date: 'aube de ce 13 juin 1830'. Yet this calendar itself was a time frame that was imported by the French and was adopted quickly by native men who came into contact with French institutions earlier than women. Women in

Algeria at the time would have been using a Muslim calendar and not this imported system.[41] In addition, the scene compares the capture of Algiers to the violation of the bride on her wedding night. We are told that 'Algiers se dévoile', like a young bride who arrives veiled at her wedding ceremony and is then unveiled by the groom.[42] The town is also decorated in a way reminiscent of a wedding dress: 'tout en dentelures et en couleurs délicates'. Djebar uses corporeal imagery to reinforce the comparison, as the town is described 'tel un corps à l'abandon, sur un tapis de verdure assombrie', like a bride awaiting her fate on the wedding mat. Djebar couples in this way the adoption of the Gregorian time frame with a feminine temporal perspective, marked by marriage or by sexual violation. The conflation of colonialism and patriarchy in this scene is undoubtedly problematic, since, together with some of the descriptions of the colonial officers' celebrations of the conflict, it sexualises colonisation in a way that becomes disturbingly seductive. The invasion and subsequent battles are likened to sexual penetration, and Djebar's response seems to be that she is both disgusted, and compelled, by this imagery. Most importantly, however, these early passages inflect the description of the invasion with a feminine idiom and recount the inauguration of colonialism in Algeria in terms of the suffering of a nation of women. The sexualised vocabulary reveals precisely the dangerous lure of the rhetoric of subjugation and Djebar's own use of the sexual metaphor demonstrates the persuasive but pernicious power of the colonial vision. Furthermore, later in the text Djebar goes so far as to literalise this sexualisation of the French presence when she narrates that Fatma and Mériem secretly entertained French officers before being killed by them.[43] This scene actively performs the co-implication of colonial and sexual violence and conveys the disturbing confusion and interpenetration of colonialism with psychoanalytic fantasy and desire.

Djebar's initial, fantastical description of the colonial invasion as a violent encounter directed particularly against Algerian women is almost immediately juxtaposed with further reflection on the tyranny of language in the face of singular atrocities. Language itself is part of the coloniser's fantasy of conquest. As a result, just as she struggles to create a coherent autobiographical narrative, be it singular or collective, so too, as in *Femmes d'Alger*, does she urge that we question the form in which wartime episodes are written. Colonialism is also a 'scriptural economy' and colonial domination is assured through the controlling and embellishment of 'official history'.[44] Passages of metadiscursive commentary reveal Djebar's troubled awareness of the seductive power of this inscription of colonial glory, as she overtly criticises, as well as performs, its deceptive rhetoric. Examining accounts by higher French officers written after the invasion, for example, Djebar notes the way in which language becomes an aesthetic ornament, a rhetorical device that paints the exploits of the army in grandiose terms but that connotes only its own pure form. She reminds us that a plethora of versions appeared in the immediate aftermath of the capture of Algiers, but these artificial narratives, each competing with the other, mask more than they reveal. Some officers embellish accounts to such an extent that the reality of their unfolding is lost:

> Le mot lui-même, ornement pour les officiers qui le brandissent comme ils porteraient un œillet à la boutonnière, le mot deviendra l'arme par excellence. Des cohortes d'interprètes, géographes, ethnographes, linguistes, botanistes, docteurs divers et écrivains de profession s'abattront sur la nouvelle proie. Toute une pyramide d'écrits amoncelés en apophyse superfétatoire occultera la violence initiale.[45]

Furthermore, reading the general Bosquet's letters recounting the attack on Oran in 1840, she notices his cursory treatment of the detail of a woman's foot, severed from her body so that her anklet can be stolen. As Elaine Scarry points out, war narratives frequently back away from such physical details, and Bosquet passes flippantly over this image, attempting to absorb it into the 'scrofules de son style'.[46] Yet for Djebar, the detail stands out; it reveals the horror of the atrocities glossed over by existing accounts and announces its own impenetrable presence. At times herself fascinated with colonial rhetoric, Djebar nevertheless sets out to denounce it precisely by shifting its emphasis and illuminating its half-concealed kernel of brute reality.

It is Pélissier's report on the asphyxiation of an entire tribe in the caves of Nacmaria in 1845 that most shocks the narrator of *L'Amour, la fantasia*, however, because here the false rhetoric gives way to a horrific realism, while at the same time presenting the event as part of a narrative of colonial victory. If most of the reports on the occupation celebrate the triumph of the coloniser in order to hide the suffering of the natives, Pélissier's frank, direct description shamelessly offers an unprecedented insight into the physical horror of the scene even as it records the triumph of the attack. Djebar suggests that language risks distorting its referents, but, curiously, she is tempted to thank Pélissier for allowing an alarming lucidity to glimmer in the interstices of the extant reports, as if to indicate the falsity of their surrounding rhetoric and to critique their own celebratory purpose more clearly. Reading this singular report, Djebar reflects that 'écrire la guerre, Pélissier, qui redige son rapport du 22 juin 1845, a dû le pressentir, c'est frôler de plus près la mort et son exigence de cérémonie'.[47] War narratives such as this are torn between the necessity, and the impossibility, of grasping death and the inevitable imposition of a constructed artifice, of ritualised, ceremonial language that deforms the intractable horror it set out to recount. Pélissier's recollections of convulsions, bleeding and starvation cut through the edifice of false rhetoric, even as they recuperate the event into a meaningful story recording the cause of the French victory over the natives.

The sections narrating Chérifa's experiences in the maquis further demonstrate the difficulty associated with trying to find an appropriate language, and they also show quite explicitly that Djebar's own language risks distorting its singular subject in the same way as that of the generals she herself critiques. She is anxious to denounce the excessive grandiosity of Bosquet's accounts, but in spite of herself her writing shares with them, and with the work of Pélissier, Delacroix and also Fromentin, a frustrated desire to convey the particularity of a violated Algeria whose history in the end resists straightforward narration.[48] On one level then, Djebar tries to recount Chérifa's history in clear terms, providing her with a strong character and a powerful sense of agency. She stresses the importance of her role in the context of the rest of the war, linking her actions to their greater causes and implications. Despite this drive to specify her precise position in history, however, Djebar also finds that much of the substance of Chérifa's story escapes the narrative that sought to depict it. The apparently lucid report presents the facts in no uncertain terms: the moment when Chérifa finds her brother's dead body, as well as the sequences of torture, are baldly recounted. Nevertheless, Djebar's narrative is punctured with gaps; impressions and sensations are largely omitted. Language can offer a formal report, but it also glosses over the contingent substance that it struggles to encapsulate. Djebar's project may well have been to 'give voice' to characters whose experiences have so far been occluded, but at the same time she finds that the singularity of the moment is betrayed and reformed as soon as it is pinned down in language. She writes: 'petite sœur étrange qu'en langue étrangère j'inscris désormais, ou que je voile. La trame de son histoire murmurée, tandis que l'ombre réengloutit son corps et son visage, s'étire comme papillon fiché, poussière d'aile écrasée maculant le doigt.'[49] The language of social and political identification dissolves in favour of a more allusive evocation of the complicity between exploration and destruction. The bare, stark language breaks down before the report is completed, giving way to a series of more elusive images that offer no resolution or certainty.

While narratives of war are shot through with breaks and silences in this way, descriptions of intimacy and love also elusively both point to and move past the singularity of their referents. If she dared, unsatisfactorily, to attempt to voice the experiences of women subjugated and abused by French soldiers and officers, both at the time of the invasion and during the war of independence, Djebar also endeavours and struggles to capture their own repressed and occluded experiences of desire. Initially, for example, the narrator is concerned to elucidate the complex position of the young Arab girl in the face of the language of love, drawing attention to the factors that define her unease and advocating a renewed sense of agency and control. Reflecting on the position of three young girls who write letters in secret to men from the Arab world and beyond, she notes the transgressive nature of their gesture but also the self-affirmation that it manifests. The girls believe that, in corresponding with these men, they are less likely to be married to a stranger, and in this way they covertly rebel against a tradition of arranged marriages that denies them their agency. Furthermore, considering her own experiences of love, Djebar expresses a sense of the urgency and necessity for self-expression. Indeed, in *Ces voix* she asserts that the autobiographical project itself stemmed from the realisation that she had never spoken words of love in the French language. As a result, she writes 'je me suis plongée, de plus en plus totalement, dans cette auto-analyse, moi comme femme, également comme écrivain – et ce «*dit de l'amour*» qui se bloquait mystérieusement!'[50] In this sense, the text becomes an enterprise of self-investigation, whereby the author endeavours to understand and define her uneasy position as well as to overcome her reticence and voice affects that always seemed inaccessible.

Once again, however, this self-assertion dissolves into a plurality of singular affects that shatters rather than creates a coherent sense of subjectivity. On one level, this is because the narrator's experience of marriage is still governed by a tradition in which the feminine position is silent, passive and frequently uncomprehending. She experiences 'le cri, la douleur' of her wedding night in secret, reflecting at the same time on social repression and the way in which taboo exacerbates women's confusion and discomfort.[51] On another level, however, when actually attempting to express a sense of intimacy, the weight of such traditions, and the foreignness of the French language in relation to them, once again confuses and silences her. The language with which she tries to express herself is unable to access the infinitely contingent kernel that she wants to describe. Djebar's narrator quickly interrupts her own love story and expresses doubts and dissatisfactions that prevent the reader from accessing the scene in an unmediated way. Words are seen to efface the identities of the lover and the loved one, and she asks: 'comment avouer à l'étranger, adopté quelquefois en camarade ou en allié, que les mots ainsi chargés se désamorçaient d'eux-mêmes, ne m'atteignaient pas de par leur nature même, et qu'il ne s'agissait dans ce cas ni de moi, ni de lui?'[52] Love becomes a knot at the centre of the self that resists definition. Although this singular core is in a sense formed by the cultural environment that surrounds it, its substance eludes and transcends any attempt to circumscribe it. Language moves past and around it, veiling its singularity rather than exposing its specificity. It is in this sense that, though in some sense 'Westernised', Djebar's narrator here does describe herself as a 'femme voilée', as if the language of flattery and romance masks her rather than aptly describing or indeed moving her. As a result, she later explains:

> L'amour, si je parvenais à l'écrire, s'approcherait d'un point nodal: là gît le risque d'exhumer des cris, ceux d'hier comme ceux du siècle dernier. Mais je n'aspire qu'à une écriture de transhumance, tandis que, voyageuse, je remplis mes outres d'un silence inépuisable.[53]

Here again, words replace affects rather than organising them and incorporating them into the subject's sense of self. Djebar's narrator experiences such anxiety regarding the language of love that she pushes the reader away, refusing to describe her experience and rendering her own language opaque. The hazy outlines of the narrator and her characters reinvent themselves before language can demarcate and freeze their limits.

Djebar encapsulates this tension between the specific and the singular-plural most dramatically in the self-reflexive narrative structure of her work. Her narratives of war and love are repeatedly interrupted by the self-conscious reflections of the narrator, who strives endlessly to analyse and refine the narrative she constructs. As I suggested, both her wartime memories and confessions of affection are always succeeded by expressions of dissatisfaction and doubt. These sections seem to want to attain further lucidity, as if to redefine the author's position in relation to the contexts she examines in ever more precise terms. This desire to delineate the relation between language and the contingent affects that underscore the sense of self nevertheless results in further occlusion, since the addition of another level of analysis can only distance the narrator further from the kernel that she wishes to reach. If Djebar complains that language obscures or deforms the experiences she hoped to encapsulate, then further commentary can only exacerbate this obfuscation. Djebar at times explores her position in relation to history, culture and society, but each attempt adds another layer of opacity that further freezes the singularities beneath the surface of the text.

Djebar's text presents the reader with a series of layers. If she embarks in *L'Amour, la fantasia* on a quest for identity, she stops to analyse and redefine that quest at the first hurdle. Realising that her narrative distances her from the singular plurality of its referents rather than helping to specify and understand their position, she begins writing on another level in order to shed light on the particularity of that distance. Each time she reflects on the problems of masking and occlusion, however, she adds another layer that further screens the process of masking that she wants to describe. Each attempt to gloss the text results in the further occlusion of its singularity. If Djebar constantly comments on her own work, repeatedly explaining both within and outside the text the specific mechanisms of its creation, she also in the same process detaches herself further from the singular substance that resides elusively at its core. In her desire to identify her position she further effaces the kernel that she wanted to explore. The addition of further descriptions only emphasises more markedly the intractability of singular-plural being.

Finally, Djebar's self-analysis is itself troubled by the multiplicity of interruptions that break up the text. The narrative is punctuated not only with meta-commentary from the narrator but also with interjections made by other voices, as a profusion of interlocutors jostle for position in the text. If on one level Djebar's narrator finds that specificity dissolves into an infinite regress of singularity, then this singularity is also surrounded by a proliferation of alternative positions. The multiplication of narrative voices itself illustrates the continual interaction of singular being with diverse influences and contacts. It is this combination of strategies and levels that demonstrates the subtlety of Djebar's conception of individuation. She privileges unconditionally neither the concrete agency of Ahmad's thinking nor the hybridity proposed by Bhabha, referred to in my introduction. Instead, she exposes the limits of any fixed or specified position while also refusing to celebrate trans-culturation to such an extent that it connotes fusion, becoming a value in itself. The search for identity is coupled with reflections both on contingent singularity and on a form of plurality that resists totalisation.

Femmes d'Alger and *L'Amour, la fantasia* introduce into Djebar's corpus a new level of philosophical complexity, and she goes on to perform this complexity in the very self-conscious fabric of the writing. Experimenting with various models of individuation, Djebar at the same time distances herself from her own experiments by commenting on and revising them in the self-reflexive passages, and her writing is itself a site of contestation and debate. It is in this sense that the form of her novels, and the very multifaceted, literary texture of her writing, are actively used in order to reflect back on the potential dogmatism of any single theoretical model of postcolonial individuation. In the next group of works, however, Djebar looks not only at Algerian women in the aftermath of the war of independence, but on the active creation of some form of feminist critique. The focus on anti-colonialism that dominates *Femmes d'Alger* and *L'Amour, la fantasia* shifts also to incorporate an anti-patriarchal strategy, though once again Djebar's project will be to explore, to test and stretch various available approaches, rather than to offer a specified political stance.

CHAPTER THREE

Feminism and Women's Identity

> Je me présente à vous comme écrivain; un point, c'est tout. Je n'ai pas
> besoin – je suppose – de dire «femme-écrivain». Quelle importance?
> Dans certains pays, on dit «écrivaine» et, en langue française, c'est
> étrange, *vaine* se perçoit davantage au féminin qu'au masculin.[1]

The notion of womanhood or femininity occupies a fraught position
in Djebar's work. She is on the one hand clearly preoccupied with
Algerian women's particular experiences, narrating numerous scenes
of female oppression and liberation occurring at different moments
in the history of the country. She sets out to retrieve suppressed
feminine voices as she reflects on the relation between women and
writing, and on the importance of creating a sense of agency through
self-expression. On the other hand, however, Djebar also unsettles
the very category of femininity, dissociating herself from women's
writing movements and contesting the validity of any specified notion
of feminine experience. She retells the history of women in Algeria
while simultaneously questioning whether 'woman' names a meaningful position or a coherent mode of identification. Rejecting the term
'écrivaine', she seeks to transcend conventional gender distinctions
and to overthrow the attribution of divisive, classificatory labels such
as 'feminist'. If *Femmes d'Alger dans leur appartement* and *L'Amour,
la fantasia* set up a quest for (post)colonial Algerian women's identity
only to present their diverse female characters as unique, singular and
resistant to appropriation, then in the next group of texts this tension
comes both to structure and to complicate the author's development
of a feminist critique.

As her career progresses, Djebar increasingly experiments with
the construction of a political stand on the position of women in
Algeria. She seeks to criticise the repressive structure of the society
she examines and to promote the increased emancipation and liberation of Algerian women. In embarking on such a challenge, however,
she must struggle to negotiate a series of complex and contradictory

ideological positions. First, she is swayed by the need to emphasise feminine unity, stressing links between women in order to strengthen her own resistant voice. She participates overtly in a wider feminist movement, aware of the political necessity for solidarity and mutual support. This search for community ties in closely with the (unsatisfied) 'quête de l'identité' set up, and deconstructed, in the preceding texts. Despite these requirements, however, Djebar is also at pains to subvert modes of criticism that homogenise the feminine community, emphasising individuality, mobility and freedom of choice. This tension then itself ties in with the apparent division between Islamic and Western thought, and Djebar's contradictory strategies unravel the stereotypes associated with each position. While Islam is usually seen as a collectivist religion where personal opinion is a possible threat, Western thinking has been associated with the prioritisation of the individual. Challenging this simplistic polarisation, Djebar intermingles a search for community with a discovery of singular-plurality, and she troubles the conception of the individual as a coherent, self-contained agent while also disrupting assumptions regarding feminine sameness or community. She struggles to dissociate herself from the discourses of both Islam and Western secularism as they are conventionally perceived, exploring by turns both singularity and alternative forms of collectivity and revealing the ways in which these modes of thinking become intertwined. In doing so, she stresses how the opposition between the individual and the community, and its association with Western versus Eastern thought, is an artificial one, and she engages both with elements of Arab feminism and with the open-ended structures of French 'écriture féminine'.

Djebar's writing is clearly linked to its Islamic context and all that this implies regarding the position of women. Most notable here is the segregation between men and women that Muslim society commands. Djebar's writing is moulded, she insists, by this dichotomous structure and by an awareness of the strict division of roles. She notes that her language is marked both by a split between French and Arabic influence and by this opposition between the sexes. She differentiates 'masculine' and 'feminine' languages and stresses how one connotes the public domain while the other remains more elusive, consigned to the private sphere and more difficult to access and pin down:

[Je viens] d'un monde et d'une culture profondément marqués par une traditionnelle ségrégation sexuelle (les femmes au-dedans,

séparées des hommes au-dehors, le «public» masculin opposé à
l'intime et au familial, le discours monotone des lieux d'hommes,
différent de la polyphonie féminine – murmures et chuchotements
ou au contraire vociférations en société féminine…), [je viens] donc
de cette fatale, de cette mutilante dichotomie.[2]

Djebar's novels frequently illustrate the repressive nature of this
polarised structure by stressing the rigidity of the barriers enclosing
women within domestic space. At the beginning of *L'Amour, la
fantasia*, for example, Djebar describes the boundaries confining
women behind closed doors, and femininity is associated with interiority. Metaphors of 'le geôlier' and 'un mur orbe' emphasise the sense
of enclosure and sequestration that traditionally define feminine existence. Similarly, *Ombre sultane* explores this interiority further, and
though both novels seek to challenge this segregated structure, both
underline women's restriction of movement and the monotony of the
domestic routine.[3] As Fatima Mernissi describes, the public universe
of the *umma* is separated from the domestic universe of sexuality,
and spatial rules are so fundamental to the Muslim order that there
are few patterns for interaction between unrelated individuals.[4] The
sexes are separated by a rigid frontier that can be traversed only in
accordance with a narrow set of regulations.

This duality results in the restriction of freedom for women. It
is worth noting, however, that the extent to which this restriction
is bound up with a conception of female inferiority is a subject of
contention. Certainly, the much debated verse 4.34 of the Koran seems
to advocate male superiority, but many thinkers affirm that this is not
moral or religious superiority, but rather part of an economic system
instructing men to support their wives financially.[5] Despite her viru-
lent critique of the rules and regulations of Muslim society, Fatima
Mernissi stresses that these are not based on a conception of female
inferiority but on an understanding of the specificity of gender roles
and of the need to maintain this specificity as a means of controlling
and organising society.[6] Mernissi reminds us that women in Muslim
society are seen as powerful, but men have the authority to regulate
that power, enforcing the subordination of women within the family
structure. It is men, therefore, who make decisions and engage in
public life, while women occupy the domestic sphere. Oppression
results from this strict social segregation and from the limitations
placed on female activity, rather than from moral subordination.
Similarly, social divisions in Djebar's work are presented as adopted

conventions that do not stem from a history of negative judgements towards women, but from a renewed sense of gender roles proper to postcolonial Algerian society. These conventions, and their relationship with the early texts of Islam, will be analysed in the section on *Loin de Médine*.

Islamic feminist thinkers frequently comment on the contradiction and ambivalence towards women's roles within Muslim societies, and Djebar's work should be read against the background of diverse conceptions of femininity within Islam. Leïla Ahmed, for example, in her impressive study of *Women and Gender in Islam*, differentiates ethical Islam from the social and legal structures it can entail.[7] According to Ahmed, the Koran is highly egalitarian, addressing women directly and stressing both their spiritual equality with men and the equivalent worth of their labour. Sura 33.35 repeats that its commands refer to both men and women, and the ethical qualities cited are intended to pertain to both sexes. Furthermore, Ahmed shows how the practices sanctioned by Islam were instituted in a society that was highly androcentric, and Islam helped to ensure the protection of women, regulating and controlling practices such as polygamy. As a result, Islam now seems to be divided between this spiritual equality and the perpetuation of a set of social structures that seem entrenched and backward. Islam has 'two voices' and the ethical voice, though crucial to the religion's structure, seems increasingly not to be heard in Algeria. Political changes and the resurgence of Islamism, for example, have led to a clamping down on women's activity that distorts the implications of some of Islam's tenets regarding women. The equality of men and women before God is difficult to square with the repressive injunctions on women's social and legal position that persist in the society Djebar describes in her novels.

This divided structure leads to difficulties of interpretation, and stereotypes regarding the position of women within Islam abound. The veil becomes a central signifier for these misperceptions, and this ambivalence towards veiling will be a dominant reflection in *Ombre sultane*. Ahmed argues that during the lifetime of the Prophet only his wives were required to wear the veil and not all women in society. Mohammed suggested seclusion as a way of protecting his wives from intrusion by members of the community rather than as a universal mechanism of repression. The practice seems to evolve after his marriage with Zeinab, when a number of the male guests remained too long in her chambers. After the incident, the Prophet received the revelation recommending 'the descent of the curtain (hijab)' unusually suddenly, and the moment appears to be bound up with his own affective disquiet.[8] Furthermore, the Koran seems to recommend that women retain their modesty and keep their bosoms concealed, rather than imposing a full covering of all but the eyes.[9] The original doctrine is concerned with tact rather than with strict sequestration or with subordination. Equally, in the present day, the veil continues to contain a number of associations that vary according to the context in which it is worn. While for some its use is enforced with violence, for others it functions as a symbol of liberation, allowing freedom of movement without the imposition of the male gaze. There is also no single form of veil but a multiplicity of varying practices with divergent connotations. As the anthropologist Fadwa El Guindi writes, 'one property of the veil is its dynamic flexibility, which allows for spontaneous manipulation and a constant changing of form'.[10] Veiling practices contain a plurality of significations rather than connoting oppression *tout court*.

This openness to interpretation, however, has precisely been quashed by the recent hardening of Islamic belief and practice in Algeria in the aftermath of colonialism. Muslim societies, such as those of Morocco and Algeria, perceived colonial intervention as a threat to their Islamic identity, and a return to traditional practices is therefore associated with resistance to the legacy of the French presence. Modern changes and an emphasis on the diversity of interpretations are seen to collude with the enemy's project to undermine the religion. As a result, the subordinate position of women comes to be regarded as a symbol of tradition to be upheld at all costs. As Marnia Lazreg points out, Algerian society still clings to backward customs in order to guard against the infiltration of Western and neocolonial modes of thought.[11] Lazreg cites the Family Code of 1984 as an example of the way in which the government bought into this notion, since this further institutionalised the unequal status of women, reinforcing male authority and restricting female autonomy. The Code reasserts the importance of the family as a 'social cell' in which 'women emerge as the instruments of protection of the family headed by a man, to whom his wife owes "obedience" and "consideration"'.[12] The strict Muslim understanding of femininity has come to epitomise the religion's much treasured difference from encroaching neocolonial ideologies, and this has been reinforced in response to the increasing advancement of Western models. Significantly, Islam is also a collectivist religion and struggles for female agency are seen to participate in 'Western' individualist ideology. Women's rebellion is feared in the Muslim world because its implications are so far-reaching, disturbing not merely the family structure but communal harmony more generally, and championing the agency of the individual.[13] The subordination of women, then, continues not necessarily because of Islamic decree but because the very gesture of female rebellion is associated with the individualist psychology of Western secularism and capitalism.

The question remains as to what constitutes the most appropriate strategy for resistance or critique. What kind of feminism is required here? One Arab feminist, Nawal El Saadawi, insists above all on the importance of solidarity, asserting that individual agency will only be obtained through collective action. El Saadawi, an Egyptian novelist trained as a doctor, has campaigned for women's rights since the 1960s, and she argues repeatedly that unity between women will help to create a more formidable force of resistance. Although she is sharply aware of the differences between oppressed women, her emphasis is on collaboration and the creation of links. Women must express themselves individually, but feminist political critique relies on the assertion of a feminine community:

> Freedom for women will never be achieved unless they unite into an organised political force powerful enough and conscious enough to truly represent half of society. To my mind the real reason why women have been unable to complete their emancipation, even in the socialist countries, is that they have failed to constitute themselves into a political force powerful, conscious and dynamic enough to impose their rights.[14]

El Saadawi calls for a necessary movement from the local to the global and though she alludes to the importance of maintaining a sense of feminine diversity, she stresses the need for a unity created over and above particular differences. She speaks of women's oppression worldwide, anxious not to diabolise Islam but to show how many societies restrict or subordinate women in contrasting ways (Western societies according to El Saadawi operate a sort of 'symbolic clitoridectomy', and make-up can function in a similar way to the veil). Resistance will spring from co-operation between these different women. Similarly, El Saadawi, like Djebar, contests the division of African women into

North and South, and she champions African unity against colonial and neocolonial domination.[15]

The risk with stressing unity in this way is that femininity can start to appear as a homogeneous category. El Saadawi is aware of this danger and she emphasises collaboration and collective action rather than similarity. Nevertheless, when she advocates the alliance of all women regardless of their differences in the name of universal liberation, it can seem that patriarchal oppression is conceived as a single and unchanging force. Similarly, when at other times she focuses on Arab (and also African) women, these seem to form a deceptively unified group. Most importantly, a general investment in collective identity is to be regarded with scepticism since it could reinforce gender and cultural stereotypes. El Saadawi is conscious of these pitfalls and she manages to escape this charge, but it is worth remembering that certain Western feminists have associated Arab women with a particular identity category and as a result have simplified and misunderstood their differences. Chandra Mohanty's much-cited article warns against this temptation, criticising the notion of the 'Third World woman' and arguing that the nature of women's oppression in different societies is highly variable.[16] Similarly, Lazreg denounces the way in which women from Algeria become subsumed by the broader label 'Arab women', embodying at the same time a culture that is presumed to be self-same and 'inferior' to that of the West. Collective terms such as these serve to objectify Islamic women and posit them as an unmediated 'other'. Some degree of collective action may be necessary, but the notion of a collective feminine identity needs to be treated with suspicion.

These difficulties indicate that a more appropriate mode of reflection might emphasise individual difference. Hélène Cixous, for example, whose origins are Algerian but whose thinking is also steeped in 'French theory', proposes introspection and personal self-expression as likely tools for resistance. As she writes in *Photos de racines*, Cixous grew up in Algeria, but her migrant, hybrid origins differ considerably from those of Djebar (who, curiously, chooses not to engage closely with her work). The descendant of European Jewish immigrants, Cixous has both German and Spanish roots, and her relationship with the Algerian community is one of exile and non-belonging. Nevertheless, her particular emphasis on self-expression recalls the passages in Djebar championing feminine agency, and certainly her call for the reintegration of mind and body seems to be answered by Djebar's descriptions of corporeal harmony in *Ombre sultane* and *Vaste est la prison*. Cixous's pamphlet 'Le Rire de la Méduse' addresses itself to 'women' as a collective group, but the author repeatedly attacks any notion of typical femininity and she emphasises endless singularity and variability: 'ce qui me frappe c'est l'infinie richesse de leurs constitutions singulières'.[17] At the centre of Cixous's thinking is the concept of the feminine voice, which she urges should surge forth in writing, uniting mind and body and exploding the confines of conventional, 'patriarchal' discourse. Crucially, however, this voice is not self-same but follows the endlessly changing rhythms of the body. Women should express themselves without adhering to a fixed subject position and revealing all the mobile affects of corporeal experience. This mode of writing is deeply tied up with a reintegration of self and body, advocating a sense of harmony with the unconscious and transcending the divisions of writing that is deemed 'patriarchal'. As Toril Moi points out, however, at times this privileging of individual liberation neglects to account for the benefits of collaboration. Cixous can be seen to be guilty of reproducing a (Western?) myth of individualism while failing to analyse the importance of interactive networks.[18]

An emphasis on singularity, then, needs to coexist with an awareness of the ways in which singular women interact with one another regardless of their differences. We need to understand that the feminist 'community' is not one that privileges resemblance, membership or belonging. Rather, resistance is achieved by means of collaboration, combined with a respect for singular difference. The individual and the community are not polar opposites. Instead, allegiances can be multiple and changing, as feminist women engage with contradictory forces without affirming a fixed, collective stance. As Miriam Cooke asserts, this form of interaction across singular differences is exemplified by the new virtual networks run by Islamic feminists, where hierarchy and partisanship are replaced by a more open-ended system of connection. Unlike official organisations, which are more usually constricted by frontiers such as nationality and class, Cooke notes that 'cybernetworks construct virtual links that connect isolated individuals in a process of vital information exchange'.[19] These networks are only starting to emerge but the mode of interaction that they promote does suggest that notions of singularity and collectivity are being rethought so as to allow women of divergent backgrounds to produce a political stance without homogenising the members of the community. This open-ended mode of affiliation allows for a diversity of interpretations and works against the fixing of any doctrine into an immutable, determined stance. The term 'Islamic feminism', used provisionally by Cooke, is as a result itself misleading, implying a specific movement rather than a set of changing and possibly contradictory concerns.

Ombre sultane

Djebar's 'feminist' project consists in a similar pattern of convergence and divergence. Concerned to depict the conditions of life for women in Algeria, Djebar locates common experiences while also stressing dissimilarities, conflicts and differences. Complicity and solidarity between women is reflected at the same time as disidentification and dissent. Feminist resistance remains at the centre of *Ombre sultane*, but this entails less a specific position or agenda, upholding or refuting unequivocally either Islamic doctrine or Western feminist critique, than a series of questions regarding women's variable roles and interaction. Feminine community is explored and celebrated, but a superficial desire for unity covers over not only the singular-plurality of that community's members, but also the inequalities underpinning their reciprocal gaze. As a result, it seems that Djebar ties in with both El Saadawi and Cixous at once, reluctant to privilege a single ideology but exploring the tensions between the singular and the communal that feminist struggle involves. She fights against the restrictions experienced by Algerian women only to throw into question the very possibility of defining or categorising those women in a single, unified way. Algerian women have a 'specific' history, shaped by the mediation of a variety of influences, but singular characters at the same time critique that history and occupy a series of unique, divergent and mobile positions in relation to it.

Ombre sultane traces these paradoxical movements of identification and dissociation in the creation of a feminist critique. Dramatising the divergent forms of feminist resistance proposed by El Saadawi and Cixous, Djebar here examines the problematic minutiae of two women's shared revolt, their intimate fusion and separation, before tackling broader historical movements in *Vaste est la prison* and *Loin de Médine*. The text focuses on the singular and intimate stories of Hajila and Isma, wives of the same man. Isma, the first wife, proposes Hajila as a second wife in order to liberate herself from imprisonment within the confines of the traditional marriage structure. The text modulates between focusing on each of the women, noting the differences between their lifestyles and the contrasts between Hajila's subjugation and Isma's newly found freedom. Most importantly, however, the narrative voice is for the most part that of Isma, who narrates her own experiences of liberation while also speaking for Hajila and dictating her actions almost in the manner of a stage-director. Her tone fluctuates between one of empathy and complicity and one of control, and she seems to perceive Hajila both as a double and as a mirror image of herself before she found the courage to improve her condition. Just as Dinarzade engineers her sister Shéhérazade's survival, Isma contributes to Hajila's liberation. The characters of *Ombre sultane*, however, seem at once similar and opposed, complicitous and competitive, and Djebar traces shifting modulations between identification and divergence rather than simply celebrating feminine communion or shared history. If many critics, including Katherine Gracki, Mireille Calle-Gruber and Silvia Nagy-Zekmi, have argued that the novel champions uncomplicated female solidarity, I would suggest that this exploration of communality is at the same time underpinned by a disturbing revelation of inequality or incompatibility in the creation of a feminist strategy of resistance.[20]

First of all, many of the early scenes focus on the oppression suffered by Hajila in her husband's home and Isma's narrative minutely unpicks the inequality of their marital relations. The opening pages express her dissatisfaction in bald, frank terms, encouraging Hajila's revolt while expressing sympathy and pity. Isma notes how 'tu t'aperçois que tu as froid. Tes yeux sont inondés de larmes. Ton mouchoir ajouré, froissé, tombe', and her succession of brief, sparse sentences emphasises both the stark brutality of Hajila's situation and her co-wife's passivity.[21] The husband is denoted simply by the anonymous 'il', remaining faceless and indistinct, and Isma underlines the impersonal nature of their interaction. The bedroom scenes are similarly recounted in cold, succinct terms, as Isma describes the touch of 'une main' on Hajila's breast without sensuality, narrating again in brief, curtailed phrases Hajila's recoil from contact. Later on, in the rape scene, Isma notes this same tension and contraction, as Hajila is crushed by her husband's weight pressing down on her body and hindering her movement. Here again, he is described simply as 'l'homme', so that the focus is on Hajila and her inability to resist him, more than on his oppressive agency. Isma also indicates that Hajila is simultaneously oppressed by her mother's complicity with the patriarchal system, since Touma complains about her inability to conceive a child. This contributes to the sense that it is a general social structure that causes Hajila's misery, that women play an active part in the continuation of their own oppression. Although for the most part these scenes appear to take the side of Hajila and to denounce the horrific injustice of her situation, Isma does at times also stress the success of her own claim for agency, in contrast to what she perceives as Hajila's weakness.

The scenes of oppression, however, are interspersed with descriptions of Hajila's clandestine walks outside the home, and these offer a glimpse of her potential for self-affirmation. Here, Isma forcefully stresses the contrast between the constriction of interior, domestic space and the freedom associated with the open space of the town. As Hajila approaches the sea, the narrator comments on her actions ('avancer au bord du gouffre. Tentation de t'y plonger: s'y renverser pour flotter dans cette immensité, face à l'immensité inversée du ciel') as if to encourage Hajila to absorb the sense of freedom produced by her contemplation of empty space.[22] Again, however, Isma's insidious emphasis on Hajila's hesitation and weakness creeps through into her description of the vista, as liberation is coupled with fear and bewilderment. The unsteadiness resulting from the opening out of the horizon is also combined with an overwhelming of the senses, as Hajila struggles to assimilate all that she sees. At the same time, Hajila enjoys the act of observing passers-by and their activities, the squares, gardens, benches and cars, and she drinks in her environment with her eyes. This freedom to observe directly counteracts the enclosure imposed upon her ordinarily, and on one level Hajila's conscious, watchful gaze is itself a gesture of re-appropriation and control. Seizing on everyday details, Hajila enjoys the freedom and sense of power she derives from choosing the object of her gaze, so that perception itself becomes an instrument of affirmation. Seating herself aside from the crowd, 'tu ne saisis ici qu'une paire de souliers éculés, là une veste trop voyante, tout près une main tenant un mégot et ponctuant devant ton nez un discours déroulé loin, au-dessus de toi'.[23] Nevertheless, it is difficult to dissociate Hajila's seizing of liberation from Isma's minute charting of the objects and people scrutinised, and the narrator's own description of her co-wife's observation constitutes a further attempt on her part to catalogue and therefore master the proliferating details of the scene. Such passages clearly set out to celebrate Hajila's seizing of agency and intimate enjoyment, but Isma's control of the perspective cannot help but unsettle the surface impression of support and shared emancipation.

As in *Les Enfants du nouveau monde* and *L'Amour, la fantasia*, the veil plays a complex role in this modulation between imprisonment and liberation. If the veil is frequently seen in 'the West' as a signifier of oppression, Djebar reveals how for Hajila it is on the contrary precisely that which confers liberation. While on one level it functions as a barrier or a restriction, Hajila's use of the veil on her clandestine outings allows her to remain anonymous and to circulate freely. The veil, though associated with subordination and segregation, also paradoxically allows certain rules to be broken, since it means that the wearer can walk in the streets sheltered from the other's gaze. Thus, though she herself has shed the veil, Isma observes 'c'était comme si, avec ce tissu, tu te préparais à concocter le mensonge. Comme si le voile emmagasinait dans ses plis ta future journée. Ton échappée.'[24] The folds of the material become not so much a barrier as a form of mediation between the woman and the outside world, a point of connection rather than a symbol of separation and seclusion. Moreover, when Hajila tentatively removes her veil while walking in the street, she feels both disorientated and liberated, and the manner in which she clutches its fabric beneath her arm suggests that she wants both to reject it and to cling to it. On putting it back on, she becomes once again 'un fantôme', implying both a repressive effacement of the self and a haven of anonymity. The veil allows for Hajila's presence in the street while simultaneously assuring her absence, evoking a sort of spectral presence freed from the determinations of identity. The narrator also affirms that 'tu retrouves la voix', as if unveiling implies a visibility that renders further personal expression impossible while the veil paradoxically allows the wearer to speak.[25] Once again, however, the irony that it is Isma's voice to which the reader has access surreptitiously colours our apprehension of Hajila's veiling practices. The veil clearly is presented as both oppressive and protective, and its use can be either passively endured or affirmatively reclaimed. Yet Isma's scrutiny of Hajila's tentative retention of the veil at the same time puts her into the position of the controlling viewer and reinforces Hajila's timid and passive position in relation to her liberated co-wife. Isma's own act of observation in turn unveils Hajila again and mimics the colonial gesture of celebrating Algerian women's shedding of the veil in order to ensure their visibility.

The modulating structure of *Ombre sultane* further reinforces the persistent sense of comparison, or potentially competition, between the apparently complicit women. Hajila's position as subordinated and repressed is constantly contrasted with Isma's current emancipation. The characters seem to be diametrically opposed, signifying enslavement and liberation respectively, and the juxtaposition of chapters focusing on the activities of each intensifies the opposition. Djebar does set out to pinpoint the potential affinities between the two women, and the contrasts at times seem to be undermined by the underlying goal of patriarchal denunciation. Hajila's oppression contains moments of freedom reminiscent of Isma's descriptions of her own experience, while Isma's consciousness continues to be overshadowed by memories of her past seclusion. Nevertheless, Isma's liberation is starkly emphasised in the sections describing her new life, and Isma's narrative voice can also be seen to stress the superiority of her position. In the initial section, Isma re-imagines her walks in the streets of Paris, underlining her freedom of movement, her sensual enjoyment of the feeling of the air on her bare legs and the sharpness of her gaze. The passage contrasts with the stifling atmosphere of the section on Hajila, and Isma's appreciation of physical and sensual details at the same time foreshadows her descriptions of former's clandestine walks, as if to emphasise her appropriation of Hajila's perspective. In the next section, the description of intimacy between lovers directly opposes the coldness and anonymity of Hajila's encounters with her husband. Isma, like the narrator of the initial section of *Vaste est la prison*, revels in the details of her lover's body, she enjoys his closeness while also placing herself in a position of control:

> Chaque nuit, j'affine la connaissance de l'autre par degrés imperceptibles – éprouver le creux de son cou, la confiance de ses épaules, tâter d'un doigt qui prend son temps toutes ses côtes, percevoir les battements de son coeur tout en levant les paupières vers son visage.[26]

If Hajila experiences her husband's presence as an impersonal and indistinct source of oppression, then this detailed scrutiny and enjoyment of the other's most intimate features overtly constitutes a seizing of power. Most disturbingly, Isma seems to be setting herself up as a sexual subject, desiring and desirable, while belittling Hajila to the status of a passive object. As Anjali Prabhu argues, Isma's descriptions of her own sexuality are coupled with a questioning of Hajila's desir-ability from a male perspective.[27] These sorts of contrasts problema-tise the apparent ethics of sharing and again place Isma, paradoxically, in the position of a masculine viewer subordinating the object of his gaze. Isma's perspective seems paradoxically to promote both Hajila's liberation and her own appropriation of the position of control.

The final scene in the hammam develops and crystallises the simul-taneous mutual identification and conflict between the two women. It is here that Isma passes Hajila the key to the house, and she sets out to open the door to her freedom and to play the role of the supportive Dinarzade. Here Djebar seems to evoke a fleeting moment of femi-nine harmony that would transcend the very division between self and other. The pattern of reflection and opposition culminates in a moment of communion that aims to overcome ordinary divisions, as well as the conventions and norms of social discourse. The hazy atmosphere blurs recognition, as the narrator reflects: 'ne plus dire «tu», ni «moi», ne rien dire; apprendre à se dévisager dans la moiteur des lieux'.[28] The boundaries between Isma and Hajila become indis-tinct, as the characters release themselves from the determinations of their everyday lives into this alternative form of communality.[29] Furthermore, this blurring evokes a renewed system of communi-cation, which consists less of a convention-bound relation between signifier and signified than of a series of more immediate and visceral sounds. We are told that 'la voix des visiteuses du jour – éclats de fatigue prolongés, soupirs et rires brefs en échos persistants – emplis-sent la gravité de ce monastère: brouhaha, ombres lovées, furtives'.[30] Social language is replaced with a form of expression that is closer to the body, implying a more intimate sharing than that sanctioned in public space. This most intense, pre-linguistic and psychic form of communion can be read, however, as both complicitous and appro-priative. Isma stresses her sense of fusion with Hajila and sets this up as a symptom of her desire to help her co-wife, but the seizing of the other's perspective and the blurring of self and other could also be seen as a further controlling gesture. Isma's subsequent, renewed scrutiny of Hajila's actions, her unannounced pursuit as Hajila walks in the town, again designates her as the silent *voyeuse*.

This subtle game of fusion and separation, complicity and control, is played out in Djebar's series of references to the inter-text of the *Arabian Nights*. On one level, as I have suggested, Isma plays a supportive role, since she provides Hajila with the key that will secure her liberation. Her position mirrors that of Dinarzade, the faithful sister who witnesses 'la fête sensuelle' and whose proximity to the conjugal bed ensures the survival of the sultan's wife. Just as Dinarzade's vigilant presence in Shéhérazade's bedroom provides the key to her sister's survival, so Isma's watchful gaze over Hajila's domestic scenes seems to lead to the liberation of the subjugated woman. In addition, Djebar plays with this comparison even further, blurring the identities of the sisters. Isma mirrors Dinarzade, but she is also the story-teller, recalling Shéhérazade and her use of invention and creativity as a means of survival. Isma's creation of a narrative, as for Shéhérazade, is itself a tool for self-affirmation and resistance. Djebar alludes to the feminine complicity demonstrated in the *Arabian Nights*, but she also goes one step further, showing how Isma plays both roles at once and succeeds in fusing the identities of the sisters. Moreover, Isma and Hajila both shift disconcertingly between assertion and occlusion, blurring the positions of the characters of the *Arabian Nights*: 'Isma, Hajila: arabesque de noms entrelacés. Laquelle des deux, ombre, devient sultane, laquelle, sultane des aubes, se dissipe en ombre d'avant midi?'[31] The characters modulate between exposure and concealment, and the roles of Shéhérazade and Dinarzade become indistinct. As Calle-Gruber argues, 'aucun de ses personnages n'est véritablement un sujet – défini selon les conventions romanesques, ce solide *character* des fictions réalistes', and both women are indistinct shadows of one another.[32]

Once again, however, despite Djebar's apparent celebration of complicity and doubling, closer reading uncovers the inequality of their interaction, and Isma's ongoing control of the narrative perspective places her in a disturbing position of dominance. She engineers Hajila's liberation but she also takes the latter's position to such an extent that she directs and manages her actions. The blurring of self and other leads to an overwhelming sense of appropriation, as Isma speaks for Hajila, as well as appearing to determine her responses. Again, as Prabhu argues, the text reveals the violence of written narrative as the narrator fixes and reduces meaning in her painstaking tracking of the other's movements.[33] The repeated use of the pronoun 'tu' contributes to this sense of stage-direction, as Isma narrates Hajila's actions and her affects as if dictating their unfolding. Isma writes the script of the 'mélodrame', projecting herself into Hajila's position and overtly stealing her voice. This appropriation of the other's position results in the sense that Isma is the sole creator of the story as she

moulds Hajila in her image regardless of the other's singular difference. On the one hand, Isma describes her attempts at self-effacement
before Hajila, but on the other she comments on the dissolution of
Hajila's subjectivity beneath the autonomy of her own narrative. She
affirms 'c'est toujours moi qui te parle, Hajila. Comme si, en vérité, je
te créais. Une ombre que ma voix lève', revealing the ways in which
her text determines Hajila's character, which was otherwise indistinct.[34] Despite her desire to provide Hajila with a voice and a means
for achieving freedom, she finds that her language creates and appro-
priates the latter's identity in terms which are not hers. Her discourse
tries to give form to, but also deforms, a subject whose singularity
remains in shadow.

In a final twist, the doubling of identity figures both complicity
and effacement, and the interplay between Hajila and Isma also
evokes for both characters the fragility of the supposed boundary
between the secure individual and community with the other. The
mutual identification of the two women reinforces solidarity, but it
also risks leading to the dissolution of a sense of self. The identities of
the characters risk becoming blurred and the search for solidarity can
lead not only to power imbalances, but also to the dissolution of individual agency. Isma provides Hajila with a means of resistance but
her presentation as Hajila's mirror image entails a dangerous form
of occlusion and disorientation. This effacement is emphasised when
the husband on two separate occasions confuses Hajila with Isma,
addressing Hajila with the name of his former wife. It is as if women
are thoroughly interchangeable; one replaces the other and little
attention is paid to the change. If Isma's identification with Hajila is
on the one hand a symbol of communal strength, Djebar suggests on
the other hand that this fusion risks denying each character her own
individual identity. The fusion of self and other becomes a threatening confusion, a confusion that leads Isma to appropriate Hajila's
position and that leads Hajila to abdicate a sense of control. For both
characters, putting oneself in the position of the other results in the
loss of a firm grasp of what that position might be.

The interjection between the first and second parts of the text
pinpoints precisely this indeterminacy. Reflecting on the use of the
word 'derra', denoting the new wife, Djebar uncovers the multiple
implications it contains. First, 'derra' connotes rivalry and competition, evoking the conflict arising between the wives of one man. The
word implies a 'blessure' inflicted by the second wife upon the first,

suggesting that patriarchal society also succeeds by pitting women against each other. At the same time, however, the passage hints at the threat that their identities become blurred: '*la seconde épouse qui apparaît de l'autre côté de la couche n'est-elle pas semblable à la première, quasiment une partie d'elle, celle-là même qui n'a pu jouir et vers laquelle l'époux dresse ses bras vengeurs*'.[35] The second wife is a reflection and a projection of the first, extending the limits of her sense of self. Furthermore, Djebar notes how the first wife withdraws on the presence of the second in order to reappear on the following night. The women come and go, continually swapping positions and modulating between presence and absence, self-affirmation and effacement. Mirroring and complementing one another, the women are bound up in a game of assertion and withdrawal and the man rhythmically drifts back and forth from one to the next. At once the same and different, present and absent, the identities of the wives remain suspended in this indeterminate space. Isma's relationship with Hajila is both complicitous and rivalrous, but in both cases it heralds a threatening dissolution of self and other and an exposure of the limits of individual control.

Ombre sultane on one level suggests that complicity and mutual support between women can function as a vital tool for resistance. Djebar's novel does retain an active, political feminist agenda, and it does to a certain extent promote collective action regardless of the singularity of each character. Nevertheless, the text also reaches beyond this at least partially politicised reflection and probes the shifting, disturbing processes of identification that can underpin such communality. If insubordination and critique require a sense of feminine solidarity and an affirmation of shared experiences, Djebar also draws attention to processes of fusion, effacement and possible re-appropriation subtending this collaborative structure. Women derive strength from working together but mutual identification threatens the self with dissolution and loss. Moreover, if on the one hand this blurring of self and other evokes a unique form of harmony that challenges conventional understandings of the individual and proposes alternative forms of intersubjective communication, on the other hand it could lead to an appropriation of the other's voice. Speaking with and for Hajila, Isma paradoxically affirms the former's position while depriving her of her agency, and her openness to the experience of the other also leads her to reassert her control over the otherness encountered. The relationship between the women performs this continuing conflict between communion and singularisation, sharing and individual control.

Vaste est la prison

The composite demands of singular and collective identification are further explored and unsettled in *Vaste est la prison*. Shifting the focus away from the intense intimacy of *Ombre sultane*, *Vaste est la prison* explores the broader links between Algerian women at different moments in the history of the country. Anxious not to privilege the individual to the detriment of communal relations, Djebar seeks connections between women of different epochs and laments their common plight. She traces similarities across generations and constructs a sort of genealogy of Algerian women in order the better to challenge the oppressive structures with which they contend. Despite this project, however, she also again reveals her scepticism regarding feminine identity, and she troubles the possibility of conceiving 'woman' as a particular group starkly differentiated from 'man'. Moreover, Djebar moves away from the stifling interaction of Isma and Hajila's relationship in *Ombre sultane* and emphasises that what is shared by the women of *Vaste est la prison* is precisely their unique and singular experiences of evasion or flight, their resistance to containment. Feminine community connotes not sameness but common currents of self-affirmation and resistance. Djebar's characters here are also less imprisoned than forgotten, and she rescues them not so much from domestic oppression as from historical occlusion and false generalisation.

In *Vaste est la prison*, Djebar on one level creates links between the women of the past and those of the present, evoking a shared sisterhood that transcends apparent divergences. The legend of Tin Hinan, narrated at the centre of the novel in among fragments from the present, serves as a focal point for this genealogy. Djebar recounts the flight of the Berber princess from the North, the trials of her journey and her death at Abalessa. Most significant, however, is the discovery in 1925 of archaeological remains, including the stele with inscriptions in the tifinagh alphabet that had been presumed lost. This writing, which we are told was maintained and guarded by the women while the men were occupied on the battlefield, becomes for Djebar a sort of feminine language that she connects with the

rhythms of women's voices in the present. Djebar hopes to gather
together these linguistic traces in order to revive the past and to
establish its renewal in modern Algerian life. Her own writing constitutes '*[un] rêve tenace qui tente de rassembler les cendres du temps,
de s'agripper aux traces autour des sépulcres par miracle conservées*',
building a bridge between epochs and drawing out common traits.[36]
The sounds and texture of Tin Hinan's writing are for Djebar repli-
cated in contemporary women's idiolects, linked to the past not so
much through meaning as through musical echoes and reflected
images. Djebar concludes with the following description: '*notre écriture la plus secrète, aussi ancienne que l'étrusque ou que celle des
«runes» mais, contrairement à celles-ci, toute bruissante encore de
sons et de souffles d'aujourd'hui, est bien legs de femme, au plus
profond du désert*'.[37] This notion of a common women's language
consisting of transported echoes announces the establishment of
some form of feminine communion. Modern, male archaeologists,
however, struggle to decipher this language, implying that it contains
a feminine idiom beyond their grasp.

At the same time, however, Djebar is not interested in 'Arab
women' as a unified cultural community, but in the partial transmission of traces from diverse origins and in the recurrence of echoes
across temporal and cultural frontiers. She explores the passage of
idioms from one generation to another without suggesting that this
linguistic exchange signifies homogeneity. In the section following the
legend of Tin Hinan, Djebar presents a series of fragments narrating
women's flight and describing the fleeting, partially preserved
languages they spoke. The first of these fragments relates to Zoraidé
from *Don Quixote*, who frees a slave and flees her own captivity,
and whose writing, used in the escape plot, is described as ephemeral
and largely obscured. This feminine evasion, and the accompanying
loss of Zoraidé's language, mirrors according to Djebar the plight of
contemporary Algerian women. Furthermore, the narrator's mother
remembers and passes on traces of feminine dialects that weave unset-
tlingly in and out of the centuries. As I suggested, these consist not of
a coherent system of signification but of disparate remnants:

> *Quelques détails dans les broderies des costumes féminins, quelque
> accent déformant le dialecte local et gardé comme seul résidu, parler
> arabo-andalou maintenu le plus long possible... Surtout la musique
> dite «andalouse» et que l'on nomme «classique», elle que de simples
> artisans – savetiers, barbiers ou tailleurs musulmans et juifs – prati-
> quaient avec conscience dans les veillées.*[38]

Fragments of images and musical cadences carry through history and re-emerge in modern practices. Djebar herself writes, she affirms, in the light of these influences, inflecting her modern histories with the language of the past.

The text of *Vaste est la prison* itself connects a series of diverse narratives and moments. Djebar's own work is situated at a crossroads, highlighting links that may not previously have been identified and constructing a form of genealogy out of the traces that she finds during her research. This feminine collectivity is consciously built using disparate fragments, figuring as a result not original membership or belonging but common threads reminiscent of Nancy's relationality. If Djebar uses the term 'genealogy', in this case it does not connote a rooted structure or an organic, homogeneous community. Rather, it denotes a means of tracing how past events subtly come to overshadow present experiences and modes of speech. Critics have emphasised this collective construction in Djebar's work, describing the feminine genealogy as an alternative form of community that does not rely on plenitude or organic identity but on suppressed echoes and hints of affinity. As Katherine Gracki points out, Djebar's collectivity transcends blood ties and ethnicity, exploring partial links that traverse diverse spaces and epochs.[39] Even more radically, Miriam Cooke argues that Djebar's feminine language escapes some of the difficulties experienced by writers such as Derrida, Khatibi and Memmi when analysing their disjunctive relationship with their mother tongue.[40] For Djebar, unlike for the male writers, language is dissociated from a desire for self-presence or possession, and the traces of feminine language that transcend the epochs are treasured for their creative power rather than for their (lack of) ability to evoke an originary communality.

Fleeting visions of created unity are, however, constantly threatened by fragmentation. While the writing of the past is to a certain extent refigured in present discourses, its resurgence is also fragile and tenuous, connoting rupture as much as continuity. The constructed community between women is dispersed and fractured, and the writing that it is hoped will serve as a point of connection is for the most part obscured or extinct. Linguistic resurgence to a certain extent emphasises continuity and sharing, but the language of the present is simultaneously always marked by the absence of the past, its eradication from modern narratives. Damaged and pillaged during the Algerian war, the narrator's mother's Andalucian music is consigned to oblivion and she can remember only curtailed phrases that become impossible fully to reconstruct. Furthermore, this loss colours Djebar's language even as she strives to accomplish its revival. Written in French, the text is immersed in the culture of the coloniser, and the traces of an alternative feminine language murmur tacitly beneath this imposing edifice. Djebar reflects '*j'écris pour me frayer mon chemin secret, et dans la langue des corsaires français qui, dans le récit du Captif, dépouillèrent Zoraidé de sa robe endiamantée, oui, c'est dans la langue dite «étrangere» que je deviens de plus en plus transfuge*'.[41] The French narrative evokes the absence of that which the author set out to recapture and the feminine community represented by linguistic resurgence falters and breaks down. The narrative both seeks and undermines the communication between past and present.

Djebar's evocation of the fugitive as a common motif itself troubles notions of a stable collective identity. The women of Djebar's narrative share not a fixed position but the experience of evasion, as they question the notion of a secure home in favour of personal reinvention. Feminine identity is not rooted in a specific place but is endlessly mobile and subject to renewal. Characters derive a sense of self not from habitation and belonging but precisely from their ability to break away from home and roots. If there is any broader feminine community evoked in Djebar's text, then this is not a genealogy that is securely located and positioned but one that champions self-invention and rebirth. As Chandra Mohanty and Biddy Martin argue in their essay on feminist politics, with reference to an autobiographical narrative by Minnie Bruce Pratt, the desire for a secure place from which to speak is constantly undercut by an awareness of the limitations that such a position would impose.[42] Similarly, despite the search for a feminine collective voice, Djebar's characters ultimately refuse to be contained within static social and cultural structures, asserting movement and choice in a multiplicity of different ways. Furthermore, feminism itself is not a 'home' for Djebar, as she does not argue for a single cause or present a particular set of issues, but focuses rather on the dynamism of male/female relationships.

The middle section on the fugitives of the past is both preceded and succeeded by extracts of women's lives in the modern era. In the first part of *Vaste est la prison* the narrator traces her thoughts and emotions during a brief love affair with a younger man and her subsequent separation from her husband. Here, the focus echoes once again the analysis of the action of departure and reinvention in the 'historical' sections, yet it is personal identity and agency that are foregrounded, despite the obvious affinity between the narrator's liberation and the flight of the women recorded in the other sections. As I have suggested, comparable experiences link different generations of women, but here the highly introspective and self-analytical reflections of the narrator suggest that her emancipation is an intensely private process. Significant here, as in *L'Amour, la fantasia*, is also the intimacy of the first-person narrative, since Islamic women are traditionally deprived of the privilege of self-expression. In this case, however, Djebar's narrator scrutinises her own affects and emotions with such precision that other characters appear as hazy outlines, apprehended only through the prism of the narrator's own psychological trajectory. In the first scene, for example, the narrator minutely charts the sensations she experiences on awakening from a siesta into a new life, and there are no other characters present. The scene takes place after the conclusion of the events of the following pages, recording the narrator's restoration of a sense of self and agency. Even her environment is bathed in an atmosphere of regeneration, 'tout apparaît irisé d'un éclairage vierge', and she notes the overflowing of the sensation of revival onto surrounding objects. In addition, other characters remain foggy and indistinct, 'des simulacres, projections funambulesques, mouvantes, se complaisant dans l'éphémere'.[43] Her heightened awareness of her own condition makes her focus on physical sensations, sounds and visual details rather than on social interaction.

This self-affirmation arises from the liberation she experiences when falling in love. The object of her affections is himself indistinct, referred to simply as 'l'Aimé', as if to foreground the importance of her perception of him rather than his particular individuality. The episode is formative because it helps the narrator to reintegrate self and body, building a sense of harmony with herself more noticeably than with the other. She frequently speaks of a return to childish sensations, for example, as she seeks to shake off the shackles of self-consciousness and to follow the rhythms of her body. In the section on the dance, she forgets social norms and expectations, allowing herself to be carried by the music and using that rhythm to suspend consciousness and artificial control. Cutting herself off momentarily from her companions, she remembers 'je me croyais en même temps seule, surgie d'une longue nuit, et abordant enfin, sous ces projecteurs rougis, le rivage'.[44] This communion between mind and body, and the self-expression reflected in the dance, recalls the exhortations of Cixous's work, symbolising the transcendence of ordinary divisions between the mental and the physical, conscious mind and unconscious affect. The passage is also reminiscent of one of the early sections in *Le Blanc de l'Algérie*, where the narrator describes not only a similar corporeal liberation but also the trace of the connection between her movements and those of Mahfoud. Here again, the complicity achieved does not connote fusion but the partners' synchronised communion with their own bodies. The dance is bound up with communication with the other, but also with a more general search for wholeness and with a refusal of the artificial separation between expression and the body. In turn, writing itself, for Djebar as for Cixous, is situated 'entre corps et voix'.[45]

Agency is equally achieved in this section through the narrator's appropriation of the gaze. If Muslim women are traditionally sequestered behind closed doors, in this novel the narrator revels in visual description, surreptitiously savouring the details of her loved one's face and appearance. This description again recalls the work of Cixous in that it aims at an exact transcription or incorporation of the other's body into language, though in this case the gesture also connotes a curious seizing of possession. Keeping herself at a discreet distance, she secretly delights in noting

> le dessin de ses sourcils, l'ourlet de l'oreille, la légere pomme d'Adam, la lèvre supérieure un peu en avant, et je remarquais comment le reflet du vert, ou du bleu-vert de la veste, de la chemise, de quoi... peu importait, comment ce reflet pouvait jouer sur la peau du visage épié.[46]

Lingering longingly on his features in the way that the camera often dwells on the heroines of French films, the narrator manages to place herself in the position of the controlling viewer. This domination achieved through the visual results in a drive for more power, again reversing male and female roles and privileging feminine agency: 'une violence me saisissait de devoir contrôler son existence, par mes yeux, en primitive et quasiment sur-le-champ'.[47] By seizing control of the gaze in this way, Djebar rebels directly against feminine subordination and masculine authority. If women have repeatedly been objectified by the male viewer, Djebar turns the tables and regards the object of her affections in a similar, consuming manner.

The second half of Djebar's text recounts her experiences as a filmmaker, developing further the notion of the female gaze and its role as a symbol of resistance. Here the very gesture of controlling the camera signifies self-affirmation and rebellion. Significantly again, however, self-expression is a collective project, undertaken explicitly in the name of all the women who suffered repression in the harem. Asserting that 'ce regard, je le revendique mien. Je le perçois «nôtre»', Djebar uses the camera to break down the walls that divide Muslim society and that keep women cloistered away from the light.[48] The photographic lens is compared to the small gap in the veil that traditionally masks the woman's face, though in this case Djebar's professional use of the camera asserts the power of her gaze openly and regardless of social taboos. Her filmmaking is concerned with expanding and broadening the woman's field of vision, tearing back the curtains of the veil and releasing the viewer into the light. Furthermore, the role of 'director' itself implies power, the active creation of images and the invention of a woman's narrative that subverts accepted versions of 'history'. Unlike the traditional 'patriarchal' gaze that objectifies its subject, however, Djebar remains open to the women that she photographs, asserting the importance of receptivity and the ability to see a scene anew. Filmmaking is here bound up with self-assertion but also with cooperation as opposed to appropriation.

The narrative structure of the text mirrors Djebar's dual preoccupation with the individual and the collective. The filmmaking scenes, tracing the narrator's own experience of self-assertion, are interwoven with fragments of women's narratives from recent years. Djebar's own process of self-discovery is interspersed with histories of women's resistance and flight, again continuing the genealogy that started with Tin Hinan and Zoraidé. The preoccupation with personal reinvention is broken up by testimonies from other women, unsettling the self-conscious, introspective tone of the first section and drawing attention to the ways in which individual histories overlap with and echo one another. Djebar traces a mother's journey to see her son Sélim in prison in Metz, noting her courageous departure from the familiar and her challenge to the French soldiers who guard him. In another passage, we learn of the grandmother Fatima's marriage at the age of fourteen, her subsequent departure and her attempts at remarriage. The emphasis is on the courage and independence of Fatima, her ability to care for her children and her endurance in the face of adversity. Finally, moments of the narrator's own childhood are juxtaposed with the present, as Djebar picks up on the image of the young girl walking to school with her father, familiar from the opening pages of *L'Amour, la fantasia*. The narrator also celebrates her infertility here, appreciating her ability to abstain from her expected role and emphasising liberation. In this way, common and divergent experiences of self-affirmation are narrated one on top of the other, underlining individual agency as well as communality between women.

On one level, then, Djebar's text is a force of connection, setting up links and narrating common experiences between singular women. Writing serves as a unifying force, integrating past and present and establishing an alternative, feminine history. Nevertheless, the text concludes by lamenting its own failure, alluding to absence and lack rather than creativity. The singular violence of the past stifles the narrator's voice, disabling reconstruction and excluding women once again from language and history: 'la voix me quitte chaque nuit tandis que je réveille les asphyxies douceâtres de tantes, de cousines entre-vues par moi, fillette qui ne comprenait pas, qui les contemplait, yeux élargis, pour plus tard les réimaginer et finir par comprendre'.[49] In this way, the text revolves around the desire for a collective feminine voice and the failure to locate and access such a voice. The narrator seeks to recount the histories of the women of Algeria but these women are also deprived of self-expression, lacking at the same time the self-presence and coherence that a particular voice would allow. Equally, Djebar is interested in the actual concerns of women while continuing to perceive these women as singular shadows, impossible to access using language. A political drive to reinvent history is coupled with a sense of defeat before the intransigence of French narrative, as the women of the text fade and hover elusively beneath its surface even as Djebar struggles to fight their common cause.

Foreshadowing both *Loin de Médine* and *Le Blanc de l'Algérie*, *Vaste est la prison* associates writing both with communication or translation and with effacement. Bearing witness to the violence committed against women both through history and during the confrontations of the 1990s, the final passages seek at once to rewrite the deaths of Algerian women or to narrate their shared history and to stress the resistance of such moments of singular violence to any form of linguistic explanation. Writing connotes silence as well as communication and spilt blood fails to offer any lasting commemoration, dissolving before it leaves a mark: 'le sang, pour moi, reste blanc cendre / Il est silence / Il est repentance / Le sang ne sèche pas, simplement il s'éteint'.[50] It is in the face of violence, then, that

Djebar's search for a common language of resistance falters in the most crippling manner; the pallor of 'l'Algérie exsangue' whites out its victims rather than accounting for their scars. The feminine genealogy sketched out by the text is severed by ellipses, caused by the recent, literal eradication of women's resisting voices.

Djebar's relation to feminism in this work is complex. She has no specific agenda and charts instead the difficult process of creating a concrete cause. She wants to affirm female solidarity and to sketch a coherent history of feminine oppression, but she also finds that the women about whom she writes resist straightforward forms of community, and she privileges individual agency and evasion. Furthermore, narrative is perceived as an unreliable construct, excluding as much as it reveals and failing to capture and encapsulate a particular group of women. Djebar's project therefore does not consist in criticising wholeheartedly Islamic society or in advocating an alternative set of norms, but in drawing attention to the tensions involved in the creation of collective narratives. Rather than denouncing 'Islamic tradition' as a whole, as hasty Western feminists can be tempted to do, she explores its varying effects through different epochs and champions multiple different forms of liberation as opposed to simplistic ideological revolt. She charts the fraught process of creating solidarity and linking threads, revealing the contradictions of feminist resistance and highlighting the conflicting forces with which women in Islam must engage. In this sense she refuses to propose a particular strategy in the manner of El Saadawi or Cixous, but explores the necessary contradictions involved in the process of critique. Women's resistance consists of a continual process of convergence and divergence, solidarity and dissociation. Djebar's novel modulates between these contrasting movements.

Loin de Médine

Djebar interrupted the Algerian Quartet before completing *Vaste est la prison* and published *Loin de Médine* in 1991, a less introspective work, even broader in historical scope. Written in response to the riots of October 1988, the novel shifts the focus away from colonialism and modern patriarchy in order to reflect on the origins of Islam and the disputed position of women during the early years of the religion. Shocked by the outburst of violence and oppression surrounding the resurgence of Islam, Djebar delves into the early chronicles in order to unravel both the repressive and the liberatory elements in Islamic doctrine, and to problematise further the possibility of establishing a coherent history of collective feminine identity in Algeria. The novel overtly questions contemporary interpretations of women's roles in order to uncover the illusions of political Islamist reworkings of the past; as Djebar argues, 'j'ai voulu expliquer comment les dirigeants se servaient de l'Islam pour régler les comptes entre eux'.[51] By retracing the shifting positions of women in Islamic memory, then, Djebar subjects that memory to scrutiny and reveals it to be perforated and fractured by ellipses and disputes. Islamic women, both present and past, cannot be tied to a monolithic doctrine setting out a specified pattern of behaviour, since the early stories at the time of the Prophet's life and immediately after reveal a multiplicity of different perceptions of femininity. Furthermore, religious custom and belief are also themselves a subject of controversy and manipulation rather than a fixed doctrine based on a set of facts. Episodes focusing on the divergent experiences or practices of individual women, and the controversies surrounding their implications, replace objective descriptions and established rules. As in *Vaste est la prison*, women's positions within Islamic tradition are multiple and divergent, and notions both of a specified Muslim feminine identity and of a secure and wholly knowable religious doctrine are shown to be inaccessible.

Before embarking on a reading of the novel, it is worth recalling the troubled context to which Djebar responds. The violence of October 1988 exploded after a prolonged period of dissatisfaction and unrest, and testified to a growing sense of uncertainty concerning the postcolonial government of Algeria. The economy had been shrinking steadily through the 1980s; there was growing unemployment, wages had been frozen and even basic foodstuffs remained in short supply. The gulf between the standard of living of the Algerian masses and that of a minority group of successful entrepreneurs added to the sense of bitterness and resentment. These economic difficulties were then coupled with a wider sense of unease with Benjedid's single-party government, and there was a demand not only for an improvement in social conditions but also for democracy, debate and cultural liberation. Thus while on the surface the riots seemed to stem from economic pressures, the young population was simultaneously expressing its distaste for the regime in place. Three-quarters of the population were at that time under the age of twenty-five, and they felt suffocated by the FLN government, seen as entrenched, static and lacking in coherence.

After a series of strikes in September 1988, rioting broke out on 4 October in Algiers, Constantine and Sétif. 5 October saw thousands of men storming the centre of the capital and many residential areas, destroying government property as well as that of the privileged and the well-off. Within two days, the unrest had spread also to Oran, Mostaganem, Blida, Annaba and others, and student groups, unions, leftists and fundamentalists all offered their support. On 6 October the government declared a state of siege and clamped down heavily on the disruption. Security forces began firing on protestors and hundreds of Algerians were killed before some semblance of order was restored on the 10th. Importantly, during the period of the riots, a mysterious movement for Algerian renewal called for the dismantling of the FLN, appealing also for adherence to Islamic law. Benjedid was forced to promise reform and set about realigning the constitution in November 1988 and February 1989. The FLN ended its monopoly of power; legislation in July 1989 led to the inauguration of a multi-party system. The Front Islamique du Salut was formed and became the primary competitor to the government.

Djebar's interest in the events stems from an anxiety regarding the ways in which Islam became implicated in a conflict that was also social, political and economic. If the riots arose out of a combination of factors contributing to social and political discontent, the outlawed political opposition seized the opportunity to criticise the ingrained 'dictatorship' of the FLN and to propose another set of morals or priorities. A renewed adherence to Islam and to Shari'a law were held up as alternatives to the failing regime, promising a sense of Algerian identity lacking in the people under Benjedid. The Islamist narrative of the religion's tenets and history set itself up as a symbol of unity designed to resolve the divisions and inequalities of Algerian society. As the FIS emerged, political renewal became identified with spiritual renaissance and religious leaders appealed to the masses by promising national regeneration in the language of faith. The Islamist movement became not just a religious revival but a revolt against the inefficacy and traditionalism of the FLN. A return to the 'fundaments' of Islamic doctrine was proposed not only for moral reasons but also as a means to attain power and to suggest solutions to problems of a political and economic nature. As I have suggested, the position of women was a key issue in this resurgence, since a return to so-called traditional gender roles offered a vision of security and resistance to the ongoing legacy of colonial influence. In response to this, however, Djebar sets out to show how religious tenets on femininity were themselves deformed and redeployed so as to serve a purpose other than their own. *Loin de Médine* was written out of a desire both to expose the fallacies of modern uses of the religion and in order to uncover the complexities and loopholes inherent in the very process of interpreting Islamic decree.

The central question raised by the novel concerns the hazy relation between knowledge and interpretation concerning the position of women in Islamic doctrine. Analysing painstakingly the chronicles of Ibn Hicham, Ibn Saad and Al-Tabari, Djebar creates her own vision of the early days of Islam, but she foregrounds both the occluded perspectives of the women in these texts and the difficulties surrounding the interpretation of their relationship with religious custom. Acting contrary to the beliefs of modern Islamist activists, she uncovers not only instances of feminine subordination but also moments of women's resistance and self-affirmation. Summarising the project of the novel, she affirms that 'c'est un livre qui répond. C'est une œuvre écrite pour mettre en cause la version "officielle" de l'histoire pour qui la femme doit être envelopée, ni vue ni connue, et réléguée à la maison', and she strives actively to write against warped interpretations of women's inferior status.[52] She retraces the lives of the 'filles d'Agar', the concubine of Abraham who was exiled in the desert with her son Ishmael, and uses the figure of Hagar to symbolise all those who revolted against their exclusion or marginalisation. Most importantly, however, Djebar develops the reflections on femininity and community explored in *Ombre sultane* and *Vaste est la prison* by exploring the blurring between knowledge and amnesia, or subjective reworking, that structures our knowledge of Algerian women in history. She exposes the gaps and silences that pierce the apparently smooth edifice of the early chronicles, retracing the moments where feminine experience is glossed over and occluded and reconstructing these moments with the aid of her own imagination. Episodes that are dealt with fleetingly by Al-Tabari are re-imagined and fleshed out; characters who are scarcely named are given new life. As a result, the 'histories' of the chroniclers are revealed to be incomplete and subjective and our knowledge of the past is shown to be intricately bound up with a process of reinvention. The early texts do contain meaning, but that meaning is not finite and singular moments are shown to be subject to recreation and fictionalisation by the reader. The origins of Islam are presented as open to reappraisal and reconsideration.

Djebar's novel in this way collapses and reconfigures the division between history and fiction. Historical narrative is presented as subjective, but fiction also is redefined as a site of experimentation and interpretative exploration. Fiction is not a pure space of fantasy and invention but a site for critique and reassessment. As Beïda Chikhi points out, the fictional text is for Djebar 'un lieu de projection, de traitement, d'analyse et de problématisation de ce texte d'histoire'.[53] As a result, historical narrative is revealed as fractured and fragmented, while fiction allows for further revision and re-interpretation. Neither genre retains a hierarchical position over the other; both are involved in a process of mutual communication and continuing critique. The novel also renders the disjunction between 'history' and 'reality' explicit, exposing the resistance of the past to determination and denouncing the desire for any definitive, unmediated or uncreated truth. In this sense, Djebar's novel encapsulates Dominick Lacapra's vision of literary writing as dialogical and contestatory:

> One way a novel makes challenging contact with 'reality' and 'history' is precisely by resisting fully concordant narrative closure (prominently including that provided by the conventional well-made plot), for this mode of resistance inhibits contemporary catharsis and satisfying 'meaning' on the level of the imagination and throws the reader back upon the need to come to terms with the unresolved problems the novel helps to disclose.[54]

Loin de Médine poses a challenge directly to political Islamist thinkers who impose closure and resolution on the religion's history, and on women's position within that history. Knowledge and invention are presented as inextricably bound up with one another; Mernissi's concept of the 'récit-souvenir' replaces the notion of religious history as a source of truth.[55]

Djebar's project is in this sense a contentious one. The Koran is seen by many Muslims to be 'uncreated', the pure word of God passed down to Mohammed without mediation by the angel Gabriel. Although Djebar does not go so far as to challenge the actual text of the Koran, leaving such an audacious and controversial move to Salman Rushdie, she does raise questions concerning the difficulties of interpretation, suggesting that Islamic history and thought are subject to endless reinvention. Djebar foregrounds how the toil of *ijtihad* or 'free interpretation' resides at the centre of Islamic learning, and she presents this as a continuing process that resists resolution. Knowledge of the religion is subject to revision and dispute, and, as Fischer and Abedi point out, a reading of the Hadiths requires 'a critical sense' or an awareness of multiple shades of meaning.[56] Djebar's claimed project of *ijtihad*, which she defines as the 'effort intellectuel pour la recherche de la vérité – venant de *djihad*, lutte intérieure recommandée à tout croyant', requires an openness to the struggle of interpretation and the surrender of any attempt at interpretative mastery.[57] As Donald Wehr argues, Djebar's portrayal of the Prophet's struggle, together with the narrator's awareness of the intricacy and ambivalence of processes of reading and rewriting, can also be read to perform Levinas's openness to the 'sensible', to alterity and the limits of knowledge.[58] Wehr demonstrates how this openness to the 'sensible', to that which imposes itself on us with 'immediacy', is at the centre of the Islamic conception of religious interpretation. He argues that 'the Prophet's example reveals that vulnerability to the sensible opens us to the transcendence of the ethical, allowing the voice of God to take root within us'.[59] Both the Prophet and the central female characters of *Loin de Médine* perceive Islam as resistant to determinate knowledge and as an experience of open-ended reflection on multiple meanings. In Levinas's terms, the inaccessible potentiality of 'le Dire' informs the text of 'le Dit'; statements and propositions are overshadowed by their exposure to what we cannot know and encapsulate. The Levinasian intertext may raise questions about the provenance of her influences, and Levinas's Jewish resonances may seem to conflict with the strictly Islamic focus of Djebar's writing. This diversity, however, is itself part of Djebar's point, since she shows that Islam is subject to the same intricate processes of self-questioning as both Judaism and European philosophy. This analysis also ties in with my reading of Derridean notions of singularisation and its partial trace within the Djebar's texts. In this case, however, Djebar alludes in particular to the ways in which religious reflection requires this confrontation with what is partially inaccessible, uncertain or open-ended.

It is through this investigation of the openness of processes of religious interpretation that Djebar opens up her portrait of Algerian women's genealogy. If religious inquiry can yield new meanings and uncover unforeseen nuances, then readings of feminine identity and duty in Islamic history and doctrine also open up a plurality of perspectives rather than a specified, monolithic trajectory. Attention to the problematic definition of women's roles within the multiple texts of Islam provides a sense, as in *Vaste est la prison*, of the singular-plurality of the women who constitute the religion's past. Djebar attends to singular feminine characters who escape specified knowledge and whose lives are knowable only as a series of hints and traces. The women of the novel escape established and expected historical frameworks, and the intermingling of fact and fiction makes them appear indeterminate. Their identities are not specifically delineated but remain partially in shadow, and the text provides fleeting glimpses of their trajectories without ascertaining their particularity or historical significance. Episodes of feminine resistance and agency are carefully uncovered and tentatively held up to the light but they are never wholly exposed. For Gayatri Spivak, Djebar's novel can be read through the lens of Derrida's *Spectres de Marx*, since it is a 'ghost dance', an exploration of hidden traces, hazy figures excluded from official history but who resurface here to undermine the smooth surface of revisionist doctrine.[60] The moments in the female characters' lives to which we are accorded access are contingent and at times de-contextualised, promising a renewed sense of feminine identity while resisting the framework of a smooth chronology or ethics. Like the women of *Femmes d'Alger*, *L'Amour, la fantasia* and *Vaste est la prison*, their voices offer fleeting, singular echoes rather than identifiable positions.

The story of Mohammed's daughter Fatima and her inheritance occupies a central position in the novel, exposing both the contentious nature of women's rights within Islam and the very difficulty of historical and religious interpretation. The focus of the story is on the resistance of both father and daughter to the demands placed on them in Medina. First, we learn of the Prophet's refusal to allow Ali, Fatima's husband, to take another wife without divorcing his daughter. The emphasis here is on the intimacy of the relationship between Mohammed and Fatima, since the Prophet places his daughter's welfare above his adherence to the Islamic decree that allows polygamy. Next, Djebar narrates Fatima's defence of Ali against Abou Bekr, the first caliph and close friend of Mohammed, and most importantly, her courageous affirmation of her rights during the controversy surrounding her inheritance. Fatima is named 'celle qui dit non à Médine', as she speaks up for herself against the religious leaders when they try to deprive her of her due. Dispossessed, Fatima understands that the dispute symbolises not only the ownership of material goods but her disadvantaged position as a woman, and she stands up for her beliefs rather than allowing herself to be subjected to the governance of men with whom she disagrees. Speaking in the name of all Muslim women, Fatima argues that the very achievement of Islam was to cater more equitably for the provision of women: 'la révolution de l'Islam, pour les filles, pour les femmes, a été d'abord de les faire hériter, de leur donner la part qui leur revient de leur père!'[61] Fatima's story reinforces the egalitarian side of Islam and it reveals how those who read the religion as oppressive to feminine rights misinterpret its original doctrine and purpose. The Koran is seen by many to look after women's interests in a society that was inegalitarian and polygamous, rather than actively perpetuating their subordination.

The episode turns on the question of interpretation. Djebar shows that the dispute is centred on how the successors understand Mohammed's declaration 'on n'hérite pas de nous'. While Abou Bekr and the others assume that this means that the Prophet will not pass his wealth and belongings on to his offspring, Fatima asserts on the contrary that it is the Prophet's position as Prophet that cannot be inherited: 'je sais bien que la prophétie ne s'hérite pas, mais tout ce qui est autre chose qu'elle, est permis, est transmissible!'[62] While the successors of Mohammed interpret the utterance in an absolute way and legislate against Fatima accordingly, she herself asserts that the Prophet was concerned with the material provision and comfort of his daughter. Furthermore, if the single phrase quoted above gives rise to these difficulties of interpretation, then this in turn reveals how the status of women in Islam as a whole is subject to dispute. The sayings of the Prophet are revealed not to be transparent but open to debate. Djebar seems to be arguing that the subordination of women is not itself inherent in Islamic decree but results from a highly particular interpretation of a set of ambiguous statements. Islamic custom originates not in truth but in this series of early controversies.

The character of Fatima is also itself hazy and uncertain. Djebar depicts her story as a succession of traces and fragments that reside beyond the framework of a specified history. Fatima herself is not dealt with in detail in Al-Tabari's chronicle, where the focus remains on Abou Bekr and Ali. Al-Tabari does not quote Fatima directly, voicing the words instead of Abou Bekr and according Fatima's dispute less space than that of Ali.[63] Indeed, Djebar notes that she features in the chronicles only after she is the mother of Hassan and Hossein. *Loin de Médine*, on the other hand, insists on Fatima's articulate and poetic rhetoric at the time of the dispute, creating a lucid feminine language of revolt. Nevertheless, Djebar is also at pains to stress the inaccessibility of Fatima's idiom and the uncertainty that surrounds her own portrayal. Fatima is not a rounded character with a particular identity but a faint outline, whose precise form Djebar struggles to delineate. Pausing in her narrative, the narrator at one point suggests that Fatima is at once daughter and son, but she also qualifies this suggestion with further doubt. In marrying her cousin, Fatima could be seen to approach the position of a male successor, but the narrator immediately pulls back from the suggestion:

> Est-ce par trop librement façonner une «idée» de Fatima? Est-ce par trop l'animer d'une pulsion de masculinité ou d'une ferveur filiale si forte que cette fiction se déchire? Risque l'invraisemblable, tout au moins l'anachronique, par l'accent mis sur la frustration supposée...[64]

Hints at Fatima's character are followed by revisions and her nature and actions are explicitly fictionalised. Djebar adds further emphasis to events that are dealt with in the chronicles scantily and with haste, but she also hesitates in producing an alternative portrait. If, for those in power at the time, 'Fatima représente le doute', if she symbolises uncertainty over the question of inheritance, then she also personifies the narrator's own doubt concerning her provisional, imperfect history.[65]

Alongside the story of Fatima, Djebar also recreates the character Aïcha, one of the Prophet's wives. The scene of the Prophet's death, for example, recounted at the beginning of the novel, is narrated through Aïcha's eyes in a drive to re-appropriate the masculine perspective of the chroniclers and to reinforce the importance of the women's active roles. The scene is also significant in that it anticipates the problems of succession that ultimately divided the Sunni' and the Shi'ite communities, again foregrounding division and dispute. Djebar begins, however, by focusing on Aïcha's personal life, and she recreates the moment of her engagement to the Prophet at the tender age of nine. While in Al-Tabari the Prophet's marriages are narrated in sparse and factual terms, in *Loin de Médine* the perspective shifts in order to stress the particularity of feminine experience. Djebar focuses on Aïcha's tumult and confusion, presenting the marriage

not as a business matter but as a moment of disorder and bewilderment for the frightened young child: 'je ne suis plus une enfant! Je ne
suis plus inconsciente!'[66] Furthermore, while Aïcha's vulnerability is
emphasised here, Djebar later draws attention to her political importance and to the influential role she played during the days of the
establishment of Islam. Indeed, as Mernissi recounts, Aïcha's role in
leading the army against Ali during the Battle of the Camel testifies
further to women's active participation in political life. Aïcha is also
significant since, as Leila Ahmed describes, many of the Prophet's
wives transmitted a large number of the Hadiths, and Aïcha herself
testified to the recitation of some of the Prophet's verses.[67] She was
seen as a source of knowledge regarding the intricacies of the Koranic
suras and as an important link in the 'isnad', the tracing of the origins
of the Hadiths. In *Loin de Médine*, she is set up as the transmitter of
the word, appropriating the utterances of the Prophet and passing
his verses down to subsequent generations. The remaining traces of
Aïcha's speech are, however, subject to questioning, consisting of
fleeting echoes and sayings that cannot be seen as definitive or true.
Her utterances are themselves indistinct and partially lost, presented
as singular idioms that slip beyond the reader's reach: 'elle source un
début de transmission: non pas conservation pieuse et compassée.
Plutôt une exhumation lente de ce qui risque de paraître poussière,
brume inconsistante.'[68] The Islamist return to the past is in this passage
refigured as a shaky chain of transmission, part of an ongoing process
of *différance*, in which women's word becomes progressively more
fragile.[69] The passing on of religious knowledge does not consist in
the straightforward communication of an original sense but in an
open-ended transcription and reinvention of meaning.

   Loin de Médine also depicts a number of female fighters who
were similarly accorded little time in Al-Tabari's chronicle. The role
of such characters is to demonstrate the active position of certain
women in the early days of Islam, though once again Djebar stresses
that this is not highlighted by Al-Tabari and belongs to the realm of
interpretation rather than fact. Djebar's own fictionalised version of
these battles serves as a commentary or a critique of accepted notions
of women's roles. One such episode involves a 'Yemenite queen', who
remains nameless in both Al-Tabari and Djebar. The queen is the wife
of Aswad, a rebel and false prophet, though importantly she uses her
position not to support him but to bring him down in defence of the
new religion. In Al-Tabari, the Yemenite queen plays a minor role in

the plot contrived to foil Aswad.[70] We are told that she participates in the conspiracy, coaxing him to sleep unwittingly in a room where some soldiers will find and kill him. Nevertheless, she is presented as a passive observer rather than an active participant, submitting to the command of the male fighters. In *Loin de Médine*, however, the queen is situated at the centre of events, and Djebar concludes:

> L'épisode du palais de Sana'a illustre la ruse des femmes d'alors et leur décision. Ou bien les femmes bédouines se mêlent aux hommes dans les combats, les suivent, tuent sauvagement elles aussi, avec une allégresse élargissant le masque de la mort; ou, à l'opposé, par la ruse du faux amour et dans le lit, elles le défendent, femelles douces, insinuantes – lit de l'amante, mais aussi lit d'accouchement et de délivrance, maintenu tenacement présent par les mères, plus tard, comme lieu symbolique de la dépendance définitive et inversée...[71]

The story for Djebar represents a forgotten moment of feminine resistance and it illustrates the inaccuracy and distortion of conceptions of Islam that foreground simply the passivity and subordination of women. Consciously fictionalised, Djebar's contentious interpretation of Al-Tabari stresses the ambiguity of the early chronicle and shows how fleeting images of the past lead to a network of stories sketching a variety of gender positions.

Other strong female characters include Oum Hakim, the wife of Ikrima, who travels for miles to find her husband and inform him that he has been pardoned by the Prophet. Oum Hakim also participates in the battle of Yarmouk, and Djebar describes her bravery and fervour assertively:

> se battre, se battre à cheval, ou à dos de chamelle, et pour l'Islam dorénavant. Leur montrer à eux, les chefs de Médine, les fameux Compagnons que, même du clan vaincu, ces femmes de La Mecque restaient des dames. A la fois des épouses, des maîtresses de maison, mais aussi des combattantes.[72]

Once again, however, the intricacies of Oum Hakim's thought processes are fictionalised, since Al-Tabari glosses over her contribution to the battle in the space of two lines. Djebar, on the other hand, stresses her passion and devotion both to her husband and to Islam, but she also ends her narrative with a series of questions, lamenting Al-Tabari's neglect and alluding to the uncertainty and ambivalence that surround her partially fictional history. In addition, Oum Temim is recalled as a darkened silhouette lingering in the margins of Al-Tabari.

The wife of the warrior and leader Khalid ibn el Walid, Oum Temim is reduced to 'celle qu'on épouse après la bataille', and Djebar again recreates her thoughts in the form of a series of hesitant and tentative questions. A further character, Oum Keltoum, is recalled in Djebar's text for her capacity for flight and resistance. Fleeing her family and resisting the demands of husbands who seek to control and restrict her, Oum Keltoum pronounces her desire to live among the Muslims. Her faith, her tenacity and self-assurance are again testimony to the insubordination of Muslim women. As with Oum Hakim and Oum Temim, however, Djebar punctuates her narrative with hypotheses and doubts.

Throughout the novel, Djebar also seeks both to reconstruct and to question the notion of a specific feminine language. Aïcha is associated with the transmission of the Hadiths, and Fatima's rhetoric, as I suggested earlier, is celebrated both for its poetic qualities and for its assertiveness and courage. Both of these feminine idioms remain elusive, however, and Djebar implies that only sparse echoes and broken rhythms can be recreated in the present. As in *Vaste est la prison*, Djebar seems to want to relocate a feminine language while also remaining wary of any sense of identity or specificity, emphasising singular traces more markedly than any shared structure. Solidarity between women is crucial, and the novel does advocate feminine dialogue in its juxtaposition of different women's interventions, but there is no determinate 'women's language', no gendered discourse of feminine identity or positionality. As in *Les Alouettes*, any possible 'parler femme' is not knowable or essential but openended, allusive, or again, 'singular-plural'. Similarly, like Fatima and Aïcha, Sadjah is remembered for her linguistic abilities, and Djebar celebrates her poetry even as she wonders at its strange opacity: 'elle crée des images, elle invente des rythmes, elle débite, sans qu'elle fasse effort, des grappes de stances obscures mais étincelantes; sa prose coule haletante ou limpide'.[73] But though these idioms are hinted at by the chronicles, their substance remains beyond the modern reader's grasp. Djebar also recalls the 'chanteuse des satires', a poetess whose name is forgotten but whose verses anchored and gave form to the resistance of her allies. Feminine poetry is here not only evocative and mysterious but also influential beyond the boundaries of the poetess's tribe, and it is glorified at the time with more enthusiasm than victory in war. Language functions as a tool for attack in this instance, symbolising mastery and resistance. Once again, however, Djebar celebrates the feminine poetic voice only to question its unique substance and to reinforce its resistance to appropriation in the present.

Rather than speaking for her female characters, Djebar's narrator frequently alters her stance or withdraws. She senses that the substance of these feminine idioms remains beyond her grasp, and she does not endeavour to recreate them but alludes tentatively to singular idiolects that resist elaboration in modern French. Rather than 'giving voice' to the women of the past in a straightforward way, Djebar's narrator demonstrates their achievements while refraining from speaking in their place. The text is not controlled by a stable and authoritative narrator; instead, the narrative voice surrenders its authority in its confrontation with the religious 'sensible', the open-ended text both of religious interpretation and of women's memory. The evolution of religious knowledge is presented as an exposure to otherness, and Djebar's literary rewriting also involves the abandonment of narrative control. To use Levinas's terms again, used to describe readings of the Talmud but perhaps relevant to Djebar's apprehension and recreation of Islamic texts, or Fatima and Aïcha's poetry:

> Dans l'imagination poétique, l'inouï peut s'entendre, s'interpeller et se dire; un texte s'ouvrir à l'herméneutique plus largement que les intentions précises qui l'avaient fixé; la métaphore conduire au-delà des expériences qui semblent l'avoir engendrée. Le symbole y donnerait à penser speculativement.[74]

In addition to this, no over-arching perspective links the episodes of *Loin de Médine*, nor establishes a clear chronology with a particular argument or purpose. The narrator juxtaposes a series of fragments and scenes while hesitating in providing a 'grand narrative' of their significance. Assertions of women's insubordination are coupled with a sense of uncertainty, as divergent episodes make it impossible to define the Islamic feminine condition in a single and unified way. The narrator constantly reveals her anxiety over the question of interpretation, uncovering moments of women's rebellion while struggling to provide a conclusive 'reading' of their status. She presents herself as ill at ease with her own project, with the search for Islamic memory and with the version that she herself tentatively offers.

Finally, the structure of *Loin de Médine* is itself polyphonic, and the narrator's voice is also only one in a series of available perspectives. Recreations of occluded episodes are interspersed with interjections made by alternative voices, enigmatic interventions whose origins remain unclear. *Rawiyates*, female transmitters of the life of the Prophet such as Aïcha, interrupt the more conventional narrative scenes, and these interventions remind us again that Islamic history is also oral and dialogic. The first *rawiya* speeds up the narrative, listing the women who travelled from Mecca to Medina and noting the experiences and sufferings of some of the Prophet's wives. The fragment stands out, briefly providing a more synthetic view before tailing off and leaving the narrator to pick up the inconclusive pieces. The second refers to the fictional character Habiba, a woman without children who arrives in Medina rootless and unknown. She is described as restless and disconsolate, at times withdrawing from contact with the women of Medina and retiring to live with Oum Ferwa, the solitary sister of Abou Bekr. Once again, knowledge of her condition eludes us and her character remains enigmatic. The third *rawiya*, Oum Harem, similarly expresses her hesitation in providing an acceptable or certain version of events. She believes she witnesses a miracle, when the Prophet feeds his companions out of supplies that seem to be too sparse. Within these sections, however, feature moments of debate and uncertainty, as rumours are passed around and various other characters air divergent perspectives. Interrupting the narrator in order to add an alternative viewpoint, these *rawiyates* do not provide a concrete truth of their own.

Djebar's *Loin de Médine* proposes not a coherent argument for the assertive position of Muslim women in Algeria but a series of possible interpretations of women's roles within the multifaceted texts of Islam. Islamists reconstruct the role of women and use this reconstruction to define the postcolonial Islamic community, but Djebar shows that the history of gender roles within the religion is disjointed, contradictory and at times inaccessible. Djebar does not trace a neat trajectory of early Muslim women's lives but offers a collection of fleeting glimpses of divergent feminine experiences. She investigates the multiple ways in which Islam has been lived and interpreted by various women in history, juxtaposing divergent fragments without imposing a wider theoretical agenda. No fixed set of doctrines is upheld or challenged and no specific principles are used (falsely) to define the nation in relation to its past. Rather, Islam is presented as multifaceted and continually mutating, Muslim women are by turns liberated and oppressed, self-assured and submissive. Most importantly, moreover, this is *both* a deconstructive project, that can be seen to develop the ideas of Derrida and Levinas, and a mode of reflection that is wholly faithful to the tradition of debate within Islam. Djebar's critique is not in this sense necessarily 'Western' or European, though it is undoubtedly influenced by her education within the French system. On the contrary, her aim is precisely to reveal that the very opposition between Eastern and Western thought, 'fundamentalism' and debate, is a false one. Any reference to Derrida and Levinas in my reading therefore serves to bring out the spirit of questioning that Djebar shows to be present in Islamic history and thought. It respects the sanctity of the Islamic texts while also showing that their interpretation is an arduous, intricate and irresolute process.

CHAPTER FOUR

Violence, Mourning and Singular Testimony

Le Blanc de l'Algérie

During the 1990s Djebar's work becomes increasingly, immediately politically engaged. While *Loin de Médine* returns to the early days of Islam in order to denounce the misuse of the past by resurgent Islamists at the end of the 1980s, Djebar's next group of texts focuses overtly and pointedly on the present. As the political climate in Algeria becomes steadily more fraught, reflections on femininity and genealogy are superseded by a direct engagement with current confrontations and losses, and Djebar's horror at the upsurge of Islamist terrorism leads her to interrogate more pointedly the contemporary disintegration of her native land. Bearing witness to a sudden swathe of murders and attacks against writers, journalists and many others who dared to speak out against the newly oppressive interpretations of Islamic doctrine, Djebar criticises forms of religious and political discourse that prescribe an artificial, monolithic and backward-looking set of rules. Looking beyond the question of women's position in Algeria at this point, she revolts not only against new forms of gendered oppression but also against cultural and linguistic tyranny more generally. She then uses her own literary writing both to uncover the oppressed multilingualism and multicultural creativity of Algerian art and literature and to search for a narrative of mourning that might somehow encapsulate the intractable horrors that FLN or Islamist ideologies have tried to deny. It is at this point, however, that Djebar relinquishes any lingering quest for Algerian specificity as she reacts against the FIS's appropriation of Algerian identity as radically Islamic and Arabic. The Islamist resurgence for Djebar occludes and destroys her native land; their violence divides the country while their false rhetoric of spiritual unity renders its culture unrecognisable. In this next group of novels, Algeria is presented as war-torn, in mourning and lacking a language with which to make sense of and resolve that process.

Le Blanc de l'Algérie focuses on the loss of Algeria's greatest writers and intellectuals, and uses this investigation of the language of commemoration both to denounce Islamist rhetoric and to question the capacity of any written narrative to attend to the singularity of the deceased. Djebar's critique in this important 'récit' in this sense has two sides.[1] First, in her portrayal of the funerary rites of an array of Algerian writers, Djebar upholds unique, creative forms of commemoration that refuse to conform to the demands of Islamist ideology or sanctioned political rhetoric. She charts the fitful progress of 'une nation cherchant son cérémonial', by which she means the ongoing search for a language of mourning that might somehow do justice to current atrocities without reincorporating them into a falsely unified framework or law.[2] Algeria's losses must be remembered and expressed in the multiple, vibrant idioms of the people, whose language cannot be unified by recent demands for Arabisation and the recreation of a new Islamist Algeria. These demands indeed have severed and ravaged the Algeria whose history Djebar was trying in former novels to recount, and the oppression of Algeria's actual diversity leads to a divided society at odds with itself and with its own past. Secondly, however, Djebar's own commemorative text itself seeks a singular language, free from convention-bound formulae and able to transcend the linear progress of a narrative necessarily evolving through time. She embarks on a search for an unmediated text that might fuse past and present, stretching the limits of narrative expression so as to challenge the tyranny of existing rhetorical forms. This search turns out to be an impossible one, however, and the narrator remains troubled by an awareness of her uneasy position as a story-teller constrained by the inevitable influence of linguistic and generic norms or 'laws'. Yet in striving to account for the singularity of the deceased, and in hoping to avoid appropriating their experiences to suit the demands of the present, Djebar draws attention to the ineluctable effects of rhetorical norms while refusing the institutionalisation of those norms. *Le Blanc de l'Algérie* uses both content and form to deconstruct the layers and masks of commemorative discourse and the political misuse of those masks.

The multiple connotations of 'Algerian white' reveal the manifold facets of Djebar's contentious project. White is the colour of mourning in the Arab world and can be associated with the death shroud or with ashes. On this level, the white of Algeria in Djebar's text points directly to the deaths of a generation of free-thinking Algerians and draws the reader's attention to certain symbols or indices of loss. At the same time, however, the white of the title evokes the emptiness of a blank page, the attempted eradication of literary and intellectual resistance by Islamist terrorists, and the muteness imposed on the generation of the 1990s. It also conveys Djebar's own anxiety towards the written word and her sense of unease towards the capacity of language to testify to recent atrocities. Algeria is shrouded in white because its vitality and richness are effaced in a series of acts that themselves reside beyond the limits of communicability. White symbolises erasure and obfuscation, a sense of loss in relation to the once familiar native land, and the impossibility of making sense of that loss using narrative. In response, the text seeks singular rituals and idioms, offered as alternatives to those sanctioned either by Islamist discourse or by the official Arabisation policy, while also struggling to give a fitting form to, and to 'work through', the traumas of the past. Djebar demands that we continue to examine the process of mourning, to attend to the lost other, but that process must remain inadequate, incomplete and resistant to resolution.

The political climate in Algeria became increasingly troubled after the riots of October 1988. Growing unrest, protests carried out by a heterogeneous collection of young people, the unemployed, students and intellectuals dissatisfied with an old-fashioned government revealed a population hungry for change. The FIS, though evidently leaving many of the intellectuals behind, set out to unify this somewhat formless movement, to direct its mission and codify its demands. Founded on 18 February 1989 and achieving official recognition in September of the same year, the FIS acted as a mediator between the dissatisfied people and the authorities. Whether or not it was an open and legal organisation, however, is unclear. Led at once by Abbasi Madani, an *ancien* Messaliste who became the voice of the religious opposition to presidents Boumedienne and Chadli, and Ali Belhadj, a more radical and wayward rebel, the movement voiced its discontent using both conventional and underground means.[3] Most significantly, however, it positioned itself at the head of the resistance and aimed to bring together the nation's voices of dissent, advocating a so-called 'return' to the fundaments of Islam as the most viable alternative to a regime that had lost its way. A return to the 'fundaments' of Islamic doctrine was now proposed not only for moral reasons but also as a means to suggest solutions to problems of a political and economic nature, and to challenge a regime that had come to be seen as auto-cratic. As the FIS emerged, the necessary process of political renewal became identified with spiritual renaissance and religious leaders appealed to the masses by promising national regeneration in the language of faith. Economic difficulties, social unrest, a sense of the growing rift between rich and poor, or between the government and the masses, all led to a desire among young Algerians for an alterna-tive discourse. Islamism became the space of political dissidence, the mosque provided a place from which to speak, and religious language became the language of political opposition.[4]

Islamist discourse is ideological on two levels: in its creation of community and in its reshaping of the past. First, it offers a profound challenge to the Algerian state as it was governed by the FLN and proposes a new vision of Algerians belonging to a wider, integrated community of believers.[5] Individual memory is subjugated by a broader collective narrative, which is supposed organically to unify the Algerian people with its moral and spiritual bond. As Lahouari Addi affirms, the FIS is a populist party that views the people as 'un corps soudé' with no room for divergences or for subjective reac-tion.[6] Islamism supposedly provides the Algerians with a renewed sense of community, uniting their differences under the banner of the religion and connecting them directly with their shared roots: 'le FIS fond tous les groupes dans un vaste ensemble national dans lequel l'individu continue de s'effacer. Par lui, la nation algérienne est une vaste communauté qui a une âme collective exprimée par la langue et la religion.'[7] Secondly, political Islam in Algeria sets itself up as a 'return to the past', designed to help restore a sense of identity and origin, but its narratives are for the most part, conversely, projections into the future. Notions of Islamic 'tradition' are often constructed rather than lifted intact from the early sources. Conceptions of the position of women, for example, stem from a desire to define Alge-rian identity in contradistinction to Western, neocolonial influence rather than from careful readings of the Koran or the Hadiths. The sequestration of women serves to define Islamic culture in Algeria as well as making a moral point. Adherence to Islamic doctrine and a sense of belonging to the *umma* of believers protect a myth of an Algerian identity as distinct from the West: 'l'option culturelle et civilisationelle du Front islamique du Salut … consiste à protéger la Communauté contre toute invasion culturelle et contre les menées des civilisations adverses'.[8] The FIS is in this sense a wholly contemporary movement hoping to solve the ills associated with the stagnant FLN government and to reinvent Algerian identity as part of an Islamic *umma* opposed to the Western, capitalist world. It is created from a highly particular ideological rhetoric, enlisting religion and culture to support its political aims. Hegemony is achieved through the promulgation of an ideology that synthesises the social, political, economic and religious demands of the people.

The FIS in this way champions not only return but also renewal. Its official recognition marked the beginning of a multi-party system and seemed to contest the hitherto undemocratic behaviour of the entrenched FLN (who had remained in power since independence). It succeeded in attracting the support of a diversity of Algerians, not necessarily because of its religiosity but because it provided hope and promised an end to social discontent. In the local elections of June 1990, the party won an astounding number of votes: 54 per cent overall, 64.16 per cent in Algiers.[9] Four million Algerians altogether voted for the FIS. In December 1991 further elections were held and once again the FIS achieved a resounding success. The total number of votes declined from four million to two million, but the movement nevertheless obtained more votes than any other party. Such success, however, now gave rise to protests from the secular opposition. Benjedid resigned, but the Haut Conseil de Sécurité took charge and cancelled the elections in an effort to check the Islamist resurgence. In the name of democracy, the state paradoxically annulled the democratic elections, with the result that the FIS was outlawed and forced back underground.[10] Although popular, the movement caused acute tension and, enraged by the cancellation, its proponents began a series of terrorist attacks. Antagonism between the Islamists and the government led to violent and frequently deadly confrontations, and gradually those who challenged the authority of Islamic doctrine in any way became targets of attack.

The ensuing murders of those intellectuals, writers and journalists who contested the constructed traditions of the FIS are the focus of *Le Blanc de l'Algérie*. The clandestine Islamist movement hit out against those who rejected the most radical versions of Islamic law and allowed no space for critique. The reinvention of tradition according to a radical reinterpretation of Islamic texts excluded the possibility of debate, and those who questioned the validity of that interpretation had to be destroyed. Journalists were targeted for not denouncing seriously the cancellation of the elections of December

1991 or because they openly spoke out against the establishment of an Islamic republic.[11] Moreover, these journalists were caught between the rebels and the government, who in turn issued restrictions on freedom of expression in the hope of quelling support for the FIS. The assassinations were exploited by the government and used to provoke further dissent against the Islamists. In addition to the journalists, intellectuals were targeted not only for their political commentaries but also for their implied questioning of the culture of Arabisation, upheld by both the FIS and the government. Both parties wanted to impose Arabic monolingualism and to eradicate widespread usage of both French and diverse Berber dialects. Arabic supplanted French as the language of the nation in 1963, the judiciary has functioned in Arabic since the mid-1980s, and both the FIS and the FLN continue to promote the use of Arabic in the public arena.[12] In hoping to stave off continued French influence, however, Arabisation oppresses not only francophone authors but also the many indigenous speakers of other languages. As a result, anyone schooled in Berber or French is excluded from political and legal representation. In Ranjana Khanna's words, 'it is that language [Arabic] that is now taking over as the uncompromising and absolute law, as the Other'.[13]

Tahar Djaout, whose bravery in championing freedom of expression is noted in *Le Blanc de l'Algérie*, was one of the first and best-known intellectuals to be assassinated. Editor of the francophone journal *El Watan* and co-ordinator of the review *Ruptures*, Djaout consciously wrote in French also in order to rebel against the oppression of Berber identity by enforced Arabisation. French, though haunted by the spectres of colonialism, becomes a language of protest and Djaout explicitly divorces writing from national identity, using literature and journalism to invent new landscapes and to conceive alternative idiolects. His novels also make a number of pointed criticisms of modern Algerian society. In *Les Chercheurs d'os*, for example, Djaout uses the image of the exhumation of war victims' bones as the focus for his analysis of commemoration, and he implicitly challenges the way in which the memory of decolonisation has been co-opted and mediated by the government. The implication is that politicians have exploited the martyrs of the war of independence for their own ends, reclaiming the past in a quest for a modern Algerian identity while simultaneously masking the singularity of individual memory. Modern society is revealed to be greedy and corrupt, and politicians betray the ideals of the revolution by twisting history to suit their own requirements and to serve their pursuit of power. Similarly, *Les Vigiles* depicts Algerian society as diseased, paralysed by convoluted bureaucracies and flattening individual creativity. Aware of the controversial nature of his statements and portraits, Djaout asserted that freedom of expression should prevail. He was assassinated on 26 May 1993.

Such events testify to an attempt to control and reduce the literary expression of Algerian intellectuals, an attempt propagated both by the government and by the increasingly revolutionary FIS. Most notably, they result in a separation between literature and national identity, as writers seek less to represent the Algerian community than to affirm their detachment from it and to lament its deformation. If, earlier in her career, Djebar's literature to some extent provided a locus for anti-colonial resistance and on this level contributed to a sense of a postcolonial, national Algerian cause, the terror of the 1990s leads her to question any notion of national unity. The quest for any coherent collective identity dissolves, and Djebar uses the flexibility of the literary form to draw attention to the irrevocable dissolution of the Algerian people and the multifaceted nature of their oppressed, singular-plural culture. Djebar denounces bitterly the Islamist desire to 'viser celui qui parle', and she emphasises that literature is a space for the free expression of singular creativity rather than for the reproduction of discourses of identity imposed from the outside.[14] *Le Blanc de l'Algérie*, then, in its celebration of linguistic plurality on the one hand and in its understanding of the difficulties of creating a singular narrative of mourning on the other, invokes a language of resistance to resurgent forms of linguistic oppression. This challenge to the rhetoric of Islamism and Arabisation more generally also announces Djebar's relinquishing of 'identity politics' of any sort.

Djebar's *Le Blanc de l'Algérie* seeks a wholly singular testimony and openly denounces those grandiose or formalised discourses that hide unique, individual experiences with their official veneer. Djebar criticises versions of history that occlude the horror of their referents beneath the flowers of their rhetoric, and exposes the errors of ideologies and myths that smooth over the oppression of which they speak. The very act of narration may bring with it the temptation to 'poeticise' experience, but while Djebar herself cannot entirely avoid such a process, her text attempts to demystify the mechanics of preconceived ceremonial language. The narrator rejects the artifice of false ritual, affirming '*je dis non à toutes les cérémonies*' and concluding the same passage '*je dis non au théâtre quand il n'est pas improvisé: celui, même flamboyant, de la rage ou celui, attendu, de la componction islamique*'.[15] Any appropriate narrative of mourning cannot take the form of a rigid ideological (Islamist) formula but should find an idiom in which to convey the singularity of the experience concerned. This rejection of official or imposed rhetoric is expressed pointedly in Djebar's depiction of the funeral of the great Algerian writer Kateb Yacine. When the Imam starts speaking in classical Arabic, the crowd shouts out against the inappropriate nature of this language, since they perceive it as a symbol of both the governmental and the Islamist desire for monolingualism that oppresses speakers of Berber dialects, including Kateb himself. Multiple singular voices undermine the idea of a 'fundamentalist' law prescribing a standardised ritual for the occasion. The mourning of Kateb becomes the locus of a rebellion against the imposition of a standard and universal language, as 'les chants berbères s'élèvent de toutes parts, cette fois pour couvrir le discours'.[16] Discourses that falsely subordinate individual experience and identity beneath the uniformity of a national (and Islamist) myth are denounced and laid bare.

Djebar is concerned not only to denounce official, universalising discourses but also those that falsely glorify the past. In her discussion of the first victims of execution at Barberousse, she notes that Ferradj's cries and protestations were seen by certain chroniclers as unheroic: '«*il aurait dû mourir comme un "vrai" Algérien*»'.[17] Djebar punctures this myth of 'true Algerian-ness', asserting that Ferradj died simply 'comme un homme', an ordinary being crushed by the violence and injustice of the war. The comment contains undertones of a liberal humanism, and certainly Djebar seeks to look beyond the narrow restrictions of Algerian or Arab particularism, but her focus even here seems to centre more on persistent singularity, on resistance to containment, than on notions of a universal humanity. Most importantly, grandiloquent versions of history that gloss over and reshape the indignity of the final moments turn out to be mythologised and unreal. Djebar warns against the danger of fetishising narratives of such horrific events, of excessively honouring the fact of trauma until the unique nature of the experience is ignored.[18] In this case, singular experience is subordinated to the myth of a new Algerian identity, and the comment glosses over the true violence of the moment by covering it in grandiose and admiring rhetoric. As I have suggested, this critique does not imply the removal of all rhetoric but an awareness of the temptations and conventions that come into play when writing about horrific events. Ritualised language is a crucial part of mourning and Djebar's text constitutes an overt search for such a 'cérémonial'. Nevertheless, she remains suspicious of discourses that impose preconceived myths and formulae, governed by religious and cultural politics, and as a result skirting around the singular moments that they hoped to describe. Her project comes to resemble Agamben's 'archive', hovering between the 'déjà-dit' of traditional rhetoric and the emptiness of oblivion, of the untranslatable.[19]

Djebar's search for a language of mourning is in this sense both a political critique and a denunciation of identitarianism more broadly. She criticises Islamist discourses of national unity and points out that the crimes of the 1990s were committed in the name of political ideology rather than religion. She then asserts that Algeria's language of mourning must on the contrary be endlessly polyphonic, not politically specified or determinate but composed of the echoes and traces of different dialects, rhythms and musical forms and refusing the demands of strict Arabisation. Funereal chants are spontaneous and improvised rather than adhering to preconceived, imposed laws; they become provisional markers rather than unchanging rituals set in stone. At Mahfoud's funeral, for example, songs are sung in Arabic, Berber and French so as to reinforce Algeria's multilingualism. Similarly, the 'theatre' of Alloula's funeral mixes genres and juxtaposes extracts of different origins and tones. Indeed, what Djebar remembers most vividly about her friends is the particularity of their idiom, the different tonalities of their exchanges in French, Arabic or Berber. Later on, in her celebration of Algerian art and writing, the multilingual diversity of the singing of the Kabylian singer and novelist Taos Amrouche is treasured:

> Taos baigne dès le début dans un bain de langues: celles de la rue, l'italien, le sicilien, l'arabe dialectal tunisois, celle de l'école, le français, bien sûr, qu'elle lit et qu'elle écrit, enfin celle de l'exil et du secret familial, le berbère kabyle dans lequel chaque soir la grand-mère et son fils ont de longues palabres – langue aussi des cris, des conflits (Belkacem avec ses premiers fils), celle en somme du drame quotidien.[20]

Noting the specific implications of each idiom, Djebar celebrates linguistic diversity as opposed to the demands of monolingualism. Her text provides a space for the commemoration of languages that have been outlawed in the forum of political or religious debate.

The memory of Taos Amrouche also forms part of a short section on women artists and writers, who for the most part remain curiously absent from this text. Agnès Peysson points out that Djebar makes scant reference to women in this context in order to force the reader to experience their very 'whiting out' from Algeria's history. The section on Taos Amrouche and the others could perhaps then be seen to enact the fleeting resurgence of their voices against that oppression and occlusion.[21]

The blankness implied by the novel's title is in this way juxtaposed with a search for a satisfactory idiom, a mode of commemoration which would perhaps echo and mimic the traces of the deceased's own singular art forms. Much of the text laments the 'untranslatability' of Algeria, the effacement of intellectual creativity and the resistance of traumatic experience to straightforward narration. The colour white weaves in and out of the text, connoting the shroud, erasure and the pallor of 'l'Algérie exsangue'. In response to this silence, however, Djebar dreams of locating a hidden language that would somehow revoke and encapsulate the multiple singular voices of her divided country. Djebar concludes the text by expressing her desire for a singular language within language, an alternative idiom lingering within accepted forms of speech:

> Dans le brillance de ce désert-là, dans le retrait de l'écriture en quête d'une langue hors les langues, en s'appliquant à effacer ardemment en soi toutes les fureurs de l'autodévoration collective, retrouver un «dedans de la parole» qui, seul, demeure notre patrie féconde.[22]

This passage invokes an ideal singular language, which would somehow provide a space of belonging for Algerians alienated and excluded by existing nationalist and Islamist rhetoric. The 'dedans de la parole' might be a hidden recess within speech (not a 'word'), a place for the expression of the singular, and the idiom might once again convey the sense of belonging that Djebar for the most part now rejects or transcends. The fantasised 'patrie' in this sense could be an ideal but unattainable language, a set of singular echoes wholly encapsulating their meaning, rather than a rooted identity adhering to a static, monolingual culture. As for Derrida in his *Le Monolinguisme de l'autre*, language is not longer considered in terms of sovereignty and possession, but as a utopian vessel that might contain and convey the shifts and traces of singular affect. Djebar is seeking to articulate a wholly singular idiom of commemoration, one that resides beyond the limits of institutionalised rituals of mourning and that encapsulates the contingency of her infinitely private experience of bereavement. If, then, political and religious institutions try to channel and organise the process of mourning, attention needs to be paid to their repressive effects on singular affect, on forms of remembrance and melancholia that resist the resolution imposed upon them from outside. Djebar's retreat from institutionalised mourning prescribed by radical Islam and her search for a language of commemoration free from artifice testify to the limits of such external discourses of affective organisation.

This search for a pure or complete language leads, however, to a sense of temporal disjunction, a resistance to the separations of time. Commemoration does not occur through the construction of a smooth linear narrative, implying progress, resolution and completion. Rather, Djebar's work of mourning jumps back and forth in time in an attempt somehow to encapsulate past experience in the language of the present. One notable feature of Djebar's text, for example, is the repeated comparison of the events of the late 1980s and 1990s with the confrontations of the war of independence. She notes the irony that the anti-colonial movement, which championed during the 1950s and 1960s liberation and democracy, has given way to a system that mimics the rhetoric and tactics of the colonisers. There are ideological affinities between the French vision of the unity and universalism of their culture and the Islamist goal of communitarianism and monolingualism. Although these positions might initially seem to be opposed, they each paradoxically set themselves up as at once exemplary and unique. Both discourses propose a unified identity, be it secular or religious.[23] Even more disturbingly, some of the techniques of repression employed by the French, including the systematic use of torture, resurface uncannily in the 1990s.[24] Re-angled and reshaped to suit the demands of the Islamists, traces of the horror of the war eschew temporal linearity and re-emerge hauntingly in the present. Any narrative of progress, bringing catharsis, renewal or at least a strict demarcation between past and present, seems unworkable in this context of partial repetition and spectral apparition. Violence, torture, oppression and tyranny are cyclical phenomena leaving Algeria trapped in an ongoing process of mourning that resists completion and working through. Careful attention to this return of the past, however, and the rejection of false hope is, according to Elizabeth Fallaize at least, the focus of Djebar's political and ethical project.[25]

This chronological anxiety affects the structure of Djebar's testimony to the suffering of her country as a whole. Echoes of the violence of the war of independence are discernible beneath the narratives of destruction of the present. Certain memories '*refusent de collaborer*', unwilling to settle themselves within a reassuring sequence of narrative progression, and cutting across time. Moments such as the execution in June 1956 of Zabana, the first Algerian to be killed by the French at Barberousse, recur in the present with a sense of renewed immediacy. Similarly, Djebar uses Fanon's phrase '*les damnés de la terre*' in order to refer to the victims of the Islamists, and the text is punctuated with reflections on how the events of the fifties and sixties could have led, in cyclical fashion, to the aggressions of the present day. Processes of mourning and burial continue thirty years on, and the search for an appropriate language of ritual is one that remains unresolved, still resistant to the set phrases of any institutional discourse. Indeed, both conflicts somehow resist language, or are described using formulae that evacuate their content; both are referred to as 'une guerre qui ne dit pas son nom'. Seeking to 'work through' her recent losses, then, Djebar insists '*ramenons les asphyxiés, les suicidés et les assassinés dans les langes de leur histoire obscure, au creux de la tragédie*'.[26] A desire for historical closure and progression seems to be thwarted in this stubborn resurfacing of familiar patterns of oppression. The 'bourreaux d'hier' step outside time and become alarmingly re-embodied in the assassins of the present day. This temporal transgression is expanded further at the end of the text when Djebar sees the ghost of Abdelkader, who unified the tribes against the French during the 1830s, resurface to revolt against the violence of the present day.

A disruption of sequential history characterises Djebar's narratives of personal bereavement, as they weave themselves in among resurgent memories from Algeria's past. The text begins, for example, with a series of dialogues between the narrator and the ghosts of her friends, who continue to speak to her after their death. The initial pages of the novel seamlessly interweave her current experience of bereavement with memories of shared moments in the past, so that absence and presence become blurred. The spectres, to use Derrida's language in *Spectres de Marx*, set time out of joint, stretching the limits of contemporaneity and blending the present moment with its virtual simulacrum.[27] Next, Djebar goes on to recount in detail the events leading up to the assassinations of her three friends as if in a

further attempt to defy temporal distance and to re-immerse herself
in the past. She carefully notes the specific details of the days of their
death, using the present tense to record the actions of their relatives
as if to eradicate the separation between the traumatic moment and
her present self. Plunging the reader into the heart of their everyday
existence she recreates the circumstances of their passing in such a
way as to force us to experience it as if in the present. In the case of
M'Hamed, for example, the brutality of his assassination is recorded
quickly and up front: 'trois meurtriers cernent M'Hamed dans sa
chambre, au fond du couloir'.[28] The text then repeatedly rewinds
in order to note the impressions and sensations of other family
members. With Mahfoud, the details of his hospital treatment are
noted in an attempt to produce a completed medical record. In the
chapter on Abdelkader Alloula, Djebar dwells on the expression on
his face, confusing death with sleep and struggling in her imagination to revive his lifeless form. It is also significant that the section on
the 'trois journées' is preceded by an explicit announcement of this
temporal refusal. Sensing the retreat of the past and its obliteration
beneath the white of the blank page, she urges that the spirits of her
friends continue to linger despite the separations of time.

The text in this way constitutes an attempt to combat disappearance or the effacement of memory by language itself. Although
narrative itself imposes some sort of linearity and closure, forcing the
narrator to 'make sense' of her material and to create a story of sorts,
Djebar suggests that the trauma of bereavement works against the
normal progression of sequential time. While Paul Ricœur exposed
the interpenetration of narrative and temporality in his monumental
Temps et récit, demonstrating the necessary unfolding of a narrative
through time, Djebar prevents that temporality from taking a strict
linear form that adheres to the laws of the genre.[29] Images of the
friends' last moments refuse to be packaged away into the past, and
the ghosts of their living selves continue to haunt her memory: 'non:
je m'entête contre l'évidence; je refuse jusqu'au bout, jusqu'à la fin
de cette déambulation, de cette remémoration de l'«après», de ce que
j'appris d'eux dans cet après…'[30] The sudden and untimely nature of
her friends' deaths also means that they are experienced as irresolute
traumas that resist rationalisation and relegation to the past. Djebar
reflects on the intractability of 'la mort inachevée', which breaks up
the more expected rhythms of life and death and which stands outside
time. Such deaths cannot be absorbed by conventional explanatory

narratives but stick out obtusely, perplexing any desire for meaning and redemption. Comparing timely with untimely deaths, Djebar reflects: 'une telle mort glisse, comme une plie luisante, dans la rivière de notre mémoire. Tandis que celle qui survient avec fracas et dans le sang dégorgé, elle bouscule, elle viole notre durée, elle nous laisse pantelants.'[31] Horrors such as this refuse temporal progression and offer no possibility of a cleansed, alternative future.

Djebar's desire to exempt her narratives of bereavement from the constraints of linear time forms part of her attempt to hold on to the singularity of her memory. The trauma of her friends' 'mort inachevé' is inassimilable, resistant to explanation and determination, and requires a narrative that would somehow convey that singular horror. The tension between this necessity and the unfolding temporality of textual writing gives rise to an underlying struggle. There is a conflict between the intractable traumatic moment that, according to Cathy Caruth's definition, stands outside time, and the sequential progression of narrative, with a beginning, middle and an end.[32] In Lawrence Langer's terms, used to describe holocaust testimonies but perhaps relevant also here, this conflict can be theorised as a separation between chronological and durational time. According to Langer, duration names this resistance to temporal progression; it is a past that continues to be present. Chronological time on the contrary assures closure, or the separation of one temporal period from another. Langer argues that 'the duration of holocaust time, which is constantly re-experienced time, threatens the chronology of experienced time. It leaps out of chronology, establishing its own momentum, or fixation.'[33] If narrative itself moves through time, shaping events and providing them with some kind of organisational principle, the durational time of trauma can simultaneously disrupt this endeavour. Langer comments on the ways in which holocaust testimonies resist the efforts of ordinary narrative to consign experience to the past. Testimonies prevent us from seeking reassurance in the patterns of progress and chronology, and they force us to confront the unending duration of the traumatic event.

Parts of Langer's study privilege oral testimony at the expense of the written, since he suggests that spoken narratives convey durational time while written texts automatically shape and fix their referents. This opposition is schematic, implying naively that oral testimonies are free from the conventions of written language and from temporal progression, when they too are evidently rhetorically constructed and unfold themselves in time. This sense of a struggle between different temporalities, between sequence and stasis or repetition, is neverthe-less informative for a reading of Djebar. Her narratives focus not on her own survival of a horrific experience but on the difficulty of coming to terms with the trauma of bereavement, yet Langer's concept of durational time can describe Djebar's sense of discomfort with resolution and narrative linearity. While aware of the effects of rhetoric and textual convention, she struggles to extract her memories from unrelenting historical sequence in order to reveal the resistance of her experience to resolution. Djebar is unwilling to complete the work of mourning and to allow her text to separate her present self from the initial trauma. She fights against the pressures of chronology and hopes to stave off forms of closure that for her would prove artificial. Djebar keeps returning to the past in order to do justice to her friends' memory, to prevent them from being forgotten and to counter precisely the Islamist desire to eradicate them. Narrating in detail the moment of their death, continuing to speak with them and conjuring up their silhouettes in a circle around her bed, Djebar holds on to the possibility of dialogue, interaction or exchange. The narra-tive switches between moments and epochs, between memory and fictionalised recreation in the present, in the attempt to eradicate the distance and potential oblivion imposed by chronological time.

Finally, in spite of this resistance to temporal progression and the concluding evocation of 'un dedans de la parole' aptly adhering to the experience it describes, it should be noted that the narrator does remain conscious of the limitations of the memory narrative she creates. In hoping to resurrect the past and to locate a language that could fuse with the memories she struggles to recapture, Djebar's text also repeatedly confesses its own ineluctable limits. The narrator wants not only to avoid the constraints of narrative convention but also to understand her necessary engagement with those constraints. She negotiates an ongoing conflict between an ideal 'dedans de la parole' and a more uneasy language of mourning, 'qui saurait sa fragilité, et même son inanité, s'il est vraiment trop tard'.[34] In this sense, Djebar perhaps seeks to 'work through' rather than 'act out' the trauma she recounts. According to Dominick Lacapra, narra-tives that 'act out' the past are those that pander to the self-fulfilling desires of the narrator, perpetuating fantasies that suit that particular speaker or writer's demands. Certain narratives 'act out' a desire for 'identity-forming meaning', which means they create sense so as to fulfil a need for coherence or reassurance rather than genuinely to do justice to the traumatic moment. Those narratives that 'work through' memories, however, recognise the transferential positions that we find ourselves in when reading about the past, and they seek to counteract the projective reprocessing of past events. Djebar's desire for a pure 'dedans de la parole' certainly seems idealised, in that it connotes some sort of comforting homeland, an idiom belonging unproblematically to its speaker. Yet in expressing this ideal precisely as an ideal, Djebar conveys perhaps a more rigorous need for a form of testimony that accesses the traumas to which it refers while also remaining aware of its own position and analytical effects. While a narrative exempt from any 'acting out', from any search for meaning, is clearly impossible, Djebar's text struggles both to return fully to the past and properly to negotiate its own mechanisms as a discourse of memory. The narrative wants both to immerse itself in the moment and to resist the temptations of ideology by remaining self-aware. In Lacapra's words:

> Working-through also requires a sustained, problematic relation between witnessing in Langer's sense and a critical comparative history that marks differences, including those between the present and the past; it also involves the attempt to acquire some perspective on experience without denying its claims or indeed its compulsive force.[35]

Criticising those discourses that impose heroism or national identity on the memories they recount, Djebar's work wants to approach authenticity while remaining fully aware of its own fraught position. In this sense, her work is now a self-consious memory narrative rather than an alternative 'history', as in *L'Amour, la fantasia*. Djebar describes the text as a subjective project to 'translate the untranslatable', and she struggles to encapsulate the traumas of the past while remaining self-conscious regarding the restrictions imposed by narrative, rhetoric and genre.

Djebar's text in this sense explores and plays with the very limits of singular testimony. On the one hand, *Le Blanc de l'Algérie* makes a statement against the entrenchment of both ideological and rhetorical norms and challenges any artificial formulation of an Algerian national language of commemoration and identitarianism. Exposing the violence of the Islamist resurgence, Djebar paints a destroyed Algeria, unable to make sense of its losses using the false rhetoric of Arabisation prevalent at the time. Islamism crushes and severs Algeria both because it silences those who believe in freedom of expression and because it reduces both their creativity and their funerary rites to the stultifying rhetoric of a monologic, ideological law. On the other hand, however, Djebar also explores the invention of an alternative form both by reaching beyond traditional constraints and by assessing the limits of her own desired critique. In her efforts to testify adequately to the horrors of Islamist violence, she advocates the necessity of a return to the past, of a renewed interaction with the deceased, and she simultaneously critiques her own perspective and the ever-present constraints of her form. The work of mourning demands an impossible openness to the singularity of the other and to the moment of their passing, and Djebar's narrative struggles against itself to counteract false impressions of reassurance, progress and resolution. *Le Blanc de l'Algérie* ultimately attempts to mourn the loss of Algeria and to recover the oppressed or extinguished singular-plurality of its cultural expression. But it also conveys a sense of disillusionment towards its own status as a testimonial narrative, towards the possibility of doing justice to the singular losses at its core.

Oran, langue morte

Djebar's following text, *Oran, langue morte*, continues this reflection on bereavement and loss and takes the form of a series of brutal depictions of political violence in Oran since decolonisation. While *Le Blanc de l'Algérie* concentrates on the fraught search for an Algerian liturgy after the assassination of a generation of writers and thinkers, *Oran, langue morte* focuses more particularly on diverse, singular experiences of violence and mourning in the ravaged city of the title. The stories again juxtapose murders resulting from contemporary unrest with scenes from the war of independence, tracing at the same time the combined impressions of separation and retroaction experienced by the victims' bereaved friends. A series of narrators struggle against the progress of linear time, seeking an appropriate way to mourn their companions while resisting both their relegation to the past and the temptation to recuperate their memory according to present demands. Most importantly, in setting the stories in the city of Oran, Djebar interrogates their destructive effects on notions of local and communal identity, and demonstrates both the association and the curious dissociation between the trauma of loss and the place and time of its occurrence. If, in the rest of her work, Djebar struggles to make sense of Algerian history and increasingly represents Algeria as disintegrated and different from itself, she uses *Oran, langue morte* to interrogate further the effects of repeated, cyclical violence on the relation between place, identity and historical continuity. As in *Le Blanc de l'Algérie*, processes of mourning after past and renewed conflicts resist completion, and Oran, like Algeria itself in the former text, is portrayed as caught between oblivion and an endless, melancholic contemplation of its irresolute losses. Mourning for Oran takes the form of a call for continued attention to the deceased other, coupled with an awareness of the singularity and inaccessibility of that other. The narrators of Djebar's stories here are conscious once again of the limitations of their testimonies (though perhaps less obsessively than in *Le Blanc de l'Algérie*), but Djebar seems to suggest that such processes of reflection are the only possible form of 'working through' the fantasies and frustrations associated with loss.

The first story, 'Oran, langue morte', depicts the struggle between commemoration and oblivion associated with the eponymous city. As I have suggested, this threat of obscurity and occlusion in Oran recalls Djebar's increasing sense of loss and erasure in relation to her homeland, Algeria, more generally, though the text also refers to Oran's particular silence during the period of commemoration immediately following the war. The text tells the story of the recent death of the narrator's aunt, but this present loss is haunted throughout by the memory of the loss of her parents thirty years earlier, in 1962, during the horrific attacks of the OAS at the end of the war of independence. As in *Le Blanc de l'Algérie*, then, there is a close relation between the violence of the past and the political unrest of the 1990s, as the ghosts of the war come back to haunt the commemorative rituals of the present. Yet Djebar's interweaving of present bereavement with memories of the violence of the past is prefaced by a reflection on the difficulty of accessing and attending to singular moments in that past. Oran is a city of forgetting that endeavours to bury past confrontations and that lacks an appropriate narrative of mourning that might make sense of historical events and situate them meaningfully in relation to the present. Memories of the horrors of the OAS attacks, just at the time when Algerians were approaching independence and victory, are silenced and buried since they cannot fit into any reassuring narrative of Algerian reinvention. Rather than 'working through' its losses, the city shrouds the violence of the war

beneath a veil, just as the Algeria of *Le Blanc de l'Algérie* was bleached
or whited out: 'A Oran, on oublie. Oubli sur l'oubli. Ville lessivée;
mémoire blanchie.'[36] Djebar also notes that official mourning lasts
just three days and each victim of assassination is remembered for a
brief moment before time is allowed to continue its relentless movement forward. Murders succeed one another in a sinister sequence,
and the accordance of just three days of mourning allows each victim
to be forgotten before the death of the next. Rigid conformity with
linear time gives rise to occlusion and amnesia, and the horrors of the
past are stored away behind the surface of the city's elegant architectural edifice and the movement of its daily life in the present.

This sense of oblivion nevertheless exists in tension with the
narrator's attempts to hold on to the past, to rescue her parents'
singular memory from the amnesia of contemporary Oranais culture.
This conflict expresses itself in succinct form at the moment when the
narrator's aunt sees Habiba's and Abbas's bodies during the scene in
the cemetery. First, the soldiers reduce the bodies to numbers, organising them and classifying them in order to package them away into
the past. Just as the narrator of *Le Blanc* sought life in the slumbering
face of Alloula's corpse, however, once again this narrator notes that
her aunt believes her sister continues to speak to her after her death.
Removing the identification plaques marked with the numbers 66
and 67, she treasures them and invests them with significance so as
to counteract the enumeration and relegation that they nonetheless
imply. These objects come to signify, metonymically, the individuals
that they initially effaced. Furthermore, during the principal narrator's present return to Oran, and the intervening years in Paris, she
continually searches for gaps in the oblivion surrounding her parents'
past:

> Je cherche ici, comme à Paris: je quête leurs traces, leurs ombres,
> je scrute les rues où ils ont circulé, plus souvent encore qu'à Paris.
> Je voudrais flairer leurs espoirs, leur peur aussi caracolant dans ces
> avenues surpeuplées, ces places bruyantes, désertées de la foule des
> 'pieds-noirs' qu'ils côtoyaient, où se trouvaient certains de leurs
> collègues, quelques-uns de leurs amis, et bien sûr le groupe des trois
> assassins du 2 février![37]

Wandering the streets of both Paris and Oran, she perceives traces of
her parents' presence that transcend both temporal and geographical
boundaries, hints of singular shadows that resist the separation of
one moment and one location from another. Noting the significance

of the date of their deaths, 2 February, she also suggests that the moment slips outside the chronological sequence of the calendar, since each recurrence of the date is accompanied by a sense of return, of the halt of progress. This return and partial reapparition nevertheless refuses to provide any meaning or reassurance; it signifies a curious combination of repetition and distancing rather than commemoration. It calls for ongoing attention to the shadows of the past while presenting these as insubstantial, inaccessible and beyond the limits of the city's contemporary culture of denial.

The rejection of temporal sequence in favour of a cyclical structure of partial return characterises the narrative of this story as a whole. The horrors of the war of independence are interwoven with reflections on loss and oblivion in the present day, and the narrator maps past and present experiences of bereavement onto one another while refusing to incorporate a sense of progress or cure. Rather than neatly separating the memory of her parents' deaths from that of her aunt, she continually interrupts the narrative of the present with divergent echoes of her former bereavement that do not fit into a tidy chronological sequence. Memories of the aunt's night in the cemetery, when Habiba's and Abbas's bodies were brought out to be buried, precede reflection on their resistant wartime activities, and this is in turn followed once more by recollection of the OAS attack in the hospital. All these episodes are interspersed with reflection on the narrator's relationship with her aunt, the sense of the connection she offers to her parents, and the role of memory in the development of their relationship between 1962 and the present. The aunt's death, then, gives rise to this pattern of circular remembrance, where moments from the past linger at the time of narration and a new experience of loss reactivates past moments that have themselves never been resolved or worked through. Again recalling *Le Blanc de l'Algérie*, the inevitable linearity of narrative and the pressure of chronological time are counteracted by repeated patterns of resurgence.

This cyclical reworking of past moments of trauma is nevertheless always fragile and incomplete, and the moments that resurface can only ever be singular fragments rather than historical truths. Traces of the lead-up to her parents' assassination are constantly interspersed, as I have suggested, with evocations of Oran as oblivious and cut off from the past. It is important that it is also the narrator's young age at the time of her parents' deaths that gives rise to this particular cycle of amnesia and partial return. She herself does not remember the scene and learns the details of its unfolding through the fractured narratives of her aunt. As a result, the moment that she mourns is always already occluded and unknown, perceived through an inherited discourse rather than fully experienced at the time. It is this initial absence that leads the narrator to experience time in a circular fashion, constantly returning to a moment to which access is barred rather than completing her mourning and 'working through' her loss. The moment of bereavement is a 'trauma' in the Freudian sense, an event that was not fully experienced as it happened and which as a result is not wholly known. As Cathy Caruth asserts, the trauma consists 'not in the forgetting of a reality that can hence never be fully known, but in an inherent latency within the experience itself'.[38] Similarly, the narrator's return to the past and the jumbled episodes that break up the narrative can be seen as 'flashbacks', hopelessly seeking to make sense of an event that was never properly absorbed in the first place. The narratives of her parents' assassination, due to the originary inaccessibility of that moment to the narrator, resist ordinary patterns of resolution and acceptance.

This originary absence at the moment of bereavement is specific to 'Oran, langue morte', but the rest of the stories in the collection reflect a similar anxiety with chronological time. Past and present violent events in Oran are not commemorated in such a way as to position them securely within a particular moment in history; instead the city is continually unsettled, divided from itself by the resurgence of singular moments of trauma. In 'La Fièvre dans des yeux d'enfant', for example, this resistance to sequence manifests itself directly in the narrator Isma's address to her dead friend, Nawal. As in *Le Blanc de l'Algérie*, the narrator speaks to the dead, hoping to bridge the gap between the world of the living and the ghosts of the past by narrating her present experiences to an absent companion. At the moment of Nawal's death, for example, the narrator is unable to believe in her loss, and after explaining the circumstances of her assassination, she intersperses the rest of her narrative with revocations of her image and her voice. Sharing her thoughts on her complex relationship with her husband Ali and with a Somali man, Omar, for example, she continues to seek advice from her friend, constructing an empty and impossible place from which she might speak. Most hauntingly however, the text ends with news of Isma's own assassination, so that the narrative contains the double absence of both narrator and addressee. Isma's letters provide fleeting insight into her experiences, but the writing signifies her absence as much as it offers any lingering hints of her memory. Isma's initial reflection on her own singular record of the ongoing cycle of violence in Oran in this sense also describes Djebar's narrative of forgotten violence and its partial resurgence. Isma questions the capacity of her letters to commemorate and do justice to contemporary violence, and wonders why she should write 'quand tout, de ces lieux, sera détruit et que ne resteront, de moi en tout cas, que ces griffonnements sur un cahier jeté, oublié, dont l'auteur à son tour sera...'[39] Similarly, then, Djebar's own stories, brief transitory glimpses of moments of violence that have never been explained or acknowledged, convey amnesia and loss despite their call for singular remembrance. The writer's self-consciousness about this duality is the only possible, hesitant step towards some form of 'working through'.

The longest story in the collection, 'Le Corps de Félicie', charts a similar pattern of amnesia and the continuation of an incomplete process of mourning. The first part of the narrative concentrates on the characters' impressions of separation and fusion as their unconscious mother approaches death, yet the second part again questions the possibility of an appropriate form of commemoration to account for her eventual loss. Félicie's children, first Armand/Karim and next Ourdia/Louise (each retains two names reflecting their dual French/Algerian identity), chart the details of their hospital visits while also interrupting their fascination with her present state with memories of the distant past. Armand/Karim in particular strives continually to blur the gap between himself and his mother and to prolong their communication. Continuing to address all his thoughts to her, he conjures up visions of her past self and resuscitates her so as to counteract her impending demise:

> Je stationne devant ton corps: je lui apporte à mon tour mon trop-plein de souvenirs d'enfance, de scènes réveillées que j'avais crues dissoutes... Peut-être que je t'encombre moi aussi, que même je te bouscule: tu les perçois en effet mes appels et injonctions: 'Réveille-toi, souris-moi, dis-moi que tu m'as aimé, moi le préféré, parmi tes enfants!'[40]

This collapsing of the boundary between self and other, past and present, at the same time borders on appropriation or ventriloquism as Armand/Karim begins speaking in the place of his silenced mother. Furthermore, when she appears suddenly to revive in the moment before her death, Armand/Karim attempts to extract that very moment from chronology, to hold on to her life by transforming the moment into a paradoxical state of permanence. Denying temporal progression, this Rimbaldian perception of the moment replaces sequential, chronological time with endless duration and collapses the boundary between life and death. While witnessing the very transience of his mother's life and the unstoppable momentum of her passing, Armand/Karim himself steps outside time and paradoxically stills this moment of transition.

Temporal disjunction is coupled with spatial displacement in this text. Félicie is of French origin, but she married an Algerian and spent much of the latter part of her life in Oran. This duality divides the memories of the children, and the transportation of their mother to France for hospital care means that their mourning is inscribed in both places. The transfer also carries associations and memories of Oran across geographical frontiers, and Armand/Karim finds that traces of one location become intermingled and grafted onto another. The streets of Barbès are confused with the poor areas of Oran:

> je suis vivant à Barbès et je traîne au 'marché des voleurs'. Mais non, je me trouve à Oran, à la périphérie de quartier pour mauvais garçons, du côté du Petit Lac, là où j'ai acheté mes premiers jeans. Je traîne chez les pauvres, ou chez les voyous, mais là-bas![41]

This interpenetration also gives rise to a prolonged discussion between the children regarding where to bury their mother after she dies. Unsure where her identity is rooted, they struggle to find the appropriate location for her commemoration and the memories enlisted in their debate cross both temporal and spatial boundaries. Although they ultimately decide to transport her body back to Algeria, in order to commemorate her struggles during the independence movement and her support for a decolonised, reinvented nation, this does not signify any straightforward sense of identification or belonging. The gesture of a return reveals the family's desire for a form of commemoration that might record and account for their own search for a reinvented Algeria in the troubled aftermath of decolonisation, but the narrative ends with an admission of the impossibility of any such quest. Armand/Karim's stubborn holding on to the living image of his mother despite her passing triggers a return to Algeria, a desire to revivify and make sense of both the country's and his mother's past, but once again, the text presents that process as unfulfilled. Oran, his city of origin, and Algeria more broadly are unrecognisable. Félicie herself becomes a resuscitated Algeria, but this image is then immediately destroyed: 'un meurtrier, un second, un troisième la bouscule, la violente, la tire par ses cheveux. Les yeux exorbités, elle voit s'approcher la lame... Qui va la préserver? Quel mot, quel objet va pouvoir faire reculer le dément qui attaque?'[42]

As in many of the texts, then, past struggles are partially echoed in the traumas of the present, and 'Le Corps de Félicie' ends with this juxtaposition of Félicie's narrow escape during the horrific confrontations with the OAS in Oran and an image of the ravaged Algeria of the present. These processes of projection and retroaction between the 1960s and the 1990s, however, broaden to incorporate a much larger scope in 'La Femme en morceaux'. Here, as in *Ombre sultane*, Djebar does not merely look at recent history but creates connections between modern Oran and the mythical stories of the *Arabian Nights* in order to reveal how old patterns of horror repeat themselves uncannily in the present. In this example, the effacement and silencing in particular of women is transported and reinscribed from the folktale to the present day. The text begins by recounting a tale from the *Arabian Nights*, where the body of a woman is found divided into pieces in a trunk at the bottom of the Tigris. We are told that the woman was unwell and asked for apples, which her husband brought to her only for them to be taken by a slave. Believing, however, that his wife had given them to another man, the husband kills the woman in an act of jealous fury. In Djebar's story, this account of feminine silencing is the object of study for a class of modern Algerian students, taught by the lively Atyka. The destruction of the original story, however, is mimicked at the end of Djebar's tale when Atyka is murdered by Islamist extremists, apparently for contradicting their understanding of women's roles. This mirrors the assassination of Mourad in 'L'attentat', a teacher who is punished because 'il s'est battu toute sa vie pour une "école, disait-il, de la modernité"'.[43] As in *Le Blanc de l'Algérie*, Djebar criticises the effacement of creativity and freedom of expression.

Despite the motif of silencing, however, the interweaving of the original tale with a modern setting conveys a desire for renewed attention to feminine agency and the importance of at least attempting to resuscitate the feminine voice in a gesture of resistance to past and present effacement. Djebar notes that in the original tale, although the woman's body resides technically at the centre of the narrative, it is also curiously forgotten. While 'The Story of the Three Apples' begins with the discovery of the sinister basket at the bottom of the river, much of the rest of the tale concentrates on the obligation placed upon Djaffar by the caliph to find the man responsible.[44] The crime around which the tale revolves is the brutal murder of the woman, but she herself is marginalised by the male characters discussing the circumstances of the crime. Djebar's explicit goal in 'La femme en morceaux' is thus to retell the story in such a way as constantly to remind the reader of the occluded woman. In the initial pages, the image of the mutilated body is repeated, and more attention is paid in the following pages to the victim's experience. Furthermore, Djaffar's investigations are interrupted with another description of the waiting body, reminding us of its continual presence and conferring upon it a form of agency:

> Et le corps, le corps en morceaux de la jeune femme découverte depuis trois jours, attend, réenveloppé dans le linge de lin blanc, le fil de laine rouge dénoué, la couffe de feuilles de palmier ouverte, le tapis déroulé, la caisse d'olivier descellée...
>
> Depuis trois jours, sous les yeux du calife, on a allumé des brûle-parfums qui fument autour du corps de la femme non inhumé.[45]

We are also told that Atyka aims to '*renverser le conte*', to re-angle the original text so as to focus more emphatically on the woman at its centre. She herself foregrounds feminine self-expression and her analysis is a gesture of resistance against female subordination and patriarchy in both its past and present forms. Atyka's discourse is one of commemoration and unveiling, shedding light on the feminine experience occluded by the tale while also asserting its political resonance in the present.

The connection between Atyka's voice and that of the woman of the original tale also operates on a structural level. In the first part of the tale, the sections on the *Arabian Nights* and those focusing on Atyka's class are alternated and distinguished by regular and italic type. Although juxtaposed, the two contexts are kept separate and we are invited to draw parallels between these different scenes. The style of the two narratives also varies. The initial section on the original tale is told using shorter, balder sentences, narrating events while keeping the reader at a distance. The sections focusing on Atyka, however, are more affective and focus more precisely on atmosphere and perception, drawing the reader in to involve her in the discussion. However, this dissociation collapses at the moment of the arrival of the armed men into Atyka's class. This section is presented in regular type and the fractured sentences mimic those that described the 'femme en morceaux' at the beginning of the text. The clauses are brief and curtailed, as we are confronted with 'quatre imposants, en uniforme de gendarmes ou de soldats, et le cinquième, maigrelet, seul à être sans barbe et sans armes, seulement un couteau, ou plutôt un poignard court dans la main'.[46] Djebar purposefully confuses the settings, suggesting that the violence of the past is repeated in the present and partial echoes of forgotten narratives transcend temporal barriers. Indeed, one of the students believes for a moment that he is in the court of the caliph, identifying the actions of soldiers with the cruel designs of the sultan Haroun. The following section in italics describes Atyka herself as 'la femme en morceaux', and the analysis that sought to commemorate feminine experience comes instead to fall in with the repeated pattern of silencing and occlusion.

In addition, this troubled quest for the preservation of the female voice is subversive in its depiction of gender roles. The strict division of male and female roles and the transgression of that law was a preoccupation in *Loin de Médine* and *Ombre sultane* and it resurfaces now in a more politicised form. Atyka's students' commentary on 'The Story of the Three Apples' gives rise at one point to a discussion of Islam's egalitarian implications, as Atyka points out that Mohammed decreed: *'le meilleur d'entre les Croyants dirigera ma Communauté, même s'il s'agit d'un esclave soudanais!'*[47] This in turn generates reflection on men and women's equal status, on women's active participation in public life. Furthermore, Djebar emphasises the symbolic doubling of Shéhérazade in Djaffar. Djaffar suffers the same fate as Shéhérazade, using narrative to delay his own execution, and this depiction of story-telling as both a male and a female activity challenges notions of separate roles. The blurring of Djaffar and Shéhérazade's voices also troubles the division between a masculine and a feminine identity, reinforcing how the artful Shéhérazade is able to perform both positions. And as Atyka suggests, the resemblance between Djaffar and Shéhérazade implies that the latter could also be a vizier to the caliph and would be capable of participating in his decisions.

'La femme en morceaux' rereads the *Arabian Nights* in order to foreground contradictory perceptions of feminine agency and the perpetuation of its repression. On the one hand, Atyka, Shéhérazade and Djaffar all represent how narrative, the voice, can function as a form of resistance to subordination or even execution. Nevertheless, in attempting to give a voice to the forgotten, effaced women of both the present and the past, Djebar also portrays the continued power of discourses of oppression, and it is for this reason that the text seems circular and repetitive.[48] Patterns of resistance and silencing recur in scenes both from the *Arabian Nights* and from the present, and the liberation of women is not depicted in terms of a progressive advancement from backwardness to modernity. In ending the story with Atyka's murder, Djebar returns us to the effacement of the 'femme en morceaux', remembering in her own text the suffering of generations of women and depicting their recurrent oppression and consignment to oblivion. As in *Loin de Médine*, Djebar reflects on the occlusion of feminine agency, but struggles fully to counteract that occlusion with only passing echoes of feminine assertion. Atyka, tragically silenced at the end of the story by Islamic extremists, seeks both to uncover the woman's body and to resist the restrictions of a patriarchal society that forbids women to voice their opinions. As Mireille Calle-Gruber points out, Atyka provokes renewed discussion and reflection on the original murdered woman of the *Arabian Nights*, but her voice is in turn silenced, so that the call for reinterpretation becomes itself spectral, disembodied: 'en faisant à Atyka, morte, revenante, l'implaçable place fictionnelle, sans référentialité possible, sans réalisme, le récit d'Assia Djebar choisit délibérément *l'u-topie*, ce non-lieu que seule la littérature a les moyens de convoquer'.[49] Omar, one of the pupils, contemplates this disembodiment, but his final reflections suggest that Atyka's resistant voice is lost. Images of obscurity, of the whiteness and oblivion of Oran recur in the closing pages of the story, and the feminine voice that speaks out against that oblivion seems frail. Djebar leaves hanging Omar's question, 'le corps, la tête. Mais la voix?', and though she suggests that the echoes of Atyka's voice might resonate beyond the moment of their enunciation, these echoes then lose themselves in the silence of the 'ville blanche'.

Oran, langue morte repeatedly juxtaposes evocations of the amnesia of modern Oran with fragmented memories of the singular violence it denies. The search for such memories, however, is no longer part of a search for identity, for a history of Oran or Algeria that makes sense of the progression from past to present. Oran, and more broadly Algeria, is not at ease with its own history but is figured instead as a locus of violence, disintegration and loss. Like *Le Blanc de l'Algérie*, however, this next collection ends with a utopian desire for a form of expression that would somehow fully incorporate the horrific events to which it wants to bear witness. Recalling the notion of a 'dedans de la parole', the collection concludes with an evocation of a 'lecteur absolu', a quotation from Ponge, used in a lament over the inability of language to seize the objects and sensations whose essence the poet sets out to evoke.[50] Noting that Ponge indeed visited Algeria between 1945 and 1954, and that he struggled to conjure an image of Algerian women just by glimpsing the 'rose de leurs chevilles', Djebar uses this reflection once more to theorise the evacuation of Algerian women from the language of history and commemoration. The 'lecteur absolu' then, would be one who could grasp the singular memories that Djebar strives to recover, implying the achievement of a form of communication that could hold on to the past and make sense of its relation with the present. As in *Le Blanc de l'Algérie*, however, Djebar's search again seems impossible and paradoxical, attempting to merge past and present while also seeking to understand the author's own position and the mechanics of the text's creation. Both texts also revolt against effacement while testifying to its continued victory. Fantasies of a fusion between the present and the singular past are juxtaposed both with evocations of oblivion and with an awareness of the more altruistic demands of 'working through'. The texts incorporate a struggle between these conflicting forces.

Les Nuits de Strasbourg

Published in the same year as *Oran, langue morte*, *Les Nuits de Strasbourg* again reflects on the recurrence of memories of violence and oppression, and on the uneven, halting process of acceptance. Developing some of the tensions of *Oran*, however, *Les Nuits* moves away from an immediate reflection on bereavement to consider how the intermittent resurgence of echoes from past conflicts and wars continues to destabilise a group of diverse and hybrid characters 'exiled' in the European city of Strasbourg. If *Oran, langue morte* examines the fraught modulations between commemoration and oblivion in a city whose past and present is stained by conflict and oppression, *Les Nuits* moves on by looking at the unresolved turbulence of Strasbourg's past *and* at the transportation and displacement of persistent memories of the Algerian conflict. The text evokes moments of oppression and invasion occurring in Strasbourg itself while also tracing transcultural echoes between these moments and the colonial confrontation in Algeria. This structure of parallels and echoes gives rise on one level to a sense of intercultural communication: memories of characters of diverse origins become curiously interspersed with one another. Characters from varying backgrounds also share their memories in the hope that communication will provide a focus for the working through of their losses, and to celebrate cultural 'métissage'. At the same time, however, Djebar is anxious to emphasise the limits of this gesture of 'entrecroisement', and she stresses that persistent echoes of past massacres continue to alienate and unsettle her migrant characters. Furthermore, Algeria becomes even more distant, indistinct and inassimilable in this text, separated from the Algerian heroine, Thelja, both by historical upheaval and by geographical displacement. The first of Djebar's novels to be written from this point of view of exile, the text constitutes a further movement away from the 'familiar' homeland, as well as a locus of questioning of both the healing and the alienating potential of cultural *métissage*.

The first scene of the novel recounts the moment of the German invasion of 1939 and the mass exodus of Strasbourg's threatened inhabitants. The city is portrayed as a site of repeated conflicts, recaptured from the French at the time of the Franco-Prussian war in 1870, returned to the French under the Versailles treaty in 1918, and invaded again by the Germans at the start of the Second World War. Situated on the border between France and Germany, it is a site both of cultural interaction and of recurrent, violent and irresolute confrontation. It is significant also that this initial passage closely recalls the opening pages of *L'Amour, la fantasia* narrating the capture of Algiers by the French in 1830. Both passages depict a city ravaged and divided from itself, made unfamiliar to its inhabitants and expropriated by a foreign power. In both cases, the description stresses at once the destruction of the city, the sapping of its life, and the curious resistance or defiance of its architectural structures – its traces of permanence. Just as Algiers is described as 'imprenable', impenetrable in the face of the enemy, the statues and churches of Strasbourg bear witness to the exodus of their inhabitants while remaining steadfastly unchanging: 'indifférentes aux hommes seront les statues, les églises et, de même, les ponts de l'Ill ainsi que les placettes étroites, chaudes et intimes à force d'avoir été désertées'.[51] These images of an impenetrable exterior nevertheless testify at the same time to amnesia, as the statues also perceive the passage of time and the disappearance of the past beneath continual scenes of renewal. Statues and buildings bear witness to conflicts only to hide the singularity of the event of invasion beneath an opaque and lifeless edifice. In both novels the inaugural scene sets up an ongoing tension between commemoration, the city's quiet resistance to the burial of the past, and an admission of its irrecuperable losses, its difference from its former self. It is perhaps also significant that the comparison reminds us that, like Algeria, Alsace has been both French and not French, and the internal otherness and plurality of Algerian culture is in fact structurally similar to divisions within metropolitan France.

If the city of Strasbourg, like Algiers and Oran, is associated for Djebar with this struggle between memory and amnesia, it is also a crossroads where characters explore their disjunctive relationship with traumatic memories rooted both in the city and elsewhere. Strasbourg is a site of interaction and 'passage' and the diverse characters who meet there seek to share and 'work through' their own displaced origins against the background of the city's own traumatic history. The collection in this sense explores the healing potential of cultural interaction while in that very process producing a further sense of disjunction and alienation in relation to an increasingly distant homeland (most importantly for my current purposes, Algeria). The text focuses on three cross-cultural couples, French and Algerian, French and German, Jewish and German, and the city bears significance for each couple while their relationship with it is at the same time disjunctive and unsettled. Each character is a migrant, signifying openness to intercultural communication, and each at the same time carries within his or her memory the irresolute legacy of a history of oppression. Eve, for example, the daughter of an Andalusian Jewish father and a Berber Jewish mother, is portrayed as an incessant nomad who refused any attachment to Germany until meeting her current partner, Hans, a German and the father of her child. Having spent her childhood in Tébessa, before moving to Marrakech and then to Holland, she is continually uprooted and nowhere at home. Describing her photographs of Rotterdam, she laments that specific people and locations slip between her fingers: 'je n'immobilise que des ciels, de l'eau, des quais à l'infini, de temps à autre, un paquebot dans le brouillard!'[52] Residing in different locations, she retains no sense of identification or belonging while remaining scarred by the memory of the persecution of the Jews during the war. The scene with Hans mimicking the recitation in Strasbourg of sermons by Charles le Chauve, commander of the army of the Franks, and Louis le Germanique, leader of the soldiers 'd'au-delà du Rhin', functions as an attempt at resolution but seems more symbolic than effective. If each leader spoke in the language of the other, symbolising reconciliation, Eve's recitation in German signifies a recognition of past conflicts as well as an acceptance of cultural integration. Nevertheless, the persistent memory connotes an irresolute preoccupation rather than acceptance, and commemoration is always presented as partial and incomplete.

Knowledge of the conflicts of history is coupled in this text with a hesitant desire for transcultural communication, though this is in turn still stained with irresolute and untranslatable traces of each character's singular past. François, the French lover of the central character, Thelja, for example, struggles to recollect the effects of the exodus from Strasbourg and to form a coherent narrative out of the fractured images he retains. Seeking in his nights with Thelja a fresh union and celebrating the contingent, fleeting unity of their communion, he also haltingly unearths buried souvenirs of the German invasion and his subsequent exile. A series of fragmented images evokes the disruption of those initial days, and François tries to work through this past trauma by narrating its disparate fragments to Thelja, punctuating his speech at the same time with hesitations and doubts:

> Je me souviens du tocsin le 2 septembre, à l'aube... Nous étions à Oberhoffen: les villages devant être évacués n'étaient pas tellement loin de nous... Des paysans stupéfaits envahissent nos routes: leurs charrois de bœufs, leur bétail en file derrière, commencent à défiler... Je me trouve près du grand-père, à l'entrée du bourg; nous sommes spectateurs.[53]

Years of amnesia in this way break up the stilted resurgence of these unsettling recollections. A similar pattern emerges when another character, Karl, suddenly alludes to his disrupted origins. Karl's partner Irma had believed him to be 'Alsacien de souche', and the discovery of the family's exile in Algeria, at the time of the Franco-Prussian war, upsets her sense of a coherent relationship between past and present. These memories are also presented as disparate fragments, as Karl focuses for example on the scent that his mother used to clean his clothes in Algeria. The Proustian recollection of this scent transports this trace of the past into the present, while also stressing the difficulty of piecing together such remnants to form an ordinary chronological sequence.

The central character Thelja's Algerian past, and its curious parallel with historical events in Strasbourg, receives the most attention and provides a focus for Djebar's growing sense of displacement in relation to Algeria. Thelja was married with a child in her homeland of Algeria, but uprooted herself and travelled to Strasbourg in the hope of liberating herself from the confines of her position and celebrating the freedom of nomadic life. Reflecting on her status as eternally 'passagère', she asserts that her departure 'me paraissait jaillir d'une tombe', and she insists on preserving the freedom to move on at whim.[54] Revolting against the restrictions placed upon women in Algeria, she remains in transit, disappearing at the end of the novel without a trace and savouring the spontaneity and ephemerality of her relationship with François. Even her name evokes this cultural disjunction, as it signifies 'snow' in Arabic and seems to contradict her North African origins. Despite this championing of migration and feminine agency, however, transculturation again hides remnants of the colonial past. Early in the text, Thelja dreams of finding the dead body of a close friend or relative, and the moment evidently reflects a sense of anxiety as a result of the rupture between past and present. References to the Algerian war crop up intermittently in the narrative, and Thelja's attempts at continual renewal are overshadowed by traces of past violence. Halim's photographs of the Casbah in Algiers at night recall the description of Strasbourg at the beginning of the novel, and Thelja dwells on the haunting traces of past and future confrontations lingering behind opaque walls. Her own disappearance also uncannily foreshadows that of Berkane in *La Disparition de la langue française*. And although the implication is that Thelja is asserting her freedom and independence, while Berkane might be a victim of the FIS, the parallel once again reinforces the haunting of the process of migration by a history of intercultural oppression.

The curious interpenetration of Algeria and Alsace, then, evokes at once a search for innovation and intercultural exchange and a sense of loss in relation to a homeland that is no longer familiar. Memories of oppression weigh heavily on the present in both locations, and the legacies of the Algerian conflict and the Second World War inevitably colour relations in the present day and unsettle each city's capacity to signify a home. As the critic Michael O'Riley points out, 'the text interweaves the historical mementoes of imperialisms, resistant stains lodged in the zones of hybridity, through the historical framework of intertextual reference'.[55] The ongoing interweaving between Algeria and Alsace offers a sense of cultural dialogue while uncovering the shadows of upheaval that separate each location from itself. The text does transgress national frontiers, championing the importance of intercultural exchange and upholding *métissage* as a symbol of liberation – not least for Algerian women constrained by Islamic doctrine in their native land. Nevertheless, hybridity is not celebrated as an uncomplicated fusion but instead continues to bear traces of the separation and conflict imposed by imperialism, and fails to offer an alternative, identifiable position. The blurring of the very names in Irma's neologism 'Alsagérie' bears the mark of this modulation between communication and separation. Irma reflects on the echo of Alsace in Algérie, dwelling on the musical harmony and murmuring 'ces deux noms de pays, de terroir noir, lourd d'invasions, de ruptures ou de retours amers', and this combination of harmony with shadow evokes the continued tension between *métissage* and imperial oppression.[56] Furthermore, during Thelja and François's final night together, the couple associate the 'z' sound of 'Alsagérie' with 'zina', the Arabic word for a couple or a liaison, celebrating the blending of cultures mimed by their own interaction. Again, however, this final scene functions as a fleeting symbol of communion between characters or nations preoccupied and alienated by their loss and unable to forge an alternative, affirmative hybrid position.

The passages in italics evoking Thelja and François's nine nights together similarly connote at once fusion and separation or alienation. These passages are distinct from the rest of the text, set out in italics to highlight their separation from their context and the fleeting vision of contingent communion they contain. The nights stand outside time – indeed the first night begins with an image of time stood still – bringing the characters together in a spontaneous union divorced from roots or restrictive ties. On one level, then, they do provide an image of harmony reaching across cultural frontiers and offer a glimpse of an alternative form of communality. The narrator describes the characters' love-making in detail, exploring the nature of their intimacy without seeking any restrictive form of similarity. This intimacy, however, also displays the simultaneous union and dissociation that the characters share. Creating singular moments of intimacy and harmony, they are also divided by their different cultural histories, and their togetherness is precisely, inevitably transitory. The nights offer fleeting glimpses of communion that stand out from, but are also wholly informed by, the characters' dissimilar memories and origins and the divergent concerns they retain. At one moment, for example, Thelja feels compelled to address François in Arabic, hoping to convey the intensity of her emotion and the extent of their closeness, but she also remains aware of the separation her language creates: '*le mot d'amour, plein à craquer, se coagule dans la bouche de Thelja. L'emplit. S'élance, tournoie au-dessus de leurs visages, revient en vrille et s'épuise, se ratatine...*'[57] At this peak of their intimacy there is also a sense of incommunicability, and even as they share the fullness of the moment, language barriers mark their separation. The nights evoke an ephemeral, inessential sharing marked at the same time by distance and dissociation.

Just as the characters throughout the text modulate between a celebration of hybridisation and a lamentation on the legacies of past conflicts, so Thelja and François's interaction shifts rhythmically between communication and alienation. While on one level Djebar investigates through all the characters the tension between the persistent residue of buried traumas and the joyful, if tentative, embrace of new connections, the nine nights focus intensively on the fusion and separation of desire. Thelja describes love in terms of these rhythmical movements of metamorphosis: '*chaque fois inventer, trouver l'approche lente ou brusque, nous entrepénétrer, nous éloigner, nous frôler à nouveau, nous sentir, nous pressentir de loin...*'[58] Fusion and intimacy are balanced against distance and separation, and desire is structured by this duality rather than by a static or unchanging bond. Similarly, then, intercultural communication does not give rise to a new fused identity but is structured by interruptions and hiatuses, moving towards hybridity while simultaneously testifying to traumatic histories that are never fully overcome. Commenting implicitly on theoretical trends celebrating the dynamism and richness of migration, Djebar reminds us of the contradictions and uncertainties that underpin the gesture of fusion.

The characters' theatrical project of presenting 'Antigone en banlieue' also symbolises this tension between renewal and past oppression. First, the choice of the name 'la Smala' for the theatre group conveys both memory and forgetting. The characters choose this name because it is an Arabic word that has passed into French; it evokes cross-cultural exchange and the transportation of references across cultural frontiers. Nevertheless, Thelja wonders whether the others comprehend the full resonance of the name, reminding us that it is the Arabic term for the encampment of Emir Abdelkader in 1843 during the French conquest of Algeria. The term signifies in this way both a move towards hybridisation and a relic of colonialism that overshadows present identity politics. Furthermore, the play itself is equally significant. Antigone is seen as a figure of sacrifice, the victim of a patriarchal society whose fate prefigures precisely the death of the actress Jacqueline. Antigone's solitude at the grave of her brother also, according to Jacqueline, mirrors Djamila's isolation or, even more, the grieving isolation of the Antigones of contemporary Algeria, 'accompagnés par nul fiancé à la tombe, vivante[s] pour y attendre la mort'.[59] This isolation then echoes the solitude of those women, such as Thelja, who choose to resist the social structures that sought to restrict their agency but who find themselves as a result separated and alienated from the community they had considered was theirs.

The intertextual reference to *Antigone* resonates in Djebar's novel on two levels. First, in Sophocles' play, Antigone challenges Creon's tyranny and insists on giving her brother a proper burial, but her journey to his tomb leads her also to her own death. Resisting the autocratic authority of Creon, Antigone sacrifices herself in the name of family ties. As I have suggested, she functions as a symbol of individual resistance against patriarchal oppression, echoing Djebar's project of championing feminine agency and self-expression in defiance of colonialism and patriarchy. Her commemoration also challenges the desire to obliterate the trauma of bereavement, it condemns the attempt to deny the horror of death and to refuse to mourn – a trope that will of course recur in *La Femme sans sépulture*. The hidden, dark underside of Creon's palace recalls modern attempts to ignore the lost victims of colonial, or indeed Islamist, oppression. Secondly, moreover, although Anouilh's version is not mentioned by Djebar, French-speaking readers will be familiar with the 1942 reworking and its relationship with the context of the German occupation of France. Indeed, at the time of the first staging of Anouilh's *Antigone* in February 1944, Creon was seen as a symbol for the ills of collaboration and Thebes was seen as a sort of modern totalitarian state. This tacit intertext again evokes the echoes of the invasion of Strasbourg in that of Algiers, and the tyranny of Nazism as well as colonialism, both of which haunt the characters of modern Strasbourg. The Anouilh version also depicts Creon slightly differently from the Sophocles version, since it characterises him less as an absolute tyrant than as someone who places his social or political duty above family loyalty. In this sense, Djebar alludes to the difficulties associated with a transcendent politics that neglects the singularity of relationships and experiences that do not conform to a state ideology. Djebar's implicit reference to Anouilh's *Antigone* once again evokes the persistent shadow of political ideology, and Antigone's persecution poignantly signals the ongoing difficulty of resistance.

The death of the actress Jacqueline adds another dimension to the co-implication of transculturation and traumatic memory and serves to crystallise both other characters' sense of rootlessness and ongoing patterns of patriarchal violence. In response to the brutal murder of her friend (Jacqueline was killed by her lover), Djamila reflects on the difficulty of overcoming entrenched structures and describes her condition as one of exile and alienation in a society that is still unable to make her feel at home. If the production initially set out to evoke both feminine agency and the importance of an appropriate form of commemoration, Jacqueline's death questions the possibilities of both innovation and redemption and reminds us gloomily of the persistence of familiar forms of oppression. Confessing her love for Jacqueline, Djamila laments her sense of non-belonging after the latter's death and reinforces the difficulty of locating a space of resistance and agency beyond established frontiers:

> *Moi, l'émigrée révoltée contre les siens, ayant coupé les amarres, dédaigneuse de la prétendue solidarité du groupe, moi, l'émigrée de nulle part et qui commençais à respirer sur les planches d'une troupe de théâtre amateur de quartier, moi la pseudo-Djamila et Antigone pour de vrai, je m'annonce comme l'amoureuse de cette reine morte, la si belle, si ardente qui, mains ouvertes, allait vers tous!...*[60]

In this way, while the project of performing Antigone in a modern setting might have been seen to uphold feminine resistance, as well as being a pointed form of commemoration, Jacqueline's death forestalls that project and leaves Djamila struggling to confer meaning on her disrupted trajectory. Djebar picks up on terms used by Anouilh again here, as the death transforms the 'tragédie', which connotes structure and coherence, into a 'drame', an unhappy event mired in the banality of police investigations.[61] The search for innovation ends in a lamentation on exile and the loss of direction.

Finally, *Les Nuits de Strasbourg* explores the potential for enriching, innovative exchange between culturally diverse individuals passing through Strasbourg while also drawing attention to the shadows of intercultural conflict that persist in alienating the characters both from themselves and from each other. Moving on from the reflections on bereavement that traverse *Le Blanc de l'Algérie* and *Oran, langue morte*, the text hesitantly celebrates *métissage* while continuing to investigate the resurgence of traumatic memories that haunt the migrants' search for innovation. Yet if much of the text seems to have progressed to a different stage, reaching beyond the limits of Algeria itself in order to make sense of the country's unsettled past from the more distant position of exile, migration and cultural interaction nevertheless do not eradicate the country's unresolved horrors. Modulations between memory and progress are subtended by images of effacement and loss as characters recall the historical moments that haunt their consciousness only to disturb their sense of identity and selfhood. The process of mourning is never completed, the only form of 'working through' consists in the realisation of the irredeemable quality of the characters' losses, and bouts of amnesia fracture any understanding either of the colonial legacy or of the effects of Second World War in Alsace. It is for this reason that the images of whiteness or effacement prevalent in the preceding two novels continue to haunt the narrative, and are indeed exacerbated by the blurring caused by geographical distance. Thelja's vision of a 'masque blanc' covering Jacqueline's memory in the 'banlieue' recalls the white shroud of *Le Blanc de l'Algérie*, calling up disturbing associations of oblivion or of a failure to mourn.[62] Similarly, Djamila's white costume when she plays Antigone evokes the mourning robes again figured in the earlier text, connoting at once commemoration and the 'whiting out' of memory. Thelja's final contemplation of Strasbourg, evoking the effacement of François's past as well as a more general, listless emptiness, again associates the city with the oblivion of Oran. Despite the exploration of new forms of cultural encounter and the resurgence and resolution of uncomfortable memories, the text draws attention to its own occlusion of moments of trauma, and of the Algeria that slips further from its grasp.

All three of the novels in this group shift the focus away from the search for any Algerian postcolonial, or feminine, specificity, and seek instead to come to terms with the renewed violence of the 1990s, its uncanny links with the history of colonial oppression. Djebar now investigates not the potential continuities of Algerian history but the ruptures and contingencies of the present, Algeria's stasis within an unresolved process of mourning its most recent victims. The resurgent violence of the 1990s also distances Djebar from her country of origin, as it is figured as unrecognisable, torn apart and hollowed out. It may be significant, then, that the last novel of this period makes such a decisive movement away from Algeria and surveys its troubles instead from the uncertain, indeterminate position of exile in Strasbourg. Djebar's relationship with Algeria is newly dislocated, disjunctive, and her references are also European: the Algerian war is compared with the Second World War, and one of the major intertexts is Sophocles', and then Anouilh's, *Antigone*. Again, this is perhaps not so much a rejection or a betrayal of Algeria, but rather a recognition of her increasingly ambiguous relationship with it, her alienation in its newly oppressive culture of Arabisation and Islamism. Algeria is pitted less obviously against France, since we are reminded of the invasion of Strasbourg in a way that calls up echoes of the French arrival in Algiers in 1830, so that the status and position of coloniser and colonised become less distinct, or are at least revealed to be transient. It is this increased blurring that leads her to question the very ontology of Algeria, of the Algerian people, in the next two novels. She definitively abandons the quest for specificity and identification in order to conceive her native land as both the same and other, haunted by its past and unable to make sense of its history. *La Disparition de la langue française* will investigate this internal otherness, this spectrality, within Algerian culture and within the French language itself.

CHAPTER FIVE

Haunted Algeria

La Femme sans sépulture

The most recent phase of Djebar's work, including *La Femme sans sépulture* and *La Disparition de la langue française*, announces a further step towards expatriation, a break from any intended quest for identity and a reconfiguration of Algeria as necessarily lost. While *Le Blanc de l'Algérie* and *Oran, langue morte* begin a process of mourning and resuscitate the ghosts of some of Algeria's writers, intellectuals and resistance fighters, the next two novels present that process of mourning as always, inevitably incomplete. Algeria in this final phase is not merely a victim of loss but *constituted* by loss, peopled by spectres, and known only in so far as it cannot be, and was never, fully known. In *La Femme sans sépulture*, Djebar returns to the memory of the war of independence, to the nature of women's intervention and their activities in the maquis, and she seeks once again to uncover singular experiences that remain uncharted by mainstream historical accounts. Yet here, the attempt to recover Algeria's traumatic history at the time of the war demands an alternative language, a complete abandonment of 'the specific' in favour of a wholly alternative poetics of haunting, loss and partial presence. Now Derridean notions of singularity and *différance* in language are expanded and radicalised to engender a more disturbing investigation of hauntology, of deathly half-presences that throw into question the borders of life and death. The text recounts the narrator's attempts to reconstruct the history of Zoulikha Oudai, a resistance fighter, a spectral, almost mythical figure who haunts the testimonies of the women interviewed despite persistent uncertainties regarding her fate. The focus also of Djebar's investigation in *La Nouba des femmes du Mont Chenoua*, Zoulikha's story demonstrates the unyielding violence of colonial oppression while simultaneously exposing the cracks in the subsequent public denial of that violence through the heroine's recurrent reappearance even after her death. The novel is distinct from Djebar's previous investigations, however, because the evocation of the war takes the form of the ghostly reapparition of the central character who, like the spectres of colonialism, hovers between the living and the dead because she was never properly laid to rest. A resistance fighter who was tortured before she mysteriously disappeared, Zoulikha appears in the novel as a ghostly resurrection whose (fictionalised) testimony is interwoven with fragments of her daughters' memories and whose half-presence testifies at once to the persistent legacy of colonial violence and to its attempted obliteration. Djebar's war story is a study in the possibility of exhumation through writing, of keeping the ghost of both Zoulikha and colonialism alive, and of the potential, or indeed the risk, that writing itself might help to bury the dead again. The novel abandons the search for identity and belonging and figures the narrative of Algeria's colonial past as haunted by partial, inadmissible presences, at once conjured up by, and banished from, its outline.

Djebar's intervention is, she confesses, itself belated. The text was written in two stages, begun in 1981 and completed in 2001, and its creation was interrupted by a plethora of other works exploring similar themes, without, however, resolving the fate of Zoulikha. It is as if her story resists the ordinary demands of narrative progression and unfolds uneasily; it enters into Djebar's writing in fits and starts. Zoulikha is, as I mentioned, a mythical figure also haunting *La Nouba des femmes du Mont Chenoua*, and she finds her echo in the stories of characters such as Chérifa in *L'Amour, la fantasia*, but her story resists resolution and confinement within a single, completed text. Writing in response to the horrors of the French defence of Algeria and in revolt against the subsequent amnesia surrounding French practices of torture and extermination, Djebar tries to recall the injustices suffered by characters such as Zoulikha, but struggles to track the chronology of her battles and subsequent demise. Just as the collective memory of the Algerian war traversed, in Bensmaïa's words, a period of forgetting followed by the 'return of the repressed', so Zoulikha's story is occluded in Djebar's work until its eventual, partial and troubled resurgence in the final version of *La Femme sans sépulture*.[1] Djebar denounces the public amnesia that succeeded the war and criticises French attempts to deny responsibility for its 'disappeared' victims, but reminds us that their stories are, as a result of that forgetting, difficult to resolve or complete.

Zoulikha as a character is therefore herself deferred, seemingly promised but remaining nevertheless beyond the narrator's grasp, most obviously at the time of Djebar's first endeavour in 1981 but also again in the final version of the text, eventually published in 2002. In the epilogue to this completed version, the narrator continues to lament her belatedness in reproducing Zoulikha's story, and she notes that 'mon écriture, avec ces seuls mots de l'écoute, a glissé de mes doigts, différée, en retard, enchaînée si longtemps'.[2] Not only, then, is the text published belatedly after a period of public (and private) amnesia, but the writing itself is bound up in a process of *différance*, at once difference and deferral, remaining always one step behind its heroine. The version we have is necessarily the result of a delay or a time lag that separates the form from the experiences and stories it hopes to seize. The written text is a sort of revenance, the belated return of a story out of joint with itself.

The haunting of the heroine and the very text of *La Femme sans sépulture* merits comparison with the postcolonial ghosts of the work of the American writer Toni Morrison, though attention to the differences between Morrison's and Djebar's projects will also help to specify the tensions of the latter. Both writers stress how the aftermath of slavery and colonialism leads to a necessary reconceptualisation of being as at once dead and alive, in thrall to the spectres of a past that continue to alter and reconstitute the present. In Morrison's work, the ghost of Beloved returns to haunt her mother Sethe, who killed her as a baby to spare her from slavery. The haunting in the novel announces the return of a past that is partially remembered and partially forgotten, beyond concrete knowledge and understanding but resistant to oblivion and consignment to a finished past. The ghost of Beloved is both absent and present and her uncanny haunting recalls a history of violence that resists relegation to the past as well as straightforward explanation in the present. Kathleen Brogan describes Morrison's own text as an attempt to come to terms with this past and therefore to bury it after its proper commemoration. In returning to Sweet Home, Beloved seeks to work through the trauma that led to her death, and similarly Morrison's text exhumes the murdered child in order to mourn her appropriately. Brogan names Morrison's text a 'provisional burial', and argues that in recalling the child's tombstone inscribed with the single word 'Beloved' the text too tries, though is not fully able, to commemorate her death in such a way as to move into the future. Brogan concludes:

'*Beloved* records the struggle toward narrative, performs the final burial, but leaves the grave open'.[3]

Is Djebar's text a similar attempt at exhumation, commemoration or reburial? Certainly, Zoulikha's ill-recorded disappearance and lost grave form the impetus for Djebar's writing, and the narrator's attempts to reconstruct her story could be seen as part of a project to resuscitate her deceased character in order, precisely, to re-narrate her death. In a sense then, Djebar's text is another form of burial and, like Morrison's ghost story, the written work could be seen as 'a verbal tomb'.[4] Nevertheless, *La Femme sans sépulture* even at the end never offers itself as a completed work of mourning and Zoulikha's ghost is never fully laid to rest. The crimes of colonialism, the torture and disappearance of hundreds of Algerian resistance fighters, are not atoned for so easily. Rather, the novel is a process of recollection that refuses to allow its central character to reside peacefully in the past but persists in pursuing the traces she leaves so as to reinforce the resonance of her mistreatment in the present. Zoulikha is never buried again, because the narrator never satisfies her search for knowledge of her experiences, and her ongoing revenance promises further recurrence in the future, just as colonialism continues to exert its influence on the present. Djebar also explicitly linked her reflection on disappearance and reapparition with the experiences of the victims of the attacks of 11 September 2001, as if once more to bring Zoulikha's narrative into the present and to give it contemporary resonance.[5] The connection is a complex one and Djebar is hesitant in stressing too strong a resemblance between the two periods, but writing in the autumn of 2001 she notes the recurrence of unexplained disappearances and reminds us of the trauma associated with the lack of a proper burial. Djebar's comment is intriguing precisely because it again betrays this resistance to the separation of past from present, as if Zoulikha is somehow reincarnated in the victims of the terrorist attacks.

Zoulikha, then, is a spectral presence rather than a fully fleshed-out character, and the narrator repeatedly describes her using the imagery of haunting and partial presence. At the beginning of the novel we are given a brief summary history of her life, a quick sketch picking out key moments, such as when she speaks out against the way in which North African soldiers were treated when fighting for the French in 1939–40. But even here, the narrator punctuates her references to specific events with anxieties concerning the ability of her chronology to trace her character's shady outline. The evocation of her participation in the activities of the maquis is broken more than once by references to her mysterious disappearance, the memory that 'personne ne la reverra vivante', and her descriptions lament her absence as frequently as they celebrate her presence.[6] Zoulikha's life, her living character, is conjured up as 'vivante au-dessus des rues étroites, des fontaines, des patios, des hautes terrasses de Césarée'; she is a floating figure, whose presence is sensed by the narrator but whom she cannot pin down in a substantial form. In another scene, her daughter Hania remembers her so fondly and seems to desire her presence so much that she imagines 'Zoulikha restée là, dans l'air, dans cette poussière, en plein soleil', somehow suspended between living and death, between presence and absence.[7] Mina maintains this same half-belief in her ongoing presence, and both the daughters and the narrator repeatedly convince themselves that Zoulikha still participates in their lives, perhaps by talking to them or by casting her shadow over the walls of their home. Mina notes 'nos souvenirs, à propos de Zoulikha, ne peuvent que tanguer, que nous rendre soudain presque schizophrènes, comme si nous n'étions pas si sûres qu'elle, la Dame sans sépulture, veuille s'exprimer à travers nous!'[8] It is as if Zoulikha lives on by haunting the consciousness of those whom she was close to; her memory is not consigned to the past but seems to transcend the boundaries of time. Zohra Oudai dreams that 'Zoulikha l'héroïne flotte inexorablement, comme un oiseau aux larges ailes transparentes et diaprées, dans la mémoire de chaque femme d'ici...'[9]

Zoulikha's partial presence is frequently expressed as a play between light and darkness. At times, the spectre is figured as a sort of passing flash, a spark that radiates still in the present but that also flickers uncertainly and threatens at any moment to be shrouded in darkness. In one episode, the dozing Hania hears women talking about her mother, and she starts to sift through memories of rituals, of women's folktales, and of her mother's position in relation to the traditions of her community. In passing through such memories, however, Hania recalls that it is precisely Zoulikha's tentative glimmer she is following: 'oui, pour toi, là où vibre cette lumière crue qui dénude, qui brûle, pas celle qui asphyxie'.[10] Hania seems to be seeking to illuminate her mother's shadowy presence, to light up the hidden recesses of her forgotten history while also being careful not to over-expose it and destroy it in the process. Her fantasy of the tomb flashes before her, 'illuminé, isolé, un monument superbe', a brief flicker of a ritualised commemoration, before blurring and fading beneath her tears.[11] Light transcends time, then, but it is fragile and loses some of its glow; an excess of clarity would lead, as in *L'Amour, la fantasia*, to the annihilation of the subject. Similarly, the narrator expresses her search for liberation as one that would escape 'l'ombre même du passé muet', so that silence becomes associated with darkness and occlusion, while recollection is a form of illumination.[12] Finally, in the anxious, self-conscious epilogue to the novel the echo of Zoulikha's voice is figured as 'vérité nue, d'un éclat aussi pur que tel ou tel marbre de déesse, ressorti hors des ruines, ou qui y reste enfoui'.[13] The reconstruction of Zoulikha's history is set up, idealistically, as a pure spark of light which, though fragile and at risk of being smothered, radiates tentatively through the interstices of the country's ruins. In the climate of amnesia and occlusion that followed the war, Zoulikha's spectral reapparition takes the form of a passing, flickering iridescence.

As in texts such as *Les Enfants du nouveau monde* and *Ombre sultane*, this search for a subtle glimmer is constantly interrupted by reflections on obscurity, on the veil and its presence, curiously at once oppressive and reassuring, in the lives of Algerian women. Zoulikha is frequently described as veiled, both literally and metaphorically, so that the light that flickers across time is also at times shaded and reveals only bits and pieces of the past. The narrator recalls early on, for example, that 'on pouvait, dans mon quartier ancien... la confondre avec mes autres concitoyennes: couvertes du voile de soie', and in some ways, retention of the veil ensures her some anonymity.[14] As we saw in *Les Enfants*, the veil served as a useful tool for women during the war, since they were able to hide weapons in the folds of its fabric. The anonymity offered by the veil, together with its associations with traditionalism, would have helped characters such as Zoulikha to carry out their activities unnoticed. Indeed, in one of her monologues, Zoulikha remembers hiding her face with her veil so as to move about in the streets unrecognised, though once again here her evocation of herself as 'unique silhouette de femme voilée' reinforces our sense of her presence only as a hazy outline in the novel.[15] In addition to offering protection, however, the veil is also frequently associated with the shroud, with death or the metaphorical extinction brought about by sequestration and the restriction of women. Zoulikha's relationship with it is ambiguous and changeable, as she seeks both to shed its associations with confinement and to benefit from its capacity to shade her from excess visibility. The novel's imagery intersperses shadowing and veiling with illumination and exposition, but nevertheless refuses to privilege or exchange one for the other. Each necessitates the other, and Zoulikha's spectral presence plays on this interface between light and dark, the visible and the invisible. As Julian Wolfreys points out on his book on spectrality in Victorian literature, 'light, which figures the phantasm in a certain manner, is also that which makes the phantasm available to sight to an imperfect degree'.[16] The ghost is momentarily illuminated but announces merely the trace of what cannot be seen. Zoulikha is described *both* as an indistinct silhouette *and* as a flickering spark of light. Her enigmatic contour is partially suggested both through the fabric of the veil and through the obscurity of the narrative's amnesia.

This suspicion towards excessive illumination is also expressed through the narrator's anxiety concerning the effects of artifice. On one level, the depiction of Zoulikha as a spectral presence testifies to the limits of colonial oppression, since it reveals the failure of the colonial drive to efface its resistors. Zoulikha's haunting shows that the coloniser could not wholly eliminate those who fought against him, and the instability of her apparition troubles the colonial desire to control public knowledge of the war and to repress the violence of the past. At the same time, however, the text does question the process of staging the spectre, as anxieties about the influence of theatricality crop up intermittently through the narrative. The critic Michael O'Riley argues of the scene of Zoulikha's capture that 'the tortured body of resistance is transformed into both spectacle and specter of colonial technology, permeated by an ethereal "lumière blanche, irréelle" "white, unreal light", and circumscribed by an "éther scintillant" "sparkling ether"'.[17] In this passage, excessive light is associated not only with over-exposure but with falsity and performance, like powerful stage lamps that shine upon actors in order to make them hyper-real. Furthermore, O'Riley's argument suggests that the spectre could itself be depicted theatrically, that precisely colonial films 'transform the body of resistance into an aestheticized specter'.[18] Certainly, Hania confesses her misgivings about a proposed project to make a film of her mother's experiences and points out that such aestheticisation simply kills Zoulikha a second time. If, then, colonial violence is portrayed as meaningless theatre, a 'tragédie éventée en plein midi qui prête à l'éther une vibration sourde et argentée', the reconstruction of Zoulikha's shadowed history must similarly lend itself to the distortions of artifice.[19] The heroine's ghost could conjure up theatrical visions of a false, staged haunting. The figure of the spectre is designed precisely to resist demands of clarity and knowledge, but perhaps it in turn risks falling in with stock, aestheticised notions of a dramatic ghostliness. These could in turn be informed by the coloniser's dream of the effacement of the insubstantial colonised. Djebar needs to resist the twisted influence of hackneyed spectres produced, at their worst, by European colonial stereotypes.

While continued veiling is one way to avoid the falsity of any exhibition, Djebar also sets about structuring her entire narrative in such a way as to deflect our attempts to turn Zoulikha's story into an aesthetic stereotype. On one level, her project is compromised in that it records the triumph of colonial ideology in partially effacing the memory of its victims, and Zoulikha's spectral interweaving in and out of the text risks poeticising the horror and violence of her elimination. Yet the narrator is nevertheless conscious of the need for an alternative mode of representation and tries to structure the work in ways that do not collude with the colonial vision. These techniques may have their own artificial aesthetic effects but can nonetheless be understood as part of an attempt to establish an alternative structure that criticises the drive towards excessive clarity and knowledge. Evidently, the division of the narrative into testimonies by different narrators undermines any attempt to secure conclusive or definitive knowledge. Each witness offers a different facet of Zoulikha's experience, but these visions cannot be knitted together to form a chronology and each contains its own gaps. Djebar's transcriptions of the memories of Hania and Mina, Zohra Oudai and Dame Lionne, are always punctuated with attention to the psychological state of the speaker, of her omissions and digressions, and personal affects that colour her representation of the past. The texture of Hania's narrative, for example, is evoked as powerfully and as minutely as its hesitant content, as we are told:

> Ainsi, une parole menue, basse, envahit la fille aînée de Zoulikha, dans l'étirement de son insomnie. Elle parle sans s'arrêter, pour elle seule. Sans reprendre souffle. Du passé présent. Cela la prend comme de brusques accès de fièvre. Une fois tous les six mois; quelquefois une seule fois par an; cette maladie a tendance à faiblir.
>
> Il y a dix ans tout juste, germa en elle cette parole ininterrompue

> qui la vide, qui, parfois, la barbouille, mais en dedans, comme un
> flux de glaire qui s'écoulerait sans perte, mais extérieur... A la fois
> un vide et un murmure en creux, pas seulement au fond de son
> large corps, parfois en surface, au risque d'empourprer sa peau si
> transparente; peau épuisée à force d'être tendue; gorge serrée à force
> d'être presque tout à fait noyée![20]

The physical creation of the words seems here as important, and as
troubling, as the memories themselves, and that creation occupies the
text as much as the stories Hania hopes to tell. Language is not transparent; it is an obstacle, a disturbing physical entity that intervenes
in and mediates the witness's attempted representation. Rather than
hiding such effects, however, and rather than celebrating a successful
reconstruction, Djebar's text constantly reminds us of the pitfalls
hindering its creation. Testimony never flows smoothly but emerges
in fragments, interspersed with silences, disturbances and doubts.

The narrative structure of *La Femme sans sépulture*, then, is a
mosaic of fleeting interventions. As in *L'Amour, la fantasia* or *Vaste
est la prison*, Djebar endeavours not to control the story's unfolding
herself but to allow multiple observers to offer their own partial vision.
In this sense, the text is less a performance of an existing, preconceived
sequence of events than a tentative gathering of half-forgotten traces.
The main narrator does not take on the role of a controlling director
but leaves room for singular witnesses to improvise their reconstruction of Zoulikha's life. Unlike in the preceding texts, however, the
curious position of the narrator/listener draws particular attention to
the difficult process of relinquishing control of the narrative to leave
space for alternative perspectives. On the one hand, the listener seems
highly self-conscious and repeatedly emphasises her anxieties about
her own lack of knowledge and the distorting influence of her view.
She sets her transcriptions of the interviews in the specific context of
her own interaction with the speakers and tries to make her readers
aware of the circumstances of the narration. Rather than presenting
the fragments as definitive statements, she offers them as part of
another narrative charting her own possibly troubled relationship
with Zoulikha's daughters and with the text she in turn produces as a
result of their words. On the other hand, however, she does nevertheless invent her own hypotheses and present these confidently, not as
truths, but as untheorised visions of what might have been. The voice
of Zoulikha herself is of course knowingly fictional, but is nevertheless transcribed unselfconsciously and generates some uncertainty

concerning the viability of the narrator's project. The main narrator of *La Femme sans sépulture* sets out to resuscitate her ghost, but also perhaps speaks in her place and can never escape the risk of aestheticising her experiences or reappropriating them for her own literary ends. The novel tries to regenerate the spectre without falsifying its history or reducing its commemoration to artifice, but also makes us question the eventual success of such a project. Djebar raises the question of whether the spectres of the past can reappear, whether they can then be properly remembered, or whether their evocation in narrative consists, on the contrary, in another form of extinction.

These difficulties of recall and remembrance in *La Femme sans sépulture* are, as I suggested, the result of a time lag, of a generation gap that severs the process of mourning. Produced as a result of interviews carried out significantly after the end of the war, the narrative relies on inherited knowledge, and the daughters, Dame Lionne and Zohra Oudai, are the receivers of information concerning their mother rather than eyewitnesses to her trauma. The most disturbing moments of Zoulikha's life are recounted as a result of hearsay, interrupted by temporal disjunction, and by the process of translation or transcription. First, the daughters' own memories are 'postmemories', to use Marianne Hirsch's term, in that they are produced at a temporal remove from the disturbing world they recall. This means that they are constantly mediated, they seek connections but necessarily forge these themselves, on the basis not of first-hand knowledge but of assumption or imagination. Their constant repetition or renegotiation constitutes a desperate attempt to account for their mother's loss, but the gaps in their knowledge and distance from her experience mean that their mourning is never completed or worked through but remains suspended. In Hirsch's words, postmemory 'creates where it cannot recover. It imagines where it cannot recall. It mourns a loss that cannot be repaired.'[21] It is for this reason that the text never completes its depiction of Zoulikha's life and death, but remains 'melancholic', bound to repetition and partial revocation rather than achieving satisfactory commemoration and working through its loss. Secondly, moreover, the narrator's transcription of the daughters' 'postmemories' is once again deferred, passed further down the chain of linguistic *différance* and standing at a further remove from the haunted memories it seeks to recover. *La Femme sans sépulture* figures this double disjunction, it seeks to transfer the past into the present in order adequately to come to terms with its trauma, but is at the same time caught up in this double-layered process of displacement and deferral.

Rather than conceding its own failure, however, and lamenting the flaws in its own production, the text offers itself as a testimony to the importance of trying to allow the ghosts of the past to speak. In its echo of Sartre's *Morts sans sépulture*, it raises the question of dying for a cause and strives to fight against the futility of this act by keeping the memory of the political injustice alive. Struggling to negotiate its relationship with Zoulikha's experiences, and inevitably troubled by their distortion and partial inaccessibility, the text nevertheless does inaugurate a process of mourning even as it admits the possibility of stagnation within the melancholic. Claiming neither fully to resuscitate the past nor to succeed in reburying it, *La Femme sans sépulture* expresses the ongoing need at least to engage with what haunts us, with the flickering shadows of past atrocities, despite their dynamic and elusive relationship with the present. Zoulikha's return displays the forgotten injustices of colonialism in Algeria and the French repression of the native revolt, and her spectral reapparition seems to announce, perhaps not retribution, but the need to hold that troubled past to account. Djebar's novel may not be comfortable and resolved in its relationship with the past and seems highly aware of the entanglement of mourning with an endless, unresolved state of melancholia. Furthermore, the mourning of Zoulikha may remain deliberately deferred, precisely since the narrator is wary of burying her again, of silencing her in her attempts to come to terms with her disturbing experiences. However, in writing this fractured, uncomfortable and multi-layered account of a buried injustice, Djebar stresses that an engagement with the past, and a reflection on our uneasy relationship with it, is preferable to the amnesia that followed the Algerian war and has political and ethical value. As Avery Gordon points out, the ghostly return is often 'not a return to the past but a reckoning with its repression in the present', and Djebar's novel argues in favour of such a reckoning, despite all its anxieties concerning the viability of its own textual mechanics.[22] The novel is an exhumation, a call for renewed interrogation, and an admission that that interrogation will never be unmediated, completed or resolved.

La Femme sans sépulture figures writing simultaneously as the absence and the presence of the other, its resurgence and its loss. Writing can resuscitate the ghosts of the past but it also distances itself from them in the same moment, opening the writer up to the memory of the other *at the same time* that it alienates her from it. As Jodey Castricano writes in her exploration of 'cryptomimesis' (the writing of the spectre) in Derrida's work, writing 'draws attention to itself in terms of inheritance, legacy, and mourning'.[23] Writing is always bound up with citation, with the ghosts of other texts, though it also remains unable to assimilate and fully account for this alien presence. In Djebar's novel, writing is at once inhabited by the other and cut off from that other, or uneasy about its connection to it. To take up again the terms used earlier in this book, Djebar's characters, her narrator and witnesses, produce narratives that are both singular and plural; they resist determination and are infiltrated by partial traces of other voices, voices announcing at the same time their difference and inaccessibility. Memory, in the form of both mourning and melancholia in *La Femme sans sépulture*, is both a singular relation with the past and an awareness that the past remains other, indistinct, many-layered. In using the motif of spectrality, moreover, Djebar adds to her previous reflections on the limits of the specific and the endless proliferation of the singular-plural a more developed sense of the interpenetration of the living with the dead, of the resurgence of the not-quite-dead. The narrator's quest in the novel is both a search for an Algerian genealogy, a communion with her country's inheritance, and a discovery of the inaccessibility of that inheritance. But in figuring both the otherness of the (anti-)colonial past and its shaky resurgence in terms of the opening up of the boundaries between past and present, life and death, she pushes further her reflection on the intractability of her characters in an Algeria at once obsessed by its past and disjointed from itself. The singular being is here disembodied, otherworldly, the spectral product of a deferred narrative that throws into question the presence and immediacy of the present and the resolution of the horrors of colonialism.

Brogan writes of Morrison's *Beloved* that 'the needed "laying to rest" can take the form of a narrative deconstruction of the past that creates of its readership a haunted community'.[24] Brogan argues that the ghost's haunting in the novel becomes a sort of historical consciousness, the reminder that the reading community too inherits and springs from a traumatic history. *Beloved* introduces the spectre into the world of the novel's readers. For Djebar, I would suggest that this historical consciousness is equally urgent but less confident. *La Femme sans sépulture* demands, as I have mentioned, the recollection of historical injustice but tracks at the same time the fraught process of accessing singular events and experiences of injustice. The attempt to exhume, understand and mourn the victims of colonial oppression is not easily fulfilled, and writer and reader are called upon somehow both to resolve the past and to disallow its false resolution. Zoulikha's ghost speaks and is simultaneously silenced. She is both there and not there, she infuses the narrator's fragmented evocations while at the same time absenting herself from them. If history in *Femmes d'Alger* and *L'Amour, la fantasia* is at once specific and singular-plural, the ghost of Zoulikha in *La Femme sans sépulture* is both same and other, transferable to the present and resistant to that transfer, to translation. And, in a radicalisation of the earlier texts' anxieties concerning the singular resurgence of incomplete memories, this more recent novel throws into question the boundaries of living being to demonstrate the ongoing effects, the menacing shadow, of colonial and neocolonial violence on the life of the living in contemporary Algeria. Postcolonial Algeria has no 'identity', but is figured as the partial memory of its losses, of colonial expropriation, and the spectral, melancholic resurgence of colonialism's half-forgotten victims.

La Disparition de la langue française

If *La Femme sans sépulture* figures the interplay between memory and amnesia in the form of the apparition of Zoulikha's ghost, *La Disparition de la langue française* is itself haunted by the earlier novel in its return to and reinvention of these motifs of dislocation and disappearance. Published just a year later in 2003, *La Disparition de la langue française* again explores the disturbing resurgence of memories of the war of independence, but here the focus simultaneously shifts forwards to the violence perpetrated by Islamists during the 1990s, and the text hints, as in *Le Blanc de l'Algérie*, at an unnerving cycle of repetition. The disappearance of the central character, Berkane, in 1993 mirrors that of Zoulikha during the anti-colonial movement, and just as the coloniser denies Zoulikha a proper burial and smooths over the history of her mistreatment, so Berkane's loss is abrupt and unexplained, his life-story 'inachevé'. In juxtaposing *La Disparition de la langue française* and *La Femme sans sépulture* in this way, then, Djebar performs the temporal disjunction and revenance theorised in the earlier work. The later text uncannily transposes the traumas of the resistance fighters onto more recent confrontations between Islamist and liberal intellectuals, and shows how these new scenes reformulate past errors. Furthermore, much of the text concentrates on Berkane's own memories of the war of independence, and the 'fantôme' of his militant, adolescent self shapes his apprehension of the contemporary turmoil. These explicit references to spectrality and disappearance emerge from a background of ongoing reflections on Berkane's sense of exile and alienation in relation to his past and his homeland, on his loss of a sense of self. Berkane slips between time frames and geographical locations, and the history of Algeria, in relation to which he attempts to position himself, is depicted as lost, dispossessed. The 'identity' or genealogy sought in Djebar's earlier novels has completely dissolved.

Berkane's disappearance, as the title may suggest, is underpinned by an exploration of the initial imposition of the French language in Algeria and its subsequent occlusion as a result of Arabisation. This jostling for position between French and Arabic means that not only Berkane, but language itself becomes detached from identity, from any secure cultural and political position, and emerges as different from itself, containing unfamiliar associations. Again, recalling the fraught politics of language in *Le Blanc de l'Algérie*, French is associated both with colonial oppression and the politics of assimilation, and with Berkane's reinvented hybrid self, constructed after years in exile in France. In addition, it functions at times as an alternative to the rigid, imposed form of standard Arabic, and its intermingling with regional dialects promotes linguistic creativity and openness. If on one level, then, the novel recalls titles such as Du Bellay's *Défense et illustration de la langue française*, heralding the rise of French as opposed to Latin after the Renaissance, it also announces the end of that era and the reconfiguration of the language as unstable, uncertain of its position and status. The double echo of Du Bellay's title and Perec's *La Disparition* reinforces this process of questioning. *La Disparition* is written entirely without the use of the letter 'e', so that Djebar's title combines associations of universalist language politics with reference to the disappearance of an element at the core of language and its reconfiguration as alien to itself.[25] This displacement of the French language also throws into question the cultural politics of the novel. Berkane returns to Algeria after his period of exile hoping to rediscover his cultural heritage in the Casbah, only to find 'des retrouvailles, irrémédiablement fissurées, partant à la dérive'.²⁶ Algerian culture is not what he had believed it to be, the enforcement of a standardised Arabic alienates him, and he continues to write in French, seeking both return and renewal. The French language somehow conjures up hints of a colonial past at the same time as it is brought down from its position of hegemony by the later imposition of Arabic monolingualism, and, paradoxically, it becomes a sort of ambivalent refuge for Berkane. Caught between these shifting positions, Berkane continues to write in French, but he becomes unsure of his allegiance and finds himself unhinged from his former self. Language and identity are both ungrounded, and Djebar's call to resuscitate the ghost of her heroine in *La Femme sans sépulture* becomes in this novel an admission that both Algeria, and the French language in which she writes, contain an intractable alterity, both the spectre of a former incarnation and the glimmer of a new reinvention.

Berkane's literal disappearance constitutes the most obvious echo to *La Femme sans sépulture*, and though it occurs at the end of the novel it seems a fitting way into its theme. Berkane's final intervention follows the recollection of his period of captivity during the war of independence, when he was tortured despite being only sixteen. These final memories are themselves ghostly, disjointed, since the experience of torture is itself never rationalised but refigured as 'une composition, presque irréelle, de chorégraphie'.²⁷ Hovering between reality and fiction or artifice, a horrific theatrical performance that only masks the singular experience behind it, the torture scene uncannily foreshadows the dissimulation and inaccessibility of the event of Berkane's disappearance. Next, the narrative perspective shifts to that of Driss, Berkane's brother, followed by Marise and Nadjia, his successive lovers, who, despite interrupting his own ruminations, again do not offer any explanation for his disappearance but portray him as possibly still there, a ghostly half-presence. Since neither his body nor any clues to the identity of his attackers are found, these successive narratives are unable to provide due burial; they offer no closure but continue to describe him as a spectral figure who has not been laid to rest. Neither dead nor alive, Berkane is not mourned, but his memory is instead interrupted; in the mind of Marise he is 'inachevé mais vivant!'²⁸ In *La Femme sans sépulture*, Zoulikha was never given a proper burial and returns to haunt the present because the boundary between life and death was never securely established. Similarly, then, in *La Disparition* Berkane's unexplained absence prevents his friends from separating their memories of him from present experiences. His brutal removal, as in the case of Zoulikha, brings not his eradication but the curious, irresolute sense of an absence that must still be accounted for and explained.

Berkane's fragile, haunting presence after his disappearance in the latter sections of the novel recalls the aimless peregrinations of his uncertain shadow charted at the beginning. In a series of early passages, Berkane evolves a hazy belief in the necessity of returning to his 'homeland', yet here the use of the English term already 'foreignises' the concept and separates the word from its assumed referent. His lazy musings, while preparing for his departure, evoke not a specific image of a secure background but a series of idealised, fantastic sights, smells and sounds. At the same time, the narrator, momentarily not Berkane, describes his sense of disorientation after retirement, his wanderings in the streets of Paris and his sudden impression of inertia and emptiness, 'un désert de pierre en lui'.[29] In addition, in his letters to Marise, Berkane confesses 'une voix perdue resurgit, elle crie, elle me tire hors de moi, et si j'écris pour te le dire, cette voix dérangeante et obscure, c'est pour comprendre le pourquoi de cet effroi rallumé dans le noir'; and his return to Algeria clearly takes place as a result of a sudden and urgent process of self-questioning.[30] Interrogating his past and its relation with his present, Berkane finds himself cut off from his former image of himself, he is a mere shadow of what he thought he was, no longer present to himself. He is still alive but somehow insubstantial, ungrounded, the spectre of his former self. The sense of singular-plurality within the self is characterised as a menacing otherness in a way that foreshadows the ghostly metaphors interspersed throughout the text and literalised in the final section.

Berkane's early sense of ghostliness or estrangement from himself is heightened by his disjunctive relationship with his former lover, Marise or Marlyse, the addressee of his introspective musings, figured as half-way between fantasy and reality. On the one hand, Berkane's anxious missives seek to re-establish a sense of connection or fusion, he writes in order to ground himself in relation to Marise. Marise symbolises for Berkane a reassuring presence, another being with whom he can share his feelings of alienation until, he hopes, they dissolve. If Berkane is traversing a period of uncertainty, struggling to position himself in relation to past and present, Algeria and France, he clings to the idea of Marise in the hope that she might anchor him.

His conception of their relationship celebrates sharing, understanding, a sense of self established precisely *through* his interaction with her, and the reinforcement of their former life at the same time helps him to link past and present. It provides continuity, and the evocation of the calm rhythms of the waves bringing back his love implies permanence as well as a sense of integration with the natural environment: 'évoquer mon amour qui subsiste, qui renaît, face à la mer qui, chaque nuit, murmure en vagues lentes et répétées, comme si elle allait se glisser au-dessous de ma couche'.[31] On the other hand, however, Berkane is conscious of the illusory nature of this fused relationship, and Marise's presence remains incomplete, distanced, coupled with the knowledge of their separation and the end of their marriage. She becomes an idealised but ghostly figure, constructed by Berkane to fuel his need for a secure connection with another being, but whose singularity escapes his nervous grasp. His letters are knowingly concerned less with the addressee than with himself and his insecure position in France, and he admits that the conversation is 'silencieuse', carried out with an absent other. Berkane's letters form an encounter without fusion, a relationship with a singular, absent being that promises to provide meaning only to leave the writing subject more alienated, separated both from himself and from the world. Berkane's drama of desired fusion and inevitable separation from the ghost of the other is also played out on the level of language, as his own idioms efface his memory of those of Marise. His own dialect, from which he at the same time feels disconnected, 'se revivifie au risque d'effacer ta présence nocturne'.[32]

Berkane's sense of alienation in France and his failed rekindling of his connection with Marise induce his return to Algeria and a search for lost origins. Here too, however, Algeria is found only to be lost again and turns out to be known to Berkane only as an object of loss. Berkane resolves to revisit the Casbah where he grew up, though once again the desire for a sense of self, for a specific position and grounding, is met with the realisation that this complex network of streets contains a world that he cannot fully know. Just as Marise becomes an incomplete and ghostly figure, both absent and present, and whose partial presence is the result of an idealised fantasy, so does the Casbah both evoke Berkane's origins and heritage as well as an exoticised, imaginary location whose real intricacies escape his search for meaning and knowledge. As Réda Bensmaïa writes in describing francophone writers' perceptions of the Medina, the aim might be to free that space from overdetermination by supposedly objective norms and to realign it according to the writer's subjective imagination.[33] In one prolonged passage, for example, Berkane names the Casbah 'mon antre, ma forteresse, mon quartier, *houma*', implying solidity, permanence and an ongoing sense of possession, and he continues: 'resté le même grâce à la permanence des pierres, des maisons à terrasses, des rues d'ombre et des escaliers en paliers, et des tranches étroites de ciel qui vous suivent'.[34] At this point, Berkane's description foregrounds security and a sense of belonging, and the image of segments of sky following the passers-by evokes a harmonious relationship between the self and his environment. Nevertheless, even this passage disavows itself in its succeeding proliferation of details and images, including the chaotic maze of streets, the crowds, the cries and laughter of the women, and Berkane loses himself in his disintegrating, imagined reconstruction. Djebar compares Berkane's impression to that evoked in Julien Duvivier's classic film *Pépé le Moko*, in which the Casbah is figured as a seething, plural world, impossible to fathom. In *Pépé le Moko*, a gangster hides in the Casbah, where he is beyond the reach of the French police who cannot master its rules. Although colonialism is not dealt with explicitly in the film, the implication is that the Casbah's baroque, labyrinthine structure exceeds the rationalist drive of the coloniser. The Casbah is also, according to Mireille Rosello's reading, 'both an inside and an outside'; part of the colonial city and subject to its laws, but abiding also by its own laws and testing the limits of the colonial grasp.[35]

While Berkane's imaginary Casbah, like that of Duvivier, celebrates its plurality, the real thing perplexes him still further. No longer the centre of resistance, it has, ironically, lost its spirit and seems instead deprived and soulless. It no longer occupies its once curiously mythical position as a parasite at the heart of the colonial city. The Casbah Berkane dreamt of in France has altered, the streets and houses are more dilapidated, and his fantasised, colonised but familiar homeland has fallen to ruin. It turns out that his previous image of the Casbah was a created, exoticised, virtual vision that had become detached from its singular and inaccessible reality. What the area has lost, furthermore, is its quaintness, its decorativeness, and its maze of interlacing streets no longer connotes mystery and endless variety but lifeless anonymity: 'la localisation, parfois, des cafés maures, des petites boutiques en désordre mais vivantes, je ne la retrouvais plus, ou difficilement, et les portes anciennes, que quelquefois

je reconnaissais, étaient dépourvues de leurs linteaux sculptés fine-
ment...'[36] In a further irony, in describing his disillusionment and
alienation on returning to the Casbah, Berkane again loses himself in
the proliferating rhetoric of his description and mythologises his own
disappointment. The narrative of the Casbah's degradation is punctured with calls to 'mon royaume d'autrefois' and 'ma citadelle'.[37]
Comparing himself to Ulysses returning to Ithaca, he laments how,
unlike the mythical hero, he has no faithful companion waiting for
him at home, but the analogy narrates his own loss in such a way as
to foreground again its theatricality. Like Camus's Jacques Cormery
in *Le Premier homme*, Berkane here uses a romanticised narrative to
disguise his sense of non-belonging.[38]

As in *La Femme sans sépulture*, then, a poetics of 'hauntology' is
coupled with an investigation of deceptive artifices and false revela-
tions, and of the spectres that haunt their recesses. Zoulikha's ghost
was at times staged as a false illumination, and in *La Disparition*,
Berkane's evocations of the Casbah are similarly exoticised and
surreal. Composed of endless, proliferating sentences that pile ornate
details on top of one another, Berkane's descriptions fictionalise the
Casbah while all the time failing to encapsulate the singular-plural
life of its architecture and inhabitants. Like the veiled women who
walk its streets, the Casbah is both visible and invisible, represented
by a screen of elaborate images that mask its unknowable and diverse
interior. In this sense, Berkane's hesitant but idealised vision, which
may be called Orientalist, both reveals and conceals, it both promises
and defers a spectral world that is never entirely real or concrete. If
the Orientalist vision configures the other in terms appropriate to
the self, if Orientalism names a manner of understanding another
culture by means of fantasies constructed by the self's own cultural
baggage and assumptions, then any alternative 'real' Orient becomes
an absent spectre that lingers behind that false artifice. In Said's
terms, the Orient becomes a product of the Western imagination, a
mythical place associated with qualities chosen by the outsider, rather
than a real location or people. Orientalist discourse is external to
what it describes, it is a surface: 'all of Orientalism stands forth and
away from the Orient'.[39] Said is at times ambiguous concerning the
possible existence of a real 'Orient', but this very uncertainty suggests
that the term evokes proliferating representations, and the signified
'Orient' is the spectre that exceeds those representations and troubles
their borders. In Djebar's work, the Casbah is similarly the product of

successive fantasies or imaginary constructions that cover the shaky, unstable spectre of a world Berkane can never quite seize.

Recalling once more the novel's title, Berkane's evocations of an idealised Casbah betray both his disjunctive relationship with his native land and the faltering grasp of the French language on Algerian culture. The descriptions strive to convey the chaos and dynamism of life in the Casbah, but the rhetoric is artificial and stylised, an aesthetic ornament behind which the spectres of alternative versions continue to linger. Berkane hopes first to rediscover his origins and, secondly, to seize the complex changes occurring within the walls of the Casbah, but in both cases the language screens the indistinct, moving shadows of those who inhabit this mythical space. This linguistic drama is then developed through the unfolding of Berkane's relationship with Nadjia, who is in turn subjected to Orientalist rewriting. First, soon after meeting Berkane, Nadjia recounts her family story, this time in her Arabic dialect, yet she too seems to become aware of the danger of dramatising and fictionalising her referents. She promises to narrate not 'le dernier film' but her own singular, subjective story, but the reference to cinematic narrative betrays her sense that the language may rewrite and dramatise events for her.[40] Secondly, however, these scenes of violence during the war of independence are in turn framed by Berkane's controlling but anxious comments, as he translates her story into French in terms that seem appropriate to him: 'je saisis, j'encercle son récit, sa mémoire dévidée, en mots arabes que j'inscris, moi, en mots français, sur ma table, alors que…'[41] Berkane rewrites her story, enjoying his role as 'un petit scribe solitaire', but implicitly warning us that his transcription separates us from Nadjia's initial version and shapes events according to his own perspective.

The tenuous grasp of Berkane's language, and the distancing of Nadjia's singular story from the framework of his own version, is further exacerbated in the love scenes. Berkane describes the details of Nadjia's body, her voice and idiom, but seems aware, at the same time, that his admiration also distances her. Using terms that closely recall those used by Djebar to describe Delacroix's *Femmes d'Alger*, Berkane notes 'son regard s'absente, cherche loin', and his depiction of Nadjia *both* exoticises her *and* reinforces the limitations of his perception of her.[42] Like Delacroix, Berkane exhibits both an Orientalist drive to idealise and possess the desired object and an awareness that his portrait only hints at the mysteries of the other's inner life. Later, in resolving to write more about his experiences with Nadjia,

Berkane lingers on the sensual details of their encounter and explicitly forgets or excludes the Arabic words she used: 'soudain j'oublie ses mots de douceur, mais pas le sens, pas sa respiration, pas son parfum mêlé à l'odeur de nos draps'.[43] Berkane repeatedly reminds us of the process of translation operating within his narrative, and his celebration of her body, her voice and her stories as a result occurs at one remove from her singular being. Nadjia herself drifts away from the narrative to be replaced, fetishistically, with an Orientalist portrait that covers over the lack of Berkane's desire. Berkane's luxuriant French prose seeks to grasp on to and give coherent form to the object of his desire, but its artifice only exacerbates his struggle both to hold on to her body and to enter her story. Losing himself in his analogies, Berkane urges, 'je veux te connaître avec précision: comme une rosée le matin, une tempête à midi, un orage du soir, savoir comment ton corps est nerfs, est douceur, est mollesse, est frémissement ou même refus', but he confesses at the end of his musings that she remains 'mon fantôme'.[44] Like the narrator in Breton's *Nadja*, Berkane writes 'hanté par Nadjia', and the heroine, in turn bound up with the Casbah just as Nadja is pursued through Breton's labyrinthine Parisian streets, is fetishistically both there and not there.[45] Berkane's Nadjia is also the product of an Orientalist fantasy, a fantasy that remains haunted by her singular spectre but that reinforces her absence from its narrow confines.

Berkane's francophone rhetoric remains, however, as I suggested at the beginning of the section, inscribed in a complex set of linguistic politics that necessitates both the return to, and the reinvention of, the French language. Berkane's narratives are at times exoticised, at a remove from Nadjia's own Arabic dialect, but his ongoing use of French also symbolises a rejection of the Arabic monolingualism promoted by Islamists in Algeria. If on the one hand he laments that the French language is 'en défaillance', Nadjia retorts that it is Arabic, as spoken and enforced by the Islamists, that is the new language of oppression: 'c'est une langue convulsive, dérangée, et qui me semble déviée'.[46] The French language remains haunted by colonialism and by a sense of inadequacy in relation to Arabic culture, but the Islamists, paradoxically, learn from French colonial policy and mimic its structure by imposing Arabic as a new language of obligation. In Berkane's memories of the war of independence, for example, French terms seem unfamiliar, even untranslatable, as *laïcité* at the time is 'un vide, un non-concept', even if he realises its potentially positive resonances later.[47] More disturbingly, the torture scenes herald the breakdown of communication, the impossibility of explanation in the language associated, according to the myth, with clarity and logic. After a series of brief staccato sentences evoking his father's experience of torture, Berkane's narrative pauses and steps back from the scenes of his own humiliation, and he provides only confused memories of cries and shouts. In the passages describing Islamist violence during the 1990s, however, Arabic has become the language of oppression and Berkane's francophone diary also signifies resistance to its enforcement. The witnessing of the horrors of contemporary Algerian society forms the trigger for Berkane's project and incites his (unfulfilled) desire to relocate his singular self. Although his language is haunted by the colonial past, just as Islamist activities and politics are haunted by the war of independence, he uses French in the (ambivalent) hope of exploring his position in relation to both influences. The French language is both his, in the sense that it offers an alternative to the new language of oppression, and not his, since it is still associated with colonialism. Both languages are lost to Berkane, and indeed to Djebar, and they offer no sense of security or belonging.

   La Disparition de la langue française develops Djebar's exploration of spectrality in *La Femme sans sépulture* in order to conceive not only of singular experiences, but also of language and its relation to history, as haunted. In *La Femme sans sépulture*, Zoulikha's ghostly reappearance throws into question the boundaries between life and death and the colonial desire to package its horrors securely within a completed past. In blurring the world of the living with that of the dead, the ghost reminds us of the precariousness of existence for those living in contemporary Algeria, overshadowed by (neo)colonial violence. In *La Disparition*, it is not only the singular trajectory of the hero and his disappearance at the end of the novel that demand a vocabulary of spectrality, but also the operation of the French language itself. Berkane's francophone narrative is haunted by the experiences and individuals that slip between its interstices, and his Orientalist evocations of Nadjia and the Casbah cover a lack of knowledge, a partial, shaky apprehension of a person and a world that offer themselves to him only as half-presences. In addition, however, the language itself is both haunted and haunting; its attendant culture recalls the spectres of colonial violence, and its myths of universalism re-emerge in contemporary Islamist calls for Arabic monolingualism. The French language is 'disappearing', losing its identity and hegemonic position in relation to the (ex-)colonies, but the novel's hero insists on its regeneration, despite its ongoing failings. As a result, the French language, like a phantom, is both the same and different, both attached to its past position and resistant to confinement within that position. Berkane's francophone narratives both struggle to explore the singular dynamism of the language and perform the persistent haunting of its previous incarnation. The novel figures French as shadowed by its past identity and simultaneously under threat, unfamiliar and other to itself. Djebar inscribes language into a poetics of hauntology, where past and present linguistic identities mingle and confront one another, and where language has no established character or position, both in its disjunction from its referents and in its cyclical return and reconfiguration.

Conclusion

Djebar's trajectory and development as a writer can be conceived as a gradual movement away from any specific form of identification with Algeria towards a new configuration of her native land as severed, diverse and haunted by its past. The lingering traces of a search for the specific in the earlier works give way, by the time of *La Femme sans sépulture* and *La Disparition*, to a depiction of Algeria's culture, language and history as intractable or spectral – present but impossible to grasp. It is in this sense that her writing constitutes a hesitant 'expatriation', a movement outside the confines of any single, specified notion of Algeria, and a statement of dissociation from the visions of postcolonial Algeria propagated both by the 1990s government and by the Islamists. This expatriation, however, does not in any sense imply rejection. Djebar is emphatically not giving up on Algeria, nor does she in any way become less preoccupied with the complex weave of its history nor the meaning of its present contradictions. Her expatriation is not a refusal of identification but a reappraisal of her country's potential to provide any such secure identification. It is an engagement with Algeria's limits, with its hidden underside, rather than a statement of dissociation or non-belonging. Djebar's 'expatriation' is a partial one, it does not connote a straightforward distancing but a movement outside all that is associated with the 'patrie', the fatherland and its attendant resonances of patriotism or pride in national frontiers. It is 'un lent et progressif déchirement, un éloignement que j'ai cru volontaire et que j'ai vécu cependant comme provisoire'.[1] Djebar's journey is not a completed departure but a questioning of the rigidity of Algeria's borders, geographically, culturally, linguistically; it reveals its postcolonial evolution as one that cannot be circumscribed as inside or outside, this or that. Haunted by colonialism, preoccupied with partial memories of hidden traumas, and ravaged anew by the uncanny violence of the Islamist resurgence, Algeria remains distraught and unknowable. Caught between conflicting cultures, languages and epochs, it harbours spectres and shadows belonging to the world of neither the living nor the dead, neither the past nor the present, living on in defiance of the artifice and amnesia of French, Islamic and indeed governmental ideologies of the postcolonial state.

An easy criticism to make of such a project might, however, be that this problematisation of Algerian specificity is necessarily a betrayal of its anti-colonialism, of the country's attempt to distance itself from colonial culture by asserting an alternative position for itself. Critics might accuse Djebar precisely of moving too far from contemporary Algeria, just at the moment when she should be helping to redefine her country in a gesture of defiance against French influence. Is the movement of expatriation not necessarily disloyal, given the precariousness of Algeria's current position in relation to Europe and the West? In response to such a criticism, however, I would argue first that postcoloniality, by which I mean an understanding of postcolonial subjectivity, is by definition not specific or identifiable, since it must always involve a rejection of the sorts of categorisation and circumscription imposed by colonialism in any case. Postcolonial thought has to involve a movement away from norms, from boundaries and fixed communities, since this is precisely what the colonial power tried to impose upon the colony. Djebar's movement away from the specific, through the singular and the singular-plural, and into the alternative realm of the spectral is as a result a postcolonial gesture, since it asserts its rejection of the very narrow forms of identification, assimilation and exclusion that characterised French colonial policy in Algeria. Secondly, Djebar's 'expatriation' is also in no sense a 'repatriation'; she does not find herself at home in her exiled position outside Algeria, and continues to affiliate herself most deeply with Algeria despite her anxiety and defamiliarisation in relation to it. Her transition 'out of Algeria' is not a step into a neocolonial culture and society, but a reorientation of her relationship with Algeria, which includes an obsessive connection with it as well as a preoccupation with its uncertainty, its limits.

In addition, the potential ambivalence of Djebar's relationship with Algeria and colonial culture is both exacerbated and performed by her use of the French language and the manner in which her thinking remains steeped in the history of French literature and thought. Her position in relation to a postcolonial Algeria could be seen to be 'compromised' by her highly visible affiliation with French cultural practice. Jacqueline Kaye and Abdelhamid Zoubir famously analyse the 'ambiguous compromise' of all francophone Maghrebian writing, not only as a result of writers using the French language, but also because of their belonging to an intelligentsia that has become disturbingly removed from the concerns of most of the Algerian people.[2] Although, surprisingly, Kaye and Zoubir make no mention of Djebar, they discuss problems of alienation in the work of writers such as Feraoun and Boudjedra, and use the terminology of 'compromise' to suggest not only ambivalence but also some sort of betrayal. Certainly, in Djebar's case, though her francophone narratives are interspersed with Arabic and Berber terms and sayings, and though her references to French literature and thought are intermingled with reflections on Arabic, Berber and Islamic sources, the effects of her French education are clearly evident in the texture of her writing. Even more, parts of her work, perhaps most notably *L'Amour, la fantasia*, display a perplexing degree of fascination and intrigue towards the seductive capacity of the colonial vision. If she is writing explicitly against the horrors of colonial imposition in Algeria, her novels at the same time testify to the power of colonial influence, its successful assimilation and acculturation of the educated Algerian minority, including Djebar.

Again, the difficulties associated with this involvement with colonial culture cannot be disputed, but Djebar's writing is highly self-conscious about that positioning. Djebar may be criticised for absorbing too much of the colonial influence working on Algeria, but she is quite clearly aware of the weight of this influence, and quite knowingly grapples with her problematic 'involvement' in Algerian culture. Her work should as a result be seen as a subtle exploration of her own ambivalence as a francophone intellectual rather than as any claim for some mythical form of true Algerianness. She does not speak in the name of a new Algeria, nor, as we saw in *Femmes d'Alger*, does she claim to offer a representative voice for the community she struggles to depict. She admits the singularity of her changing stance and in no way claims to make a straightforward political statement about the necessary form of Algeria's reinvention. Although she does initially explore Algeria's potential 'specificity', she is ultimately not interested in the creation of a strategic identity designed to prove Algeria's expulsion of its pernicious colonial past, and reaches far beyond the demands of identity politics. Her project is on the contrary to explore her ambivalent position as a writer and historian trying to make sense of a history torn apart by conflicting influences and altered, time and again, beyond her recognition. Taking into account developments instigated first by the coloniser and next by the politicians, and the Islamists, of postcolonial Algeria, she traces the difficulties of writing about Algerian history as someone who belongs unequivocally to neither political group, even if she shares some of the reference points of both. Self-conscious about the anxieties of her project, she theorises the ambivalence of her positioning, even though she writes about Algeria in a broader sense. She is in no doubt about the horrors of either colonialism or resurgent Islamism, but traces their effects on the project of the francophone writer and historian rather than denying the depth of their legacy in a more confident assertion of a liberated postcolonial identity.

It is in this sense that her work should be defended for its literary sophistication, its openness to its own multiple dimensionality, and it should not be required to be positive or forthright enough to offer a clear political stand. The sorts of materialist postcolonial critics who might object to some of Djebar's indistinct and ethereal philosophical musings might be those who forget that postcolonial studies is also a literary discipline that has to remain limited in its resonance in more active political circles. Readings of postcolonial literature informed by poststructuralist conceptions of ambivalence and singularisation may, for critics such as Aijaz Ahmad and E. San Juan Jr, appear divorced from actual nationalist struggles; but frequently the texts themselves refuse to assert such a clear political position precisely because they are literary, and are using their literary form precisely to explore issues of representation rather than activism.[3] There should be a space within postcolonial studies not only for engagement with the politics of post- and neocolonialism, but also for exploration of the problems and dilemmas of literary representation and its fraught relationship with those politics. The nature and contradictions of such a space have been theorised at length by Nick Harrison in *Postcolonial Criticism*, and lie beyond the scope of the present work.[4] But one might indeed argue for an understanding of postcolonial literary work as a process of experimentation, in which notions of reference are not cast aside but where they are, precisely, interrogated and troubled. In Peter Hallward's words, 'the privilege of literary study is the privilege of that detachment which allows us as readers to step back from representation, suspend its natural flow, and pay an "artificial" attention to *how it works*'.[5] Djebar's work is experimental, many-layered, ambivalent and reflexive, and sets out to problematise the representation of postcolonial Algeria rather than to provide solutions to its dilemma or offer a cultural vision that might enhance the community's sense of self and security. Djebar's literary endeavour is also not supposed to suggest strategies, policies or promises of future hope, but to tease out the subtle interaction between historical development and philosophical inquiry in the francophone intellectual's perception of Algeria, in the wake of the ravages the country has suffered. In moving from the tentative reflection on women and resistance in *Les Enfants du nouveau monde*, through the struggle with community in *Femmes d'Alger* and *Vaste est la prison*, and finishing with the intractable ghosts of *La Disparition*, Djebar's *œuvre* performs some of the difficulties of postcolonial writing. It insists on the importance of tracing genealogies, negotiating influences and creating communities, but reveals how the loopholes of francophone writing, and the upheavals and repressions of Algerian history, increasingly haunt and disrupt the writer's initial, urgent endeavour.

Notes

Introduction

1 Assia Djebar, *Ces voix qui m'assiègent* (Paris: Albin Michel, 1999), p. 203.

2 Foucault writes, for example, 'the individual is not a pre-given entity which is seized on by the exercise of power. The individual, with his identity and characteristics, is the product of a relation of power exercised over bodies, multiplicities, movements, desires, forces.' Michel Foucault, *Power/Knowledge: Selected Interviews and Other Writings 1971–1977*, ed. Colin Gordon, trans. Colin Gordon, Lee Marshall, John Mepham, Kate Soper (New York and London: Prentice Hall, 1980), p. 73. See also Michel Foucault, 'Subjectivité et vérité', *Dits et écrits 1954–1988*, Vol. IV (Paris: Gallimard, 1994), pp. 213–19.

3 Peter Hallward, *Absolutely Postcolonial: Writing between the Singular and the Specific* (Manchester: Manchester University Press, 2001), p. 330. For Hallward, a singular mode of individuation is conceived as a continual, internalised process of differentiation, and this contrasts with Foucault's understanding of a specific subject negotiating between a series of particular positions at a point in space and time. Hallward's terminology will inform much of the discussion in this book.

4 See Derrida's famous essay 'La différance', *Marges de la philosophie* (Paris: Minuit), pp. 41–66. For more on his conception of the subject, see Jacques Derrida and Jean-Luc Nancy, '"Eating Well," or the Calculation of the Subject: An Interview with Jacques Derrida', *Who Comes After the Subject?*, ed. Eduardo Cadava, Peter Connor, Jean-Luc Nancy (New York and London: Routledge, 1991), pp. 96–119. See also Philippe Lacoue-Labarthe, *Le Sujet de la philosophie* (Paris: Aubier-Flammarion, 1979).

5 Jean-Luc Nancy, *Etre singulier pluriel* (Paris: Galilée, 1996), p. 60.

6 Peter Hallward reads Djebar as a 'specific' writer, arguing that 'Assia Djebar's fiction explores what is involved in the positioning of a perspective (French and Algerian, innovative and traditional, female and male, inside and outside, house-bound and mobile...). These perspectives are not described as static, self-sufficient windows upon the world, but as rivals within a field of interested, competitive alternatives – the field excavated by a kind of militant curiosity' (*Absolutely Postcolonial*, p. 332). My reading deliberately troubles this conclusion.

7 See Jacques Derrida, *Spectres de Marx: l'état de la dette, le travail de deuil et la nouvelle Internationale* (Paris: Galilée, 1993). Derrida reinterprets ontology as 'hauntology', so that being is not necessarily being-there (*Dasein*), it is not necessarily situated in time and space, but contains within it the haunting traces of other

moments and epochs. The present is bound up with what is not present, not contemporaneous, but virtual.

8 Ibid., p. 15.

9 There has been some work on ghosts in postcolonial thought, and critics such as David Punter elucidate the spectral, other-wordly resonances in the works of a number of anglophone postcolonial writers. Punter's *Postcolonial Imaginings: Fictions of a New World Order*(Edinburgh: Edinburgh University Press, 2000) notes how writers such as Toni Morrison figure this resurgence of an irresolute past. I want to go a little further than Punter, however, and suggest that in Djebar it alters the writer's very conception of identity and language. Another useful reference is Pheng Cheah, *Spectral Nationality: Passages of Freedom from Kant to Postcolonial Literatures of Liberation* (New York: Columbia University Press, 2003). Cheah articulates postcolonial nationality as spectral, as the nation's *Bildung* haunts the state's participation in global capitalism. Cheah's politico-economic account becomes distant from Djebar's thinking, as it places the postcolonial nation in tension with new technical advancements and globalisation, but is nevertheless testimony to the growing use of the figure of spectrality to describe ambivalent modes of resistance in postcolonial debate. Finally, see the PhD thesis by Emily Tomlinson, 'Torture, Fiction, and the Repetition of Horror: Ghost-writing the Past in Algeria and Argentina' (Cambridge University, 2002).

10 Jeanne-Marie Clerc, *Assia Djebar: Ecrire, Transgresser, Résister...* (Paris: L'Harmattan, 1997). Mireille Calle-Gruber, *Assia Djebar ou la résistance de l'écriture* (Paris: Maisonneuve et Larose, 2001).

11 Calle-Gruber, *Assia Djebar ou la résistance de l'écriture*, p. 253.

12 Debra Kelly, *Autobiography and Independence: Selfhood and Creativity in North African Postcolonial Writing in French* (Liverpool: Liverpool University Press, 2005).

13 See John Erickson, *Islam and Postcolonial Narrative* (Cambridge: Cambridge University Press, 1998). Also, Hafid Gafaïti, 'The Blood of Writing: Assia Djebar's Unveiling of Women and History', *World Literature Today* 70.4 (1996), pp. 813–22.

14 One example of this excessively positivist reading is John Erickson, who claims that 'writing and vocalization have the power to counter the aphasia that renders Algerian women silent. The space of writing so painfully carved out by the narrator offers to Algerian women the space of identity they seek.' See 'Women's Space and Enabling Dialogue in Assia Djebar's *L'Amour, la fantasia*', *Postcolonial Subjects: Francophone Women Writers*, ed. Mary Jean Green et al. (Minneapolis: University of Minnesota Press, 1996), pp. 304–20.

15 See her interview with Djebar on the early texts of Islam used in *Loin de Médine*, 'When the Past Answers Our Present: Assia Djebar Talks About *Loin de Médine*', *Callaloo* 16.1 (1993), pp. 116–31. Also, Zimra carefully unravels the interconnections between 'La femme qui pleure' and 'La femme en morceaux', reading the latter at the same time through the lens of 'The Story of the Three Apples' in the *Arabian Nights*. See Zimra, 'Sounding Off the Absent Body: Intertextual Resonances in "La Femme qui pleure" and "La Femme en morceaux"', *Research in African Literatures* 30.3 (1999), pp. 108–24.

16 Clarisse Zimra, 'Cadastre de l'imaginaire dans *le quatuor*', *Assia Djebar: No-*

made entre les murs… Pour une poétique transfrontalière, ed. Mireille Calle-Gruber (Paris: Maisonneuve et Larose, 2005), pp. 171–84 (p. 178).

17 Kelly notes that *djebar* in classical Arabic means 'intransigence', but *Assia* is dialect for 'she who consoles'. See *Autobiography and Independence*, p. 253.

18 Homi Bhabha, *The Location of Culture* (New York and London: Routledge, 1994), p. 36.

19 Aijaz Ahmad, *In Theory: Classes, Nations, Literatures* (London: Verso, 1992), p. 69.

20 Ibid., p. 70.

21 Benita Parry, 'Signs of Our Times: A Discussion of Homi Bhabha's *The Location of Culture*', *Third Text* 28/29 (1994), pp. 5–24. Reprinted in Benita Parry, *Postcolonial Studies: A Materialist Critique* (London: Routledge, 2004).

22 Azzedine Haddour, *Colonial Myths: History and Narrative* (Manchester: Manchester University Press, 2000), p. 150.

23 Arif Dirlik, *The Postcolonial Aura: Third World Criticism in the Age of Global Capitalism* (Boulder, CO: Westview Press, 1997).

24 See Gayatri Chakravorty Spivak, 'Can the Subaltern Speak?', *Colonial Discourse and Postcolonial Theory*, ed. Laura Chrisman and Patrick Williams (Hemel Hempstead: Harvester Wheatsheaf, 1994), pp. 66–111 (p. 89).

25 Spivak, 'Can the Subaltern Speak?', p. 89.

26 See Hallward, *Absolutely Postcolonial*, p. 34.

The Early Years

1 See for example the complex studies of social and sexual mores, and the repressive force of 'biopouvoir', in the *Histoire de la sexualité* (Paris: Gallimard, 1984).

2 Assia Djebar in 'Assia Djebar Speaking: An Interview with Assia Djebar', by Kamal Salhi. *International Journal of Francophone Studies* 2.3 (1999), pp. 168–79 (p. 171). Abdelkebir Khatibi also recuperates the novel by arguing that it charts a young Algerian woman's discovery of her body. See *Le Roman Maghrébin* (Paris: Maspero, 1968), p. 62.

3 Assia Djebar, *La Soif* (Paris: Réné Julliard, 1957), p. 11.

4 Ibid., p. 12.

5 Ibid., p. 14.

6 Ibid., p. 23.

7 Ibid., p. 68.

8 Ibid., p. 116.

9 Ibid., p. 31.

10 Ibid., p. 145.

11 Ibid., p. 160.

12 Ibid., p. 163.

13 Ibid., pp. 70–71.

14 Assia Djebar, *Les Impatients* (Paris: Réné Julliard, 1958), pp. 22–23.

15 Ibid., p. 35.

16 Ibid., p. 86.

17 Ibid., p. 153.

18 Ibid., p. 95.

19 Ibid., p. 107.

20 Ibid., p. 214.

21 Ibid., p. 216.

22 Ibid., p. 239.

23 Frantz Fanon, 'L'Algérie se dévoile', *L'An V de la révolution algérienne* (Paris: Maspero, 1959), pp. 13–49 (p. 46).

24 Zohra Drif, in Danièle Djamila Amrane-Minne, *Des femmes dans la guerre d'Algérie* (Paris: Karthala, 1994), p. 140.

25 Assia Djebar, *Les Enfants du nouveau monde* (Paris: Réné Julliard, 1962), p. 137.

26 Ibid., p. 73.

27 Ibid., p. 107.

28 See Miriam Cooke, *Women and the War Story* (Berkeley and London: University of California Press, 1996), p. 111.

29 Djebar, *Les Enfants du nouveau monde*, p. 32.

30 See Gordon Bigelow, 'Revolution and Modernity: Assia Djebar's *Les Enfants du nouveau monde*', *Research in African Literatures* 34.2 (2003), pp. 13–17.

31 Assia Djebar, *Les Alouettes naïves* (Paris: Actes Sud, 1997), p. 8.

32 Ibid., p. 15.

33 Ibid., pp. 27–28.

34 Ibid., p. 125.

35 Ibid., p. 37.

36 Ibid., p. 32.

37 Ibid., p. 237.

38 Ibid., p. 225.

39 Ibid., pp. 450–51.

40 See Emily Tomlinson, 'Assia Djebar: Speaking with the Living Dead', *Paragraph* 26.3 (2003), pp. 34–50.

41 Djebar, *Les Alouettes naïves*, pp. 387–89.

42 Ibid., p. 324.

43 Luce Irigaray, *Ce sexe qui n'en est pas un* (Paris: Minuit, 1977), p. 172.

44 Djebar, *Les Alouettes naïves*, pp. 70–71.

45 Ibid., pp. 114–15.

46 Ibid., p. 378.

War, Memory and Postcoloniality

1 See Djebar's own comments in 'Ecrire, filmer, à partir de langue arabe', in Calle-Gruber (ed.), *Assia Djebar: Nomade entre les murs…*, pp. 87–89.

2 A useful article on camera work in *La Nouba* is Réda Bensmaïa's 'Assia Djebar's *La Nouba des femmes du Mont Chenoua*: Introduction to the Cinematic Fragment', in Bensmaïa, *Experimental Nations or, The Invention of the Maghreb* (Princeton: Princeton University Press, 2003), pp. 83–97.

3 Assia Djebar, *Ces voix qui m'assiègent* (Paris: Albin Michel, 1999), p. 36.

4 Ibid., p. 39.

5 See Nicholas Harrison, *Postcolonial Criticism: History, Theory, and the Work of Fiction* (Cambridge: Polity, 2003). This discussion of *darstellen* and *vertreten* comes in the chapter on Chraïbi, but issues of representativity are also clearly pertinent in the Djebar chapter.

6 Assia Djebar, *Femmes d'Alger dans leur appartement* (Paris: Albin Michel, 2002), p. 9.

7 Ibid., p. 8.

8 Ibid., p. 7.

9 Djebar, *Ces voix qui m'assiègent*, p. 25.

10 Ibid., p. 31.

11 Ibid., p. 29.

12 Ibid., p. 77.

13 Djebar, *Femmes d'Alger dans leur appartement*, p. 10.

14 Ibid., p. 120.

15 Ibid., pp. 90–98.

16 Ibid., p. 57.

17 Ibid., p. 111.

18 See Elaine Scarry, *The Body in Pain: The Making and Unmaking of the World* (Oxford: Oxford University Press, 1985).

19 Djebar, *Femmes d'Alger dans leur appartement*, p. 197.

20 Ibid., p. 203.

21 Ibid., p. 45.

22 Ibid., p. 225.

23 Ibid., p. 229.

24 See Marnia Lazreg, *The Eloquence of Silence: Algerian Women in Question* (London: Routledge, 1994).

25 Harrison, *Postcolonial Criticism*, p. 126.

26 Djebar, *Femmes d'Alger dans leur appartement*, p. 245.

27 Critics such as John Erickson, as I mentioned in the introduction, tend to offer a rather positivist reading of Djebar's project. Denise Decaires Narain suggests in contrast that 'there is no definitive representation of Algerian women that can replace Delacroix's Orientalist image'. See 'What Happened to Global Sisterhood? Writing and Reading "the" Postcolonial Woman', *Third Wave Feminism: A Critical Exploration*, ed. Stacy Gillis, Gillian Howie and Rebecca Munford (Basingstoke: Palgrave, 2004), pp. 240–51 (p. 249).

28 Djebar, *Femmes d'Alger dans leur appartement*, p. 232.

29 Clarisse Zimra, 'Writing Woman: The Novels of Assia Djebar', *Sub-Stance: A Review of Theory and Literary Criticism* 21.3 (1992), pp. 68–84 (p. 69).

30 See Harrison, *Postcolonial Criticism* and Kelly, *Autobiography and Independence*. Another useful reference here is Magda Al-Nowaihi's 'Resisting Silence in Arab Women's Autobiographies', *International Journal of Middle East Studies* 33.4 (2001), pp. 477–502, which stresses that not all Arab societies have encouraged women to be silent. Al-Nowaihi also argues how writers such as Djebar, Tuqan and al-Zayyat criticise the mechanisms that forced them into silence by staging their own self-silencing.

31 See Mildred Mortimer, 'Entretien avec Assia Djebar', *Research in African Literatures* 19.2 (1988), 197–203 (p. 201).

32 Gafaïti, 'The Blood of Writing', p. 814.

33 Erickson, *Islam and Postcolonial Narrative*, p. 38. Erickson also writes that 'the space of writing so painfully sketched out by the narrator offers to these women the social-sexual-historical space that they seek as their own' (p. 40).

34 Assia Djebar, *L'Amour, la fantasia* (Paris: Albin Michel, 1995), p. 95.

35 Ibid., p. 229.

36 Ibid., p. 201.

37 See Mortimer, 'Entretien avec Assia Djebar', p. 203.

38 See Celia Britton, 'The (De)Construction of Subjectivity in Daniel Maximin's *L'Ile et une nuit*', *Paragraph* 24.3 (2001), pp. 44–58. It is noteworthy that Djebar also troubles James Olney's conception of autobiography as a means to identify one's position within a specific community. Olney notes the significance of the study of autobiography for critics in 'Black', or 'Women's' studies, observing: 'according to the argument of these critics (who are becoming more and more numerous every day), autobiography – the story of a distinctive culture written in the individual characters and from within – offers a privileged access to an experience (the American experience, the black experience, the female experience, the African experience) that no other variety can offer'. See James Olney, 'Autobiography and the Cultural Moment: A Thematic, Historical and Bibliographical Introduction', in James Olney (ed.) *Autobiography: Essays Theoretical and Critical* (Princeton: Princeton University Press, 1980), p. 13.

39 Djebar, *L'Amour, la fantasia*, p. 178.

40 Ibid., p. 241.

41 I would like to thank Sura Qadiri for drawing my attention to some of the features mentioned in this paragraph.

42 Djebar, *L'Amour, la fantasia*, pp. 14–17.

43 Ibid., p. 188.

44 The phrase 'scriptural economy' is borrowed from Adrian V. Fielder, 'Historical Representation and the Scriptural Economy of Imperialism: Assia Djebar's *L'Amour, la fantasia* and Cormac McCarthy's *Blood Meridian*', *Comparative Literature Studies* 37.1 (2000), pp. 18–44.

45 Djebar, *L'Amour, la fantasia*, p. 56.

46 Ibid., p. 68. See also Scarry, *The Body in Pain*. Scarry writes: 'the written and spoken record of war over many centuries certifies the ease with which human powers of description break down in the presence of battle, the speed with which they back away from the injuring and begin to take as their subject the most incidental or remote activities occurring there, rather than holding onto what is everywhere occurring at its centre and periphery' (p. 66).

47 Djebar, *L'Amour, la fantasia*, p. 93.

48 In the final section of the novel, Djebar tells of how Fromentin records the fate of Haouia, a young dancer who participated in the fantasia, but was knocked down by one of the officers on horseback.

49 Djebar, *L'Amour, la fantasia*, p. 160.

50 Djebar, *Ces voix qui m'assiègent*, p. 107.

51 Djebar, *L'Amour, la fantasia*, p. 124.

52 Ibid., p. 143.

53 Ibid., p. 76.

Feminism and Women's Identity

1 Djebar, *Ces voix qui m'assiègent*, p. 61.

2 Ibid., p. 72.

3 For more on the segregation of space in Djebar's work see Victoria Best, 'Between the Harem and the Battlefield: Domestic Space in the work of Assia Djebar', *Signs: Journal of Women in Culture and Society* 27.3 (2002), pp. 873–79.

4 See Fatima Mernissi, *Beyond the Veil: Male-Female Dynamics in Modern Muslim Society* (London: Al Saqi, 1985), p. 138.

5 The verse states: 'men have authority over women because Allah has made the one superior to the other, and because they spend their wealth to maintain them', *The Koran*, trans. N.J. Dawood (Harmondsworth: Penguin, 1985), p. 370. While some have interpreted this as a comment on moral hierarchy, many feminist critics argue that the Koran is egalitarian, prescribing specific social roles in order to protect women and ensure that they are provided for.

6 Mernissi, *Beyond the Veil*.

7 Leila Ahmed, *Women and Gender in Islam: Historical Roots of the Modern Debate* (London and New Haven: Yale University Press, 1992), pp. 64–67. Ahmed argues that Islam provides both an ethical and a social vision, and women's position is subordinate only in the latter. Ghada Karmi makes a similar point in the article 'Women, Islam and Patriarchalism', in *Feminism and Islam: Legal and Literary Perspectives*, ed. Mai Yamani (Reading: Ithaca Press, 1996), pp. 69-85. Karmi suggests that the Koran consists of two documents: the first deals with practical questions and can be seen to respond to the contemporary socio-policial situation; the second is concerned with spiritual, moral and philosophical issues.

8 See Fatima Mernissi, *Le Harem politique: Le Prophète et les femmes* (Paris: Albin Michel, 1987).

9 See 24.31, 'enjoin believing women to turn their eyes away from temptation and to preserve their chastity; to cover their adornments (except such as are normally displayed); to draw their veils over their bosoms and not to reveal their finery except to their husbands, their fathers, their husbands' fathers, their sons, their stepsons, their brothers, their brothers' sons, their sisters' sons, their women-servants, and their slave-girls', p. 216.

10 Fadwa El Guindi, *Veil: Modesty, Privacy, Resistance* (Oxford: Berg,1999), p. 93.

11 Lazreg, *The Eloquence of Silence*. The postcolonial critic Anne McClintock makes a similar, more general point about the association between women and nationalism. Women are often constructed as 'symbolic bearers of the nation', insofar as they signify national difference and reproduce boundaries through marital relations. See 'No Longer in Future Heaven: Gender, Race and Nationalism', in *Dangerous Liaisons: Gender, Nation and Postcolonial Perspectives*, ed. Anne McClintock, Aamir Mufti and Ella Shohat (Minneapolis: University of Minnesota Press, 1997), pp. 89-112 (p. 90).

12 See Lazreg, *The Eloquence of Silence*, p. 156. The code states, for example, that men have the right to divorce whereas women do not. Although on a few matters it did help to assure that women retained some rights, its thrust was clearly inegalitarian.

13 For more on this see Fatima Mernissi, *Women's Rebellion and Islamic Memory* (London and New Jersey: Zed Books, 1996).

14 Nawal El Saadawi, *The Hidden Face of Eve: Women in the Arab World* (London: Zed Books, 1980), p. xv. See also the essays in *The Nawal El Saadawi Reader* (London: Zed Books, 1997). Another Islamic feminist critic, Haideh Moghissi, emphasises collectivity even further in her text *Feminism and Islamic Fundamentalism: The Limits of Postmodern Analysis* (London: Zed Books, 1999). She asserts the importance of identifying women's common struggle, arguing that certain forms of oppression are universal, and the exclusion of Islamic women from Western feminist discourses means that feminism becomes the privileged domain of the West.

15 Nada Elia writes that when Djebar received the Prix Fonlon, she explicitly reiterated her connections with Africa and indicated that she did not abide by Europe's division of African between North and Sub-Saharan. See *Trances, Dances, and Vociferations: Agency and Resistance in Africana Women's Narratives* (New York and London: Garland Publishing, 2001), p. 41.

16 Chandra Mohanty, 'Under Western Eyes: Feminist Scholarship and Colonial Discourses', *Feminist Review* 30 (1988), pp. 61–88.

17 Hélène Cixous, 'Le Rire de la Méduse', *L'Arc* 61 (1975), pp. 39–54 (p. 39). The text is translated by Keith Cohen and Paula Cohen and printed in *New French Feminisms: An Anthology*, ed. Elaine Marks and Isabelle de Courtivron (New York: Schocken Books, 1981), pp. 245–64 (pp. 245–46).

18 Toril Moi writes: 'the paucity of references to a wider community of women or to collective forms of organization is not only conspicuous in the work of a feminist activist, but indicative of Cixous's general inability to represent the non-Imaginary, triangulated structures of desire typical of social relationships.' See *Sexual/Textual Politics: Feminist Literary Theory* (London: Methuen, 1985), p. 125.

19 Miriam Cooke, *Women Claim Islam: Creating Islamic Feminism through Literature* (London and New York: Routledge, 2001), p. 121. Teresa De Lauretis's more general understanding of the feminist community may also be helpful here. De Lauretis writes that 'an understanding of the feminist community whose boundaries shift, and whose differences can be expressed and renegotiated through interconnections both interpersonal and political goes hand in hand with a particular understanding of individual experience as the result of a complex bundle of determinations and struggles, a process of continuing renegotiation of external pressures and internal resistances.' See 'Eccentric Subjects: Feminist Theory and Historical Consciousness', *Feminist Studies* 16.1 (1990), pp. 115–50 (p. 137).

20 See Calle-Gruber, *Assia Djebar ou la résistance de l'écriture*, Katherine Gracki, 'Writing Violence and the Violence of Writing in Assia Djebar's Algerian Quartet', *World Literature Today* 70.4 (1996), pp. 835–43, and Silvia Nagy-Zekmi, 'Tradition and Transgression in the Novels of Assia Djebar and Aïcha Lemsine', *Research in African Literatures* 33.3 (2002), pp. 1–13.

21 Assia Djebar, *Ombre sultane* (Paris: Editions Jean-Claude Lattès, 1987), p. 15.

22 Ibid., p. 28.

23 Ibid., p. 49.

24 Ibid., p. 27.

25 Ibid., p. 43.

26 Ibid., p. 57.

27 See Anjali Prabhu, 'Sisterhood and Rivalry in-between the Shadow and the Sultana: A Problematic of Representation in *Ombre Sultane*', *Research in African Literatures* 33.3 (2002), pp. 69–96.

28 Djebar, *Ombre sultane*, p. 158.

29 Philippe Barbé also discusses the significance of the hammam, and of the patios, as feminine spaces. See 'The Closure and Opening of Domestic Space in *Ombre sultane* by Assia Djebar', in *Francophone Postcolonial Cultures: Critical Essays* (Lanham, Boulder, New York, Oxford: Lexington, 2003), pp. 28–38.

30 Djebar, *Ombre sultane*, p. 159.

31 Ibid., p. 9.

32 See Calle-Gruber, *Assia Djebar ou la résistance de l'écriture*, p. 53.

33 See Prabhu, 'Sisterhood and Rivalry in-between the Shadow and the Sultana'. Prabhu is, however, a little one-sided in her analysis of the novel, and she stresses Isma's assumption of power without showing how this is subtly coupled with a desire for complicity. Prabhu finally recuperates the novel by arguing that it portrays ethics as 'the experience of the impossible', though I would question the conclusion that the text therefore teaches us something concrete about the need for a particular form of communal political struggle.

34 Djebar, *Ombre sultane*, p. 91.

35 Ibid., p. 100.

36 Assia Djebar, *Vaste est la prison* (Paris: Albin Michel, 1995), p. 163.

37 Ibid., p. 164.

38 Ibid., p. 170.

39 See Gracki, 'Writing Violence and the Violence of Writing in Assia Djebar's Algerian Quartet'.

40 Cooke, *Women Claim Islam*. Cooke argues that Derrida, Khatibi and Memmi all continue (perhaps unwittingly) to perceive the mother tongue as the site of an authentic identity, lamenting the loss of that originarity and conceiving the acquisition of a new language as a threat. For Djebar, on the other hand, language is not associated with ownership in this way. While Cooke's argument is intriguing and informative in the context of Djebar, her reading of Khatibi in particular could benefit from more nuance, since he too seems at times to challenge the connection between language and identity, championing instead plural participation.

41 Djebar, *Vaste est la prison*, p. 172.

42 See Biddy Martin and Chandra Talpade Mohanty, 'Feminist Politics: What's Home Got to Do With It?', *Feminist Studies/Critical Studies*, ed. Teresa De Lauretis (Bloomington: Indiana University Press, 1986), pp. 191–212.

43 Djebar, *Vaste est la prison*, p. 21.

44 Ibid., p. 60.

45 Djebar makes this point in *Ces voix qui m'assiegent*, p. 86.

46 Djebar, *Vaste est la prison*, p. 26.

47 Ibid., p. 30.

48 Ibid., p. 174.

49 Ibid., p. 337.

50 Ibid., p. 347.

51 Aliette Armel, 'Assia Djebar et la mémoire des femmes', *Magazine Littéraire* 410 (2002), pp. 98–103 (p. 102).

52 This is quoted from an unpublished interview by Clarisse Zimra in 'Not so far from Medina: Assia Djebar charts Islam's Insupportable Feminist Revolution', *World Literature Today* 70.4 (1996), pp. 823–34 (p. 823).

53 Beïda Chikhi, *Littérature algérienne: désir d'histoire et esthétique* (Paris: L'Harmattan, 1997), p. 141.

54 Dominick Lacapra, *History, Politics and the Novel* (Ithaca, NY: Cornell University Press, 1987), p. 14.

55 This is Fatima Mernissi's phrase, used to describe *Le harem politique*.

56 See Michael M-J. Fischer and Mehdi Abedi, *Debating Muslims: Cultural Dialogues in Postmodernity and Tradition* (Madison, WI: University of Wisconsin Press, 1990). Fischer and Abedi go so far as to assert: 'the entire structure of the Qur'an and hadith is a fun house of mirrors playing upon appearances and resemblances (*mutashabih*) that may or may not be grounded (*muhkam*), depending upon the perspective and knowledge of the interpreter' (p. 100).

57 Assia Djebar, *Loin de Médine* (Paris: Albin Michel, 1991), p. 6.

58 Donald R Wehr, 'The "Sensible", the Maternal and the Ethical Beginnings of Feminist Islamic Discourse in Assia Djebar's *L'Amour, la fantasia* and *Loin de Médine*', *Modern Languages Notes* 118.4 (2003), pp. 841–66. Levinas's discussions of religious reflection of course centre on readings of Jewish texts and Jewish philosophy, but his philosophical openness and ongoing intellectual endeavour seem also to help to conceptualise Djebar's representation of Islamic thought.

59 Ibid., p. 865.

60 See Gayatri Spivak, 'Ghostwriting', *Diacritics* 25.2 (1995), pp. 64–84. Spivak writes, '*Specters of Marx* allows me to read *Far from Madina* as a ghost dance, a prayer to be haunted, a learning to live at the seam of the past and the present, "a heterodidactics between life and death" [SM, xviii]', p. 78.

61 Djebar, *Loin de Médine*, p. 79.

62 Ibid., p. 86.

63 See *The History of Al-Tabari. Volume IX. The Last Years of the Prophet.* Trans. Ismail K. Poonawala (Albany: State University of New York Press, 1990). The episode is narrated on p. 196.

64 Djebar, *Loin de Médine*, p. 60.

65 Ibid., p. 85.

66 Ibid., p. 268.

67 See Ahmed, *Women and Gender in Islam*. Ahmed suggests that some 2,210 *Hadiths* are attributed to Aïcha. It should perhaps also be noted here that Aïcha grows up to be an impressive warrior. Mernissi reminds us that at the age of 42 she took to the battlefield at the head of an army that challenged the legitimacy of the fourth orthodox caliph, 'Ali. See *Le Harem politique*.

68 Djebar, *Loin de Médine*, p. 300.

69 George Lang also describes the chain of transmission as open, irreversibly decentred and verging on 'différance'. See his chapter in *The Marabout and the Muse: New Approaches to Islam in African Literature*, ed. Kenneth W. Harrow (Portsmouth: Heinemann, 1996).

70 The scene is narrated in *The History of Al-Tabari*, Vol. IX, p. 27.

71 Djebar, *Loin de Médine*, p. 27.

72 Ibid., p. 141.

73 Ibid., p. 46.

74 Emmanuel Levinas, *L'Au-delà du verset: lectures et discours talmudiques* (Paris: Minuit, 1982), p. 107.

Violence, Mourning and Singular Testimony

1 That she calls the text a 'récit' rather than a novel is itself significant, since it has moved even further from the conventions of the genre of the novel.

2 Assia Djebar, *Le Blanc de l'Algérie* (Paris: Albin Michel, 1995), p. 12.

3 As a messaliste, Madani supported Messali Hadj's *Mouvement national algérien* during the war of independence. This was an alternative party fighting for independence that set itself up in opposition to the FLN.

4 For more on this see Robert Malley, *The Call from Algeria: Third Worldism, Revolution and the Turn to Islam* (Berkeley, CA: University of California Press, 1996), p. 233.

5 For more on the precise relationship between Islamism and the Algerian nation state, see Hugh Roberts, 'The Embattled Arians of Algiers: radical Islamism and the dilemma of Algerian nationalism', in his *The Battlefield Algeria 1988–2002* (London: Verso, 2003), pp. 1–33. Islamism in Algeria was not nationalist, though it clearly is bound up with alternative notions of Algerian identity and defence against European influence.

6 See Lahouari Addi, *L'Algérie et la démocratie: pouvoir et crise du politique dans l'Algérie contemporaine* (Paris: La Découverte, 1995).

7 Ibid., pp. 209–10.

8 M. Al-Ahnaf, B. Botiveau and F. Frégosi, *L'Algérie par ses islamistes* (Paris: Karthala, 1991), p. 205.

9 These statistics are quoted by Malley, *The Call from Algeria*, p. 227.

10 Derrida comments on the irony of this annulment, arguing as a result that democracy also has to rely on strategies foreign to its original tenets. The Algerian case demonstrates the aporetic structure of democracy, leading to 'un certain suicide de la démocratie'. See *Voyous: Deux essais sur la raison* (Paris: Galilée, 2003), p. 57.

11 See Hafid Gafaïti, 'Power, Censorship and the Press: The Case of Postcolonial Algeria', *Research in African Literatures* 30.3 (1999), pp. 51–61.

12 This policy was derived from the ideals of the *ulema* movement, instigated in the 1930s as part of the struggle for independence, which stated not only that Islam would be the national religion but also that Arabic was the language of Algeria. For more on the links between Islamism, Arabisation and the *ulema* movement, see Benjamin Stora, 'Algérie: absence et surabondance de mémoire', *Esprit* (January 1995), pp. 62–67; Yahia H. Zoubir, 'The Painful Transition from Authoritarianism in Algeria', *Arab Studies Quarterly* 15.3 (Summer 1993), pp. 83–110.

13 Ranjana Khanna, 'The Experience of Evidence: Language, the Law, and the Mockery of Justice', in *Algeria in Others' Languages*, ed. Anne-Emmanuelle Berger (Ithaca, NY, and London: Cornell University Press, 2002), pp. 107–38 (p. 134). Khanna analyses a mock trial held in Algiers in March 1995, in which some women from the international feminist community accused (in French) Madani and Belhadj of crimes against humanity. The event clearly raises complex questions of language

and law, and foregrounds the irony that the French language should function as a tool for the expression of dissent.

14 Djebar, *Le Blanc de l'Algérie*, p. 238.

15 Ibid., pp. 61, 53.

16 Ibid., pp. 188, 158.

17 Ibid., pp. 42, 37.

18 For more on this problem, in a different context, see Henry Greenspan, *On Listening to Holocaust Survivors* (Praeger: Westport, CT, and London, 1998).

19 See Giorgio Agamben, *Remnants of Auschwitz: The Witness and the Archive* (New York: Zone Books, 1999). Agamben writes: 'between the obsessive memory of tradition, which knows only what has been said, and the exaggerated thoughtlessness of oblivion, which cares only for what was never said, the archive is the unsaid or sayable inscribed in everything said by virtue of being enunciated; it is the fragment of memory that is always forgotten in the act of saying', p. 144.

20 Djebar, *Le Blanc de l'Algérie*, p. 202.

21 See Agnès Peysson, '*Le Blanc de l'Algérie*: une liturgie aux disparus', *International Journal of Francophone Studies* 2.3 (1999), pp. 163–67 (p. 165).

22 Djebar, *Le Blanc de l'Algérie*, pp. 275–76.

23 See Hafid Gafaïti, 'Culture and Violence: The Algerian Intelligentsia between Two Political Illegitimacies', *Parallax 7: Translating Algeria* (1998), pp. 71–77. For more on the curious contradiction within French republicanism (and Algerian nationalism) between the universal and the particular, see Peter Fitzpatrick, *Modernity and the Grounds of Law* (Cambridge: Cambridge University Press, 2001).

24 For more on this see Tomlinson, 'Torture, Fiction, and the Repetition of Horror'.

25 See Elizabeth Fallaize, 'In Search of a Liturgy: Assia Djebar's *Le Blanc de l'Algérie (1995)*', *French Studies* 59.1 (2005), pp. 55–62. Fallaize's article for the most part focuses on the absence of resolution and healing in Djebar's novel, but she concludes that nevertheless, 'her search for a liturgical form free of political theatre and capable of responding to waves of violent and innocent deaths begins the work of an urgent ethical task, one which has become especially acute in our era' (p. 62). I agree on the whole with this reading, though would insist that Djebar is at pains to stress the limits of this ethical process and the shortcomings of her own narrative.

26 Djebar, *Le Blanc de l'Algérie*, p. 123.

27 See Derrida, *Spectres de Marx*.

28 Djebar, *Le Blanc de l'Algérie*, p. 64.

29 See Paul Ricœur, *Temps et récit* (Paris: Seuil, 1983).

30 Djebar, *Le Blanc de l'Algérie*, p. 17.

31 Ibid., p. 96.

32 See Cathy Caruth, *Unclaimed Experience: Trauma, Narrative, and History* (Baltimore and London: Johns Hopkins University Press, 1996).

33 Lawrence Langer, *Admitting the Holocaust: Collected Essays* (New York and Oxford: Oxford University Press, 1995), p. 15.

34 Djebar, *Le Blanc de l'Algérie*, p. 271.

35 Dominick Lacapra, *Representing the Holocaust: History, Theory, Trauma* (Ithaca, NY, and London: Cornell University Press, 1994), p. 200. Lacapra stresses that the relationship between 'acting out' and 'working through' is not 'from/to', and the former can never be fully overcome. Both processes are at work in the production

of memory narratives. Furthermore, Lacapra notes that in Freud, working through is normative, while he prefers to see it as the ability to render explicit the question of normativity.

36 Assia Djebar, *Oran, langue morte* (Paris: Actes Sud, 1997), p. 13.

37 Ibid., pp. 32–33.

38 See Caruth, *Unclaimed Experience*, p. 17. Trauma for Caruth is defined by an event's lack of integration into the consciousness of the subject.

39 Djebar, *Oran, langue morte*, p. 72. Her ellipsis.

40 Ibid., pp. 270–71.

41 Ibid., p. 291.

42 Ibid., p. 358.

43 Ibid., p. 157.

44 The original story is to be found in *Arabian Nights' Entertainments*, ed. Robert L. Mack (Oxford: Oxford University Press, 1995), pp. 179–222, though Atyka does not complete her analysis of this lengthy section.

45 Djebar, *Oran, langue morte*, p. 192.

46 Ibid., p. 207.

47 Ibid., p. 198.

48 Clarisse Zimra comments on this structure in 'Sounding Off the Absent Body'. Zimra comments that the revised version of the story from the *Arabian Nights* is itself circular, since it begins with its own ending. This circularity is repeated when Atyka is murdered at the end of Djebar's own text.

49 Calle-Gruber, *Assia Djebar, ou la résistance de l'écriture*, p. 144.

50 Djebar, *Oran, langue morte*, p. 378.

51 Assia Djebar, *Les Nuits de Strasbourg* (Paris: Actes Sud, 1997), p. 14.

52 Ibid., pp. 65–66.

53 Ibid., p. 127.

54 Ibid., p. 51. Philippe Barbé comments on this movement, noting how Djebar's earlier texts focus on women's relationship with interior space while the current novel finds long-awaited access to the 'outside'. The 'outside' of Strasbourg is also an extraterritorial outside, figuring not only public space but a space divorced from notions of identity and belonging. See 'Transnational and the Translinguistic Relocation of the Subject in *Les Nuits de Strasbourg* by Assia Djebar', *Esprit Créateur* 41.3 (2001), pp. 125–35.

55 Michael O'Riley, 'Translation and Imperialism in Assia Djebar's *Les Nuits de Strasbourg*', *French Review* 75.6 (2002), pp. 1235–49 (p. 1243).

56 Djebar, *Les Nuits de Strasbourg*, p. 285.

57 Ibid., p. 270.

58 Ibid., pp. 116–17.

59 See *Ces voix qui m'assiègent*, p. 143.

60 Djebar, *Les Nuits de Strasbourg*, p. 330.

61 The terms are used by Djamila to describe Jacqueline's passing, p. 357. They are also used by the chorus in Anouilh's *Antigone* (Paris: Table ronde, 1946): 'c'est propre, la tragédie. C'est reposant, c'est sûr... Dans le drame, avec ces traîtres, avec ces méchants acharnés, cette innocence persécutée, ces vengeurs, ces terre-neuve, ces lueurs d'espoir, cela devient épouvantable de mourir, comme un accident', p. 55.

62 Djebar, *Les Nuits de Strasbourg*, p. 335.

Haunted Algeria

1 See Bensmaïa, *Experimental Nations*, p. 41.

2 Assia Djebar, *La Femme sans sépulture* (Paris: Albin Michel, 2002), p. 220.

3 Kathleen Brogan, *Cultural Haunting: Ghosts and Ethnicity in Recent American Literature* (Charlottesville, VA, and London: University Press of Virginia, 1998), p. 91.

4 Ibid., p. 65.

5 See Djebar's comments in the interview with Aliette Armel, 'Assia Djebar: La Mémoire des femmes', p. 103.

6 Djebar, *La Femme sans sépulture*, p. 16.

7 Ibid., p. 50.

8 Ibid., p. 87.

9 Ibid., p. 128.

10 Ibid., p. 83.

11 Ibid., p. 58.

12 Ibid., p. 129.

13 Ibid., p. 220.

14 Ibid., p. 21.

15 Ibid., p. 118.

16 Julian Wolfreys, *Victorian Hauntings: Spectrality, Gothic, the Uncanny and Literature* (Basingstoke: Hampshire, 2002), p. 21. Wolfreys goes on to discuss the emergence of the invisible within the visible in George Eliot's *The Lifted Veil*. This trace of the invisible within the field of vision also serves as a metaphor for writing, which also relies on the conjuring of what we cannot see.

17 Michael O'Riley, 'Place, Position, and Postcolonial Haunting in Assia Djebar's *La femme sans sépulture*', *Research in African Literatures* 35.1 (2004), pp. 66–86 (p. 71).

18 Ibid., p. 72.

19 Djebar, *La Femme sans sépulture*, p. 204.

20 Ibid., pp. 60–61.

21 Marianne Hirsch, 'Past Lives: Postmemories in Exile', in *Exile and Creativity: Signposts, Travelers, Outsiders, Backward Glances*, ed. Susan Suleiman (Durham, NC, and London: Duke University Press, 1998), pp. 418–46 (p. 422). Hirsch writes about the exiled children of holocaust victims, but her understanding of inherited 'postmemories' does seem pertinent here, despite the differences in context.

22 Avery F. Gordon, *Ghostly Matters: Haunting and the Sociological Imagination* (Minneapolis: University of Minnesota Press, 1997), p. 183.

23 Jodey Castricano, *Cryptomimesis: The Gothic in Jacques Derrida's Ghost Writing* (Montreal: McGill University Press, 2001), p. 20.

24 Brogan, *Cultural Haunting*, p. 92.

25 See Georges Perec, *La Disparition* (Paris: Denoël, 1969). Perec's novel tells the story of the disappearance of the central character, Anton Voyl, but the entire narrative excludes the letter 'e', with the curious effect of making the language seem opaque and alien.

26 Assia Djebar, *La Disparition de la langue française* (Paris: Albin Michel, 2003), p. 87.

27 Ibid., p. 223.

28 Ibid., p. 275. The use of this term 'inachevé' of course recalls Djebar's reflections in *Le Blanc de l'Algérie* on untimely deaths, interrupted lives, which are as a result impossible to mourn successfully.

29 Ibid., p. 18.

30 Ibid., pp. 26–27.

31 Ibid., pp. 22–23.

32 Ibid., p. 30.

33 See Bensmaïa, 'Cities of Writers', in *Experimental Nations, or, the Invention of the Maghreb*, pp. 27–46.

34 Djebar, *La Disparition de la langue française*, p. 82.

35 See Mireille Rosello, *Postcolonial Hospitality: The Immigrant as Guest* (Stanford, CA: Stanford University Press, 2001), p. 163.

36 Djebar, *La Disparition de la langue française*, p. 85.

37 Ibid., pp. 84, 87.

38 For more on this see Ernspeter Ruhe, 'Ecrire est une route à ouvrir', in Calle-Gruber (ed.), *Assia Djebar: Nomade entre les murs…*, pp. 53–65.

39 Edward Said, *Orientalism: Western Conceptions of the Orient* (Harmondsworth: Penguin, 1995), pp. 21–22.

40 Djebar, *La Disparition de la langue française*, p. 117.

41 Ibid., p. 124.

42 Ibid., p. 134. Djebar describes the women in Delacroix's painting as 'à la fois présentes et lointaines', *Femmes d'Alger dans leur appartement*, p. 241.

43 Djebar, *La Disparition de la langue française*, p. 138.

44 Ibid., p. 143.

45 Ibid., p. 180. Berkane's musings continue: 'j'espère qu'elle reconnaîtra ma voix, en me lisant, un jour, même à l'autre bout de la terre! C'est fort improbable, mais pas impossible. J'écris dans son ombre et malgré la séparation.' This evocation of Nadjia's shadow, and Berkane's sense that his writing is both directed to her and necessarily detached from her, again closely recalls Breton's narrator's uneasy pursuit of the spectral Nadja.

46 Ibid., pp. 156, 157.

47 Ibid., p. 164.

Conclusion

1 Djebar, *Ces voix qui m'assiègent*, p. 206.

2 Jacqueline Kaye and Abdelhamid Zoubir, *The Ambiguous Compromise: Language, Literature, and National Identity in Algeria and Morocco* (London: Routledge, 1990). The authors assert, 'the real problem, we believe, is not the status of French as a component part of Algerian culture but its persistence as the medium of the intelligentsia rather than being a generic expression of the national fabric' (p. 82). Their analyses of Maghrebian writing for this reason have a critical slant, though their conclusion accepts that this 'compromise' is on some level both necessary and inevitable.

3 See Ahmad, *In Theory*, and Epifanio San Juan Jr, *Beyond Postcolonial Theory*

(Basingstoke: Macmillan, 1998).

4 See 'Conclusion: Literature and the Work of Criticism', in *Postcolonial Criticism*, pp. 136–50.

5 Hallward, *Absolutely Postcolonial*, p. 333.

Bibliography

Books by Assia Djebar

La Soif. Paris: Réné Julliard, 1957.
Les Impatients. Paris: Réné Julliard, 1958.
Les Enfants du nouveau monde. Paris: Réné Julliard, 1962.
Les Alouettes naïves. Paris: Réné Julliard, 1967. Paris: Actes Sud, 1997.
Rouge l'aube. Algiers: SNED, 1969.
Poèmes pour une Algérie heureuse. Algiers: SNED, 1969.
Femmes d'Alger dans leur appartement. Paris: des femmes, 1980. Paris: Albin Michel, 2002.
L'Amour, la fantasia. Paris: Editions Jean-Claude Lattès, 1985. Paris: Albin Michel, 1995.
Ombre sultane. Paris: Editions Jean-Claude Lattès, 1987.
Loin de Médine: Filles d'Ismaël. Paris: Albin Michel, 1991.
Chronique d'un été algérien. Paris: Editions Plume,1993.
Vaste est la prison. Paris: Albin Michel, 1995.
Le Blanc de l'Algérie. Paris: Albin Michel, 1995.
Oran, langue morte. Paris: Actes Sud, 1997.
Les Nuits de Strasbourg. Paris: Actes Sud, 1997.
Ces voix qui m'assiègent. Paris: Albin Michel, 1999.
La Femme sans sépulture. Paris: Albin Michel, 2002.
La Disparition de la langue française. Paris: Albin Michel, 2003.

Translations

Women of Algiers in their Apartment. Trans. Marjolijnde Jager. Charlottesville, VA: University Press of Virginia, 1992.
Fantasia: An Algerian Cavalcade. Trans. Dorothy S. Blair. London and New York: Quartet, 1985.
A Sister to Scheherazade. Trans. Dorothy S. Blair. London and New York: Quartet, 1987.
Far from Madina: Daughters of Ishmaël. Trans. Dorothy S. Blair. London and New York: Quartet, 1994.
So Vast the Prison. Trans. Betsy Wing. New York: Seven Stories Press, 1999.
Algerian White. Trans. David Kelley. New York: Seven Stories Press, 2000.

Children of the New World; A Novel of the Algerian War. Trans. Marjolijnde Jager. New York: Feminist Press, 2005.

Films

La Nouba des femmes du mont Chenoua, 1978
La Zerda ou les chants de l'oubli, 1982

Secondary Works

Accad, Evelyne. 'Assia Djebar's Contribution to Arab Women's Literature: Rebellion, Maturity, Vision', *World Literature Today* 70.4 (1996), pp. 801–12.

Addi, Lahouari. *L'Algérie et la démocratie: pouvoir et crise du politique dans l'Algérie contemporaine.* Paris: Editions de la découverte, 1995.

Adlai-Murdoch, H. 'Rewriting Writing: Identity, Exile and Renewal in Assia Djebar's *L'Amour, la fantasia*', *Yale French Studies* 83.2, *Post/Colonial Conditions: Exiles, Migrations and Nomadisms* (1993), pp. 71–92.

Afkhami, Mahmaz (ed). *Faith and Freedom: Women's Human Rights in the Muslim World.* London and New York: Tauris, 1995.

Agamben, Giorgio. *Remnants of Auschwitz: The Witness and the Archive.* New York: Zone Books, 1999.

Ahmad, Aijaz. *In Theory: Classes, Nations, Literatures.* London: Verso, 1992.

Ahmed, Leïla. *Women and Gender in Islam: Historical Roots of the Modern Debate.* London and New Haven, CT: Yale University Press, 1992.

Ahmida, Abdellatif (ed.). *Beyond Colonialism and Nationalism in the Magrheb: History, Culture and Politics.* New York: Palgrave, 2000.

Al-Ahnaf, M., B. Botiveau and F. Frégosi. *L'Algérie par ses islamistes.* Paris: Karthala, 1991.

Al-Nowaihi, Magda. 'Resisting Silence in Arab Women's Autobiographies', *International Journal of Middle East Studies* 33.4 (2001), pp. 477–502.

Al-Tabari. *The History of Al-Tabari.* Trans. Ismail K. Poonavala. Albany, NY: State University of New York Press, 1990.

Amrane-Minne, Danièle Djamila. *Des femmes dans la guerre d'Algérie.* Paris: Karthala, 1994.

Anouilh, Jean. *Antigone.* Paris: Table ronde, 1946.

Armel, Aliette. 'Assia Djebar et la mémoire des femmes', *Magazine littéraire* 410 (2002), pp. 98–103.

Arnaud, Jacqueline. *La Littérature maghrébine de langue française.* Paris: Publisud, 1986.

Ashcroft, Bill and Helen Tiffin. *Key Concepts in Postcolonial Studies.* London and New York: Routledge, 1998.

Barbé, Philippe. 'Transnational and Translinguistic Relocation of the Subject in *Les Nuits de Strasbourg* by Assia Djebar', *Esprit Créateur* 41.3 (2001), pp. 125–35.

——, 'The Closure and Opening of Domestic Space in *Ombre sultane* by Assia

Djebar,', in *Francophone Postcolonial Cultures: Critical Essays* (Lanham, Boulder, New York, Oxford: Lexington, 2003), pp. 28–38.

Bensmaïa, Réda. 'Nations of Writers', *Studies in Twentieth Century Literature* 23.1 (1999), pp. 163–78.

——, *Experimental Nations, or, The Invention of the Maghreb*. Princeton, NJ: Princeton University Press, 2003.

Berger, Anne-Emmanuelle (ed.). *Algeria in Others' Languages*. Ithaca, NY, and London: Cornell University Press, 2002.

Best, Victoria. 'Between the Harem and the Battlefield: Domestic Space in the Work of Assia Djebar', *Signs: Journal of Women in Culture and Society* 27.3 (2002), pp. 873–79.

Bhabha, Homi. *The Location of Culture*. London and New York: Routledge, 1994.

Bigelow, Gordon. 'Revolution and Modernity: Assia Djebar's *Les Enfants du nouveau monde*', *Research in African Literatures* 34.2 (2003), pp. 13–17.

Bonn, Charles and Farida Boualit. *Paysages littéraires algériennes des années 90: témoigner d'une tragédie?* Paris: L'Harmattan, 1999.

Bouhdiba, Abdelwahab. *Sexuality in Islam*. Trans. Alan Sheridan. London: Routledge, 1985.

Braziel, Jana Evans. 'Islam, Individualism and *Dévoilement* in the Works of Out El Kouloub and Assia Djebar', *Journal of North African Studies* 4.3 (1999), pp. 81–101.

Breton, André. *Nadja*. Paris: Gallimard, 1964.

Britton, Celia. 'The (De)construction of Subjectivity in Daniel Maximin's *L'Ile et une nuit*', *Paragraph* 24 (2001), pp. 44–58.

Brogan, Kathleen. *Cultural Haunting: Ghosts and Ethnicity in Recent American Literature*. Charlottesville, VA, and London: University Press of Virginia, 1998.

Bulbeck, Chilla. *Re-orienting Western Feminisms: Women's Diversity in a Postcolonial World*. Cambridge: Cambridge University Press, 1998.

Calle-Gruber, Mireille. *Assia Djebar, ou la résistance de l'écriture*. Paris: Maisonneuve et Larose, 2001.

——, (ed.) *Assia Djebar, nomade entre les murs…: Pour une poétique transfrontalière*. Paris: Maisonneuve et Larose, 2005.

Caruth, Cathy (ed.). *Trauma: Explorations in Memory*. Baltimore, MD, and London: Johns Hopkins University Press, 1995.

——, *Unclaimed Experience: Trauma, Narrative, and History*. Baltimore, MD, and London: Johns Hopkins University Press, 1996.

Castricano, Jodey. *Cryptomimesis: The Gothic in Jacques Derrida's Ghost Writing*. Montreal: McGill University Press, 2001.

Célestin, Roger. 'Un Entretien avec Assia Djebar', *Sites: The Journal of Contemporary French Studies* 6.2 (2002), pp. 256–58.

Cheah, Pheng. *Spectral Nationality: Passages of Freedom from Kant to Postcolonial Literatures of Liberation*. New York: Columbia University Press, 2003.

Chikhi, Beïda. *Les romans d'Assia Djebar*. Alger: Office des publications universitaires, 1990.

——, *Littérature algérienne: désir d'histoire et esthétique*. Paris: L'Harmattan, 1997.

——, *Les romans d'Assia Djebar*. Alger: Office des publications universitaires, 1990.

Cixous, Hélène. 'Le Rire de la Méduse', *L'Arc* 61 (1975), pp. 39–54.

Cixous, Hélène and Mireille Calle-Gruber. *Photos de racines*. Paris: des femmes, 1994.

Clerc, Jeanne-Marie. *Assia Djebar: Ecrire, Transgresser, Résister*. Paris: L'Harmattan, 1997.

Cooke, Miriam. *Women and the War Story*. Berkeley, CA, and London: University of California Press, 1996.

——, *Women Claim Islam: Creating Islamic Feminism through Literature*. London and New York: Routledge, 2001.

Dejeux, Jean. *La littérature féminine de langue française au Maghreb*. Paris: Karhala, 1994.

De Lauretis, Teresa. 'Eccentric Subjects: Feminist Theory and Historical Consciousness', *Feminist Studies* 16.1 (1990), pp. 115–50.

Derrida, Jacques. *De la grammatologie*. Paris: Minuit, 1967.

——, 'La Différance', *Marges de la philosophie*. Paris: Minuit, 1972, pp. 41–66.

——, *Spectres de Marx: L'état de la dette, le travail du deuil et la nouvelle Internationale*. Paris: Galilée, 1994.

——, *Specters of Marx: The State of Debt, the Work of Mourning, and the New International*. Trans. Peggy Kamuf. London and New York: Routledge, 1994.

——, *Le Monolinguisme de l'autre, ou, le prothèse de l'origine*. Paris: Galilée, 1996.

——, *Voyous: Deux essais sur la raison*. Paris: Galilée, 2003.

Derrida, Jacques and Jean-Luc Nancy, '"Eating Well," or the Calculation of the Subject: An Interview with Jacques Derrida', in *Who Comes After the Subject?*, ed. Eduardo Cadava, Peter Connor, Jean-Luc Nancy (New York and London: Routledge, 1991), pp. 96–119.

Dirlik, Arif. *The Postcolonial Aura: Third World Criticism in the Age of Global Capitalism*. Boulder, CO: Westview Press, 1997.

Djaout, Tahar. *Les Chercheurs d'os*. Paris: Seuil, 1984.

——, *Les Vigiles*. Paris: Seuil, 1991.

Donadey, Anne. 'Assia Djebar's Poetics of Subversion', *Esprit Créateur* 33.2 (1993), pp. 107–17.

——, 'The Multilingual Strategies of Postcolonial Literature: Assia Djebar's Algerian Palimpsest', *World Literature Today* 74.1 (2000) pp. 27–36.

——, *Recasting Postcolonialism*. Portsmouth: Heinemann, 2001.

Elia, Nadia. *Trances, Dances and Vociferations: Agency and Resistance in Africana Women's Narratives*. New York: Garland, 2001.

El Guindi, Fadwa. *Veil: Modesty, Privacy, Resistance*. Oxford: Berg, 1999.

El Saadawi, Nawal. *The Hidden Face of Eve: Women in the Arab World*. London: Zed Books, 1980.

——, *The Nawal El Saadawi Reader*. London: Zed Books, 1997.

Erickson, John. *Islam and Postcolonial Narrative*. Cambridge: Cambridge University Press, 1998.

Fallaize, Elizabeth. 'In Search of a Liturgy: Assia Djebar's *Le Blanc de l'Algérie*', *French Studies* 59.1 (2005), pp. 55–62.

Fanon, Frantz. *L'An V de la révolution algérienne*. Paris: Maspero, 1959.

——, *Les Damnés de la terre*. Paris: Gallimard, 1991.

Felman, Shoshana and Dori Laub. *Testimony: Crises of Witnessing in Literature, Psychoanalysis and History*. London: Routledge, 1992.

Fielder, Adrian V. 'Historical Representation and the Scriptural Economy of Imperialism: Assia Djebar's *L'Amour, la fantasia* and Cormac McCarthy's *Blood Meridian*', *Comparative Literature Studies* 37.1 (2000), pp. 18–44.

Fischer, Michael M.-J. and Mehdi Abedi. *Debating Muslims: Cultural Dialogues in Postmodernity and Tradition*. Madison, WI: University of Wisconsin Press, 1990.

Fitzpatrick, Peter. *Modernity and the Grounds of Law*. Cambridge: Cambridge University Press, 2001.

Forsdick, Charles and David Murphy. *Francophone Postcolonial Studies: A Critical Introduction*. London: Arnold, 2003.

Foucault, Michel. *Power/Knowledge: Selected Interviews and Other Writings 1971–1977*. Ed. Colin Gordon, trans. Colin Gordon, Lee Marshall, John Mepham, Kate Soper. New York and London: Prentice Hall, 1980.

——, *Histoire de la sexualité*. Paris: Gallimard, 1984.

——, 'Subjectivité et vérité', *Dits et écrits 1954–1988*, Vol. IV (Paris: Gallimard, 1994), pp. 213–19.

Fromentin, Eugène. *Une année dans le Sahel*. Paris: Flammarion, 1991.

Gafaïti, Hafid. 'The Blood of Writing: Assia Djebar's Unveiling of Women and History', *World Literature Today* 70.4 (1996), pp. 813–22.

——. 'Culture and Violence: The Algerian Intelligentsia between Two Political Illegitimacies', *Parallax 7: Translating Algeria* (1998), pp. 71–77.

——, 'Power, Censorship and the Press: The Case of Postcolonial Algeria', *Research in African Literatures* 30.3 (1999), pp. 51–61.

Gauvin, Lise. *L'Ecrivain francophone à la croisée des langues: Entretiens*. Paris: Karthala, 1997.

Ghaussy, Soheila. 'A Stepmother Tongue: Feminine Writing in Assia Djebar's *Fantasia*', *World Literature Today* 68.3 (1994), pp. 457–62.

Gilmore, Leigh. *Autobiographics: A Feminist Theory of Women's Self-Representation*. Ithaca, NY, and London: Cornell University Press, 1994.

Gordon, Avery F. *Ghostly Matters: Haunting and the Sociological Imagination*. Minneapolis, MN: University of Minnesota Press, 1997.

Gordon, David C. *Women of Algeria: An Essay on Change*. Cambridge, MA: Harvard University Press, 1968.

Gracki, Katherine. 'Writing Violence and the Violence of Writing in Assia Djebar's *Algerian Quartet*', *World Literature Today* 70.4 (1996), pp. 835–43.

Green, Mary Jean and Karen Gould (eds). *Postcolonial Subjects: Francophone Women Writers*. Minneapolis, MN: University of Minnesota Press, 1996.

Greenspan, Henry. *On Listening to Holocaust Survivors*. Westport, CT, and London: Praeger, 1998.

Haddour, Azzedine. *Colonial Myths: History and Narrative*. Manchester: Manchester University Press, 2000.

Hallward, Peter. *Absolutely Postcolonial: Writing between the Singular and the Specific*. Manchester: Manchester University Press, 2001.

Harrison, Nicholas. *Postcolonial Criticism: History, Theory, and the Work of Fiction.* Cambridge: Polity, 2003.

Harrow, Kenneth (ed.). *The Marabout and the Muse: New Approaches to Islam in African Literature.* Portsmouth: Heinemann, 1996.

Hiddleston, Jane. 'The Specific Plurality of Assia Djebar', *French Studies* 58.3 (2004), pp. 371–84.

——, 'Feminism and the Question of "Woman" in Assia Djebar's *Vaste est la prison*', *Research in African Literatures* 35.4 (2004), pp. 91–104.

——, 'Political Violence and Singular Testimony: Assia Djebar's *Le Blanc de l'Algérie*', *Law and Literature* 17.1 (2005), pp. 1–20.

Hirsch, Marianne. *Family Frames: Photography, Narrative and Postmemory.* Cambridge, MA: Harvard University Press, 1997.

——, 'Past Lives: Postmemories in Exile', *Exile and Creativity: Signposts, Travelers, Outsiders, Backward Glances.* Ed. Susan Suleiman. Durham, NC, and London: Duke University Press, 1998, pp. 418–46.

Hobsbawm, Eric and Terence Ranger (eds). *The Invention of Tradition.* Cambridge: Cambridge University Press, 1983.

Hornung, Alfred and Ernspeter Ruhe. *Postcolonialism and Autobiography.* Amsterdam: Rodopi, 1998.

Irigaray, Luce. *Ce sexe qui n'en est pas un.* Paris: Minuit, 1977.

John, Mary E. *Discrepant Dislocations: Feminism, Theory and Postcolonial Histories.* Berkeley, CA: University of California Press, 1996.

Karmi, Ghada. 'Women, Islam and Patriarchalism', in *Feminism and Islam: Legal and Literary Perspectives*, ed. Mai Yamani. Reading: Ithaca Press, 1996, pp. 69–85.

Kaye, Jacqueline and Abdelhamid Zoubir. *The Ambiguous Compromise: Language, Literature, and National Identity in Algeria and Morocco.* London: Routledge, 1990.

Kelley, David. 'Assia Djebar: Parallels and Paradoxes', *World Literature Today* 70.4 (1996), pp. 844–46.

Kelly, Debra. *Autobiography and Independence: Selfhood and Creativity in North African Postcolonial Writing in French.* Liverpool: Liverpool University Press, 2005.

Khanna, Ranjana. *Dark Continents: Psychoanalysis and Colonialism.* Durham, NC, and London: Duke University Press, 2003.

Khatibi, Abdelkebir, *Le Roman maghrebin.* Paris: Maspero, 1968.

Lacapra, Dominick. *History, Politics and the Novel.* Ithaca, NY, and London: Cornell University Press, 1987.

——, *Representing the Holocaust: History, Theory, Trauma.* Ithaca, NY, and London: Cornell University Press, 1994.

Lacoue-Labarthe, Philippe. *Le Sujet de la philosophie.* Paris: Aubier-Flammarion, 1979.

Langer, Lawrence. *Admitting the Holocaust: Collected Essays.* New York and Oxford: Oxford University Press, 1995.

Lazreg, Marnia. *The Eloquence of Silence: Algerian Women in Question.* London: Routledge, 1994.

Levinas, Emmanuel. *L'Au-delà du verset: Lectures et discours talmudiques.* Paris:

Minuit, 1982.

Lionnet, Françoise. *Postcolonial Representations: Women, Literature, Identity.* Ithaca, NY, and London: Cornell University Press, 1995.

Mack, Robert L. (ed). *Arabian Nights Entertainments.* Oxford: Oxford University Press, 1995.

Malley, Robert. *The Call from Algeria: Third Worldism, Revolution, and the Turn to Islam.* Berkeley, CA: University of California Press, 1996.

Martin, Biddy and Chandra Malpade Mohanty. 'Feminist Politics: What's Home Got To Do With It?', in *Feminist Studies/Critical Studies,* ed. Teresa De Lauretis. Bloomington, IN: Indiana University Press, 1986, pp. 191–212.

McClintock, Anne. 'No Longer in Future Heaven: Gender, Race, and Nationalism', in *Dangerous Liaisons: Gender, Nation, and Postcolonial Perspectives.* Ed. Anne McClintock, Aamir Mufti, Ella Shohat. Minneapolis, MN: University of Minnesota Press, 1997, pp. 89–112.

Mehrez, Samia. 'Translation and Postcolonial Experience: The Francophone North African Text', in *Rethinking Translation: Discourse, Subjectivity, Ideology.* Ed. Lawrence Venuti. London: Routledge, 1992, pp. 120–38.

Mernissi, Fatima. *Beyond the Veil: Male-Female Dynamics in Modern Muslim Society.* London: Al Saqi, 1985.

——, *Le Harem politique: Le Prophète et ses femmes.* Paris: Albin Michel, 1987.

——, *Women and Islam: A Historical and Theological Inquiry.* Trans. Mary Jo Lakeland. Oxford: Basil Blackwell, 1991.

——, *Women's Rebellion and Islamic Memory.* London: Zed Books, 1996.

Minh-ha, Trinh. *Woman, Native, Other: Writing Postcoloniality and Feminism.* Bloomington and Indianapolis: Indiana University Press, 1989.

Moghissi, Haideh. *Feminism and Islamic Fundamentalism: The Limits of Postmodern Analysis.* London: Zed Books, 1999.

Mohanty, Chandra. 'Under Western Eyes: Feminist Scholarship and Colonial Discourses', *Feminist Review* 30 (1988), pp. 61–88.

Moi, Toril. *Sexual/Textual Politics: Feminist Literary Theory.* London: Methuen, 1985.

Mortimer, Mildred. 'Entretien avec Assia Djebar', *Research in African Literatures* 19 (1988), pp. 197–203.

——, *Journeys through the French African Novel.* Portsmouth: Heinemann, 1990.

——, 'Reappropriating the Gaze in Assia Djebar's Fiction and Film', *World Literature Today* 70.4 (1996), pp. 859–66.

——, 'Assia Djebar's *Algerian Quartet*: A Study in Fragmented Autobiography', *Research in African Literatures* 28.2 (1997), pp. 102–17.

——, (ed.) *Maghrebian Mosaic: A Literature in Transition.* Boulder, CO: Lynne Rienner, 2001.

Moura, Jean-Marc. *Littératures francophones et théorie postcoloniale.* Paris: PUF, 1999.

Nagy-Zekmi, Silvia. 'Tradition and Transgression in the Novels of Assia Djebar and Aïcha Lemsine', *Research in African Literatures* 33.3 (2002), pp. 1–13.

Nancy, Jean-Luc. *La Communauté désœuvrée.* Paris: Christian Bourgois, 1986.

——, *Etre singulier pluriel.* Paris: Galilée, 1996.

Narain, Denise Decaires. 'What Happened to Global Sisterhood? Writing and Reading "the" Postcolonial Woman', in *Third Wave Feminism: A Critical*

Exploration. Ed. Stacy Gillis, Gillian Howie and Rebecca Munford. London: Palgrave, 2004, pp. 240–51.

Naylor, Philip C. *France and Algeria: A History of Decolonization and Transformation.* Gainesville, FL: University Press of Florida, 2000.

O'Beirne, Emir. 'Veiled Vision: Assia Djebar on Delacroix, Picasso, and the *Femmes d'Alger*', *Romance Studies* 21.1 (2003), pp. 39–51.

Olney, James (ed.). *Autobiography: Essays Theoretical and Critical.* Princeton, NJ: Princeton University Press, 1980.

O'Riley, Michael. 'Translation and Imperialism in Assia Djebar's *Les Nuits de Strasbourg*', *French Review* 75.6 (2002), pp. 1235–49.

——, 'Place, Position, and Postcolonial Haunting in Assia Djebar's *La femme sans sépulture*', *Research in African Literatures* 35.1 (2004), pp. 66–86.

Orlando, Valerie. *Nomadic Voices of Exile: Feminine Identity in Francophone Literature of the Maghreb.* Athens, OH: Ohio University Press, 1999.

Parry, Benita. 'Signs of Our Times: A Discussion of Homi Bhabha's *The Location of Culture*', *Third Text* 28/29 (1994), pp. 5–24.

——, *Postcolonial Studies: A Materialist Critique.* London: Routledge, 2004.

Pears, Pamela A. *Remnants of Empire in Algeria and Vietnam: Women, Words, and War.* Lanham, MD: Lexington Books, 2004.

Perec, Georges. *La Disparition.* Paris: Denoël, 1969.

Peysson, Agnès, '*Le Blanc de l'Algérie*: une liturgie aux disparus', *International Journal of Francophone Studies* 2.3 (1999), pp. 163–67.

Prabhu, Anjali. 'Sisterhood and Rivalry in-between the Shadow and the Sultana: A Problematic of Representation in *Ombre Sultane*', *Research in African Literatures* 33.3 (2002), pp. 69–96.

Punter, David. *Postcolonial Imaginings: Fictions of a New World Order.* Edinburgh: Edinburgh University Press, 2000.

Ricoeur, Paul. *Temps et récit.* Paris: Seuil, 1983.

Roberts, Hugh. *The Battlefield Algeria 1988–2002.* London: Verso, 2003.

Rosello, Mireille. *Postcolonial Hospitality: The Immigrant as Guest.* Stanford, CA: Stanford University Press, 2001.

Ruedy, John. *Islam and Secularism in North Africa.* Basingstoke: Macmillan, 1994.

Said, Edward. *Orientalism: Western Conceptions of the Orient.* Harmondsworth: Penguin, 1995.

Salhi, Kamal (ed). *Francophone Voices.* Exeter: Elmbank, 1999.

——, 'Assia Djebar Speaking: An Interview with Assia Djebar', *International Journal of Francophone Studies* 2.3 (1999), pp. 168–79.

——, 'Chronology of Assia Djebar', *International Journal of Francophone Studies* 2.3 (1999), pp. 180–82.

——, *Francophone Postcolonial Cultures: Critical Essays.* Lanham, MD, Boulder, CO, New York: Lexington Books, 2003.

Salhi, Zahia Smail. 'Memory, Gender, and National Identity in the Work of Assia Djebar', *Moving Worlds* 4.1 (2004), pp. 17–30.

San Juan Jr, Epifanio. *Beyond Postcolonial Theory.* Basingstoke: Macmillan, 1998.

Scarry, Elaine. *The Body in Pain: The Making and Unmaking of the World.* Oxford: Oxford University Press, 1985.

Segarra, Marta. *Leur pesant de poudre: romancières francophones du Maghreb.*

Paris: L'Harmattan, 1997.

Seyhan, Azade. 'Enduring Grief: Autobiography as "Poetry of Witness" in the Work of Assia Djebar and Nazim Hikmet', *Comparative Literature Studies* 40.2 (2003), pp. 159–72.

Soukehal, Rabah. *L'Ecrivain de langue française et les pouvoirs en Algérie*. Paris: L'Harmattan, 1999.

Spivak, Gayatri Chakravorty. *The Post-colonial Critic: Interviews, Strategies, Dialogues*. Ed. Sarah Harasym. London and New York: Routledge, 1990.

——, 'Can the Subaltern Speak?', in *Colonial Discourse and Postcolonial Theory*. Ed. Laura Chrisman and Patrick Williams. Hemel Hempstead: Harvester Wheatsheaf, 1994, pp. 66–111.

——, 'Ghostwriting'. *Diacritics* 25.2 (1995), pp. 64–84.

——, 'Echo', *The Spivak Reader*, ed. Donna Landry and Gerald Maclean. New York and London: Routledge, 1996, pp. 175–202.

Stendman, Jennifer Bernhardt. 'A Global Feminist Travels: Assia Djebar and *Fantasia*', *Meridians: Feminism, Race, Transnationalism* 4.1 (2003), pp. 173–99.

Stone, Martin. *The Agony of Algeria*. London: Hurst and Co, 1997.

Stora, Benjamin. 'Algérie: absence et surabondance de mémoire', *Esprit* (January 1995), pp. 62–67.

——, 'Women's Writing between Two Algerian Wars', *Research in African Literatures* 30.3 (1999), pp. 78–94.

Tomlinson, Emily. 'Torture, Fiction, and the Repetition of Horror: Ghost-writing the Past in Algeria and Argentina'. PhD thesis, Cambridge, 2002.

——, 'Assia Djebar: Speaking with the Living Dead', *Paragaraph* 26.3 (2003), pp. 34–50.

Violet, Michèle E. 'Between Sound and Fury: Assia Djebar's Poetics of l'*entre-deux-langues*', *Symposium: A Quarterly Journal of Modern Literatures* 56.3 (2002), pp. 149–63.

Waterman, David. 'Body/Text/History: The Violation of Borders in Assia Djebar's *Fantasia*', *Studies in Twentieth Century Literature* 22.2 (1998), pp. 319–33.

Wehr, Donald R. 'The "Sensible", the Maternal and the Ethical Beginnings of Feminist Islamic Discourse in Assia Djebar's *L'Amour, la fantasia* and *Loin de Médine*', *Modern Language Notes* 118.4 (2003), pp. 841–66.

Wolfreys, Julian. *Victorian Hauntings: Spectrality, Gothic, the Uncanny and Literature*. Basingstoke: Macmillan, 2002.

Woodhull, Winifred. *Transfigurations of the Maghreb: Feminism, Decolonization and Literatures*. Minneapolis, MN: University of Minnesota Press, 1993.

Young, Robert. *Postcolonialism: A Historical Introduction*. Oxford: Blackwell, 2001.

Zimra, Clarisse. 'In Her Own Write: The Circular Structures of Linguistic Alienation in Assia Djebar's Early Novels', *Research in African Literatures* 11.2 (1980), pp. 206–23.

——, 'Writing Woman: The Novels of Assia Djebar', *Sub-Stance: A Review of Theory and Literary Criticism* 21 (1992), pp. 68–84.

——, 'When the Past Answers Our Present: Assia Djebar talks about *Loin de Médine*', *Callaloo* 16.1 (1993), pp. 116–31.

——, 'Not so far from Medina: Assia Djebar Charts Islam's Insupportable Feminist

Revolution', *World Literature Today* 70.4 (1996), pp. 823–34.

——, 'Sounding Off the Absent Body: Intertextual Resonances in "La femme qui pleure" and "La femme en morceaux"', *Research in African Literatures* 30.3 (1999), pp. 108–24.

——, 'Hearing Voices, or, Who You Calling Postcolonial? The Evolution of Assia Djebar's Poetics', *Research in African Literatures* 35.4 (2004), pp. 149–59.

Zoubir, Yahia H. 'The Painful Transition from Authoritarianism in Algeria', *Arab Studies Quarterly* 15.3 (1993), pp. 83–110.

Index